SECULAR AND CHRISTIAN
LEADERSHIP IN CORINTH

ARBEITEN ZUR GESCHICHTE DES ANTIKEN JUDENTUMS UND DES URCHRISTENTUMS

HERAUSGEGEBEN VON

Martin Hengel (Tübingen), Peter Schäfer (Berlin),
Pieter W. van der Horst (Utrecht), Martin Goodman (Oxford),
Daniël R. Schwartz (Jerusalem)

XVIII

SECULAR AND CHRISTIAN LEADERSHIP IN CORINTH

A Socio-Historical and Exegetical Study of 1 Corinthians 1-6

BY

ANDREW D. CLARKE

E.J. BRILL
LEIDEN • NEW YORK • KÖLN
1993

The paper in this book meets the guidelines for permanence and durability of the Committee on Production Guidelines for Book Longevity of the Council on Library Resources.

Library of Congress Cataloging-in-Publication Data

LC-number 93-10139

Die Deutsche Bibliothek – CIP-Einheitsaufnahme

Clarke, Andrew D.:
Secular and christian leadership in Corinth: a socio-historical and exegetical study of 1 corinthians 1-6 / by Andrew D. Clarke. — Leiden; New York; Köln: Brill, 1993
   (Arbeiten zur Geschichte des antiken Judentums und des Urchristentums; Bd. 18)
   ISBN 90-04-09862-3
NE: GT

ISSN   0169-734X
ISBN   90 04 09862 3

PRINTED IN THE NETHERLANDS

To my Mother and Father

TABLE OF CONTENTS

PREFACE

This book is a revision of a doctoral dissertation submitted to the University of Cambridge in 1991. The work was conducted under the careful supervision of Dr Ernst Bammel with further comments given by the examiners, Professor C.K. Barrett and Mr John Sweet.

The initial interest in looking at leadership in the Pauline churches was prompted by a desire to discover those areas in which the biblical text might inform an understanding and practice of leadership in churches today.

The research was principally carried out at Tyndale House Biblical Research Library, Cambridge whose resources and tools for research were invaluable for the project. In addition to the material resources, I am grateful to many who, whilst visiting Tyndale House, offered thoughtful advice. I have especially benefited from the detailed precision with which Miss Joyce Reynolds, Professor E. Judge and Dr David Gill read my discussion of Ancient History sources. In particular, however, I record my thanks to the Warden of Tyndale House, Dr Bruce Winter, who demonstrated to me the value of addressing the Graeco-Roman background to leadership in the Corinthian church, continued to take a great interest in the whole project, and offered, not only encouragement, but also considerable advice and insight. My debt to him is made plain through the footnotes of the book.

At an early stage of my research a visit to the site of Roman Corinth was influential in altering the course of the study and broadening my appreciation of the extent to which Graeco-Roman life in Corinthian high society must have influenced the Pauline community. The time afforded me by the Directors of Excavations at Corinth, Dr C.K. Williams and Dr Nancy Boukidis was most valuable.

My wife will be as glad as I am to witness this book see the light of day and I thank her for her support and confidence. This book is dedicated, however, to my parents who have watched this project for a much longer period, from its outset.

Tyndale House
Cambridge

CHAPTER ONE

INTRODUCTION

1. *The Object of the Study*

This study examines the nature of local leadership in 1 Corinthians 1-6 using the combined disciplines of social history and New Testament exegesis. Extant epigraphic, numismatic, literary and secondary sources are used to describe the structures of secular leadership within Roman Corinth. The dynamics of leadership used by the élite of Corinthian society are then described.

The thesis is that some from that élite Corinthian society also belonged to the Pauline community and that, both in practices adopted and perceptions of leadership in the church, some of these were strongly influenced by a secular model. Paul's own critique of these secular practices and, in contrast, his own non-status understanding of Christian leadership are also demonstrated.

This argument is developed by discussing: 1. the epigraphic and numismatic evidence which draws a profile of Roman Corinthian leadership; 2. the literary sources which show the dynamics of Graeco-Roman leadership; 3. the New Testament and possible extra-biblical evidence for the presence of élite members of secular society in the Christian church; 4. evidence in 1 Corinthians of the secular practice of leaders undertaking litigation in the Corinthian law courts; 5. the indications that members of the Pauline community, for reasons of status, were ignoring the sexual immorality of one of their élite fellow Christians; 6. evidence that Christian leaders had widely adopted in the church a number of secular perceptions of leadership; and finally, Paul's own critique of that secular leadership in the church and his contrasting use of non-status images of Christian leadership.

2. *The Parameters of the Study*

The limitations of a single volume necessitate the strict definition of parameters for study. A balance must be sought between covering, on the one hand, selected verses of 1 Corinthians, allowing for greater detail but no cumulative effect of the argument and, on the other hand, spanning all the relevant sections of 1 Corinthians, drawing extensive information for that cumulative picture but arguing it in insufficient detail. This study seeks to cover 1 Corinthians 1-6 in sufficient detail to provide cumulative evidence with which to reconstruct an understanding of local leadership in the Corinthian church. It does not aim to undertake a verse-by-verse exegesis of 1 Corinthians

1-6. Only those sections and verses which are relevant to this reconstruction of local leadership will be addressed.

It is only the Graeco-Roman social background for leadership which has been assessed here to shed light on the situation in the Christian church. This is the principal background for such a study, although the additional value of investigating both the Jewish and Old Testament influences on leadership in the Pauline church is not denied.

3. *The Question of Method*

a. *The Problem*

The study of the nature and development of local leadership in New Testament churches has often focused on the process of institutionalisation through the first two centuries and the antithesis between those churches emphasising the Spirit and charisma and those with formal structures and offices. Within this broader debate, the church of Corinth, and especially 1 Corinthian, have been central.

b. *The Consensus View*

The consensus view of the early Pauline churches is largely based on theological investigation of New Testament texts and is frequently traced back to the nineteenth century work of Sohm.[1] It was Sohm who coined the term 'charismatic organisation' derived from Paul's use of χαρίσματα in 1 Corinthians 12.4. This was only later taken up, and altered in meaning, by Weber.[2] In *Kirchenrecht,* 'charismatic organisation' in the Pauline churches is contrasted with the later development of Catholicism with its legal organisation and hierarchy.[3]

The consensus view of the Pauline church as a charismatic organisation without structures or offices which has developed since the work of Sohm may be characterised by the following summary statements. Bultmann argues that "The chief persons of authority are those endowed with gifts of the Spirit".[4] Von Campenhausen considers that "Paul develops the idea of the Spirit as the organizing principle of the Christian congregation. There is no need for any

---

[1]   R. Sohm, *Kirchenrecht* I (Leipzig, 1892). See also B. Holmberg, *Paul and Power. The Structure of Authority in the Primitive Church as reflected in the Pauline Epistles* (Lund, 1978), 4.

[2]   R. Sohm, *Kirchenrecht* I, 26, "Die aus dem göttlichen Wort geschöpfte, in Wahrheit apostolische Lehre von der Verfassung der Ekklesia ist die, daß die Organisation der Christenheit nicht rechtliche, sondern charismatische Organisation ist". For an illuminating discussion of Weber's debt to Sohm see P. Haley, 'Rudolph Sohm on Charisma', *The Journal of Religion* 60 (1980), 185-6, 195-7, and B. Holmberg, *Paul and Power,* 148.

[3]   R. Sohm, *Kirchenrecht* I, 26-8. This later development is seen in 1 Clement: *Kirchenrecht* I, 157-9.

[4]   R. Bultmann, *Theology of the New Testament* II (ET: London, 1955), 97.

fixed system with its rules and regulations and prohibitions".[5] Schweizer concludes that there is "no fundamental organization of superior or subordinate ranks, because the gift of the Spirit is adapted to every Church member".[6] Dunn describes the Pauline churches as charismatic communities, "characterized by mutual interdependence where each though he knows the Spirit for himself must depend on his fellow members for teaching and all sorts of other ministries".[7]

The assumption throughout is that leadership presupposes organisation: where there is little New Testament evidence for structure, offices or organisation, there must, therefore, be no leadership. The theological investigation of, for example, Paul's discussion of the church finds little mention of offices or structures. This conclusion is used as the basis for assuming the historical reality: there was no leadership.

In recent years the consensus view of this process of institutionalisation has quite rightly been challenged as being defective at these levels of presupposition and method.[8] It has been questioned whether the Pauline corpus alone provides sufficient evidence to reconstruct the situation as it existed. Scholars opposed to the consensus view argue that theologians have been guilty of an 'idealistic fallacy': ignoring the value of both historical context and social forces and, instead, defining the situation as it existed solely on the basis of the theological and corrective statements given in Paul's letters.[9]

c. *The Social Sciences*

A criticism of the presuppositions underlying the consensus view has been mounted using sociological techniques to understand the processes involved in the Pauline churches.[10] New Testament sociologists argue that the purely theological study divorces the original situation from history and that only by sociological study of the text can the Pauline church be placed within its social and historical context.[11]

---

[5] H. von Campenhausen, *Ecclesiastical Authority and Spiritual Power in the Church of the First Three Centuries* (ET: London, 1969), 58.

[6] E. Schweizer, *Church Order in the New Testament* (ET: London, 1979), 99.

[7] J. Dunn, *Unity and Diversity in the New Testament* (London, 1977), 114.

[8] Cf. B. Holmberg, *Sociology and the New Testament* (Minneapolis, 1990), 1-3. This is also extensively argued in A.L. Chapple, *Local Leadership in the Pauline churches: theological and social factors in its development: a study based on 1 Thessalonians, 1 Corinthians and Philippians,* unpublished PhD Thesis (Durham, 1984), 8-19.

[9] "The fallacy of idealism", B. Holmberg, *Paul and Power,* 205.

[10] Cf. B. Holmberg, *Paul and Power,* who uses Weber's classical sociology of authority, with modifications, 124 ff.; A. Chapple, *Local Leadership in the Pauline churches,* who uses sociology and social psychology to analyse concepts of group leadership; M. MacDonald, *The Pauline Churches. A Socio-historical Study of Institutionalization in the Pauline and Deutero-Pauline Writings* (Cambridge, 1988), who also uses sociological analysis, although she qualifies this by saying that she also places this within an historical framework.

[11] Cf. B. Holmberg, *Paul and Power,* 205.

The multi-disciplinary move to assess the New Testament data through sociological tools has generated considerable recent debate.[12] As Holmberg notes, however, the term 'sociological' describes a wide range of methods including, at one end, historical-descriptive study and, at the other, analysis of social situations using theoretical models.[13] P.J. Richter contrasts the analytical and the descriptive studies by saying of the former:

> A sociological approach to early Christianity will make use of the explanatory theories and hypotheses of the academic discipline of sociology and will be interested in explaining as well as describing the relevant social data.[14]

Frequently the sociological model which is used is that of Weber.[15] Holmberg writes: "To decide to use sociology in the interpretation of authority means to discuss *Max Weber*'s classical sociology of authority, which still dominates this field."[16] Initially derived, via Sohm, from Paul's teaching regarding the *charismata* in 1 Corinthians, this would appear to be the obvious model with which to analyse Pauline ecclesiology.

Clifford Geertz, in an important essay in 1966, however, criticises this ready return to the 'classical' sociologists. His comments are worth citing at length:

> Two characteristics of anthropological work on religion accomplished since the second world war strike me as curious ... One is that it has made no theoretical advances of major importance ... The second is that it draws what concepts it does use from a very narrowly defined intellectual tradition. There is Durkheim, Weber, Freud, or Malinowski ... But virtually no one even thinks of looking elsewhere—to philosophy, history, law, literature, or the 'harder' sciences—as these men themselves looked, for analytical ideas. ... If the anthropological study of religion is in fact in a state of general stagnation, I doubt it will be set going again by producing more minor variations on classical theoretical themes. ... In art, this solemn reduplication of the achievements of accepted masters is called academicism; and I think this is the proper name for our malady also. Only if we abandon ... that sweet sense of accomplishment which comes from

---

[12] See R. Scroggs, 'The Sociological Interpretation of the New Testament: The Present State of Research', *NTS* 26 (1979-80), 164-79; B. Holmberg, 'Sociological versus Theological Analysis of the Question concerning a Pauline Church Order', in ed. S. Pedersen, *Die Paulinische Literatur und Theologie* (Århus, 1980), 187-200; H.C. Kee, *Christian Origins in Sociological Perspective, Methods and Resources* (Philadelphia, 1980); B.J. Malina, *The New Testament World—Insights from Cultural Anthropology* (Atlanta, 1981); B.J. Malina, 'The Social Sciences and Biblical Interpretation', *Interpretation* 36 (1982), 229-42; J.G. Gager, 'Shall we Marry our Enemies?', *Interpretation* 36 (1982), 256-65; W.A. Meeks, 'The Social Context of Pauline Theology', *Interpretation* 36 (1982), 266-77; D. Tidball, *An Introduction to the Sociology of the New Testament* (Exeter, 1983); T.F. Best, 'The Sociological Study of the New Testament: Promise and Peril of a New Discipline', *SJT* 36 (1983), 181-94; A.J. Malherbe, *Social Aspects of Early Christianity* (Philadelphia, 1983); S.K. Stowers, 'The Social Sciences and the Study of Early Christianity', in ed. W.S. Green, *Studies in Judaism and its Greco-Roman Context, Approaches to Ancient Judaism* V (Atlanta, 1985), 149-81.

[13] B. Holmberg, *Sociology and the New Testament*, 4.

[14] P.J. Richter, 'Recent Sociological Approaches to the Study of the New Testament', *Religion* 14 (1984), 78.

[15] Cf. B. Holmberg, *Paul and Power*, 6; K. Giles, 'Demystifying Ordination with the help of Max Weber', *Tyndale Paper* 32 (July, 1987); M.Y. MacDonald, *The Pauline Churches*, 13-16.

[16] B. Holmberg, *Paul and Power*, 6.

parading habitual skills and address ourselves to problems sufficiently unclari-
fied as to make discovery possible, can we hope to achieve work which will not
just reincarnate that of the great men of the first quarter of this century, but
match it.[17]

It may thus be argued that analysis of leadership and the processes of institutionalisation carried out with the traditional or modified Weberian models of
social theory is likely to produce predictable results.

Furthermore, despite Richter's conclusion that "Any fully fledged sociological approach presupposes work at the proto-sociological level",[18] the data
used by those who adopt the Weberian model often remain as unhistorical as
those used to reach the earlier consensus view. This criticism is made of
Holmberg's work on authority in the New Testament church, *Paul and
Power*.[19] Judge writes of it:

> It couples with New Testament studies a strong admixture of modern sociology,
> as though social theories can be safely transposed across the centuries without
> verification. The basic question remains unasked: What are the social facts of
> life characteristic of the world to which the New Testament belongs? Until the
> painstaking field work is better done, the importation of social models that have
> been defined in terms of other cultures is methodologically no improvement on
> the 'idealistic fallacy'. We may fairly call it the 'sociological fallacy'.[20]

In the attempt to counter the 'idealistic fallacy', the proto-sociological work of
historical description has been neglected.[21] This 'historical' path is precisely
one of the avenues which Geertz suggests may prove more fruitful than returning to the 'classical' sociologists which produces predictable results.[22]

Richter recognises there is an historical problem inherent in applying
modern models of social theory to New Testament data. He writes:

> At the very least the historical distance of the New Testament data precludes
> many of the typical empirical techniques of sociology ... Sometimes there is
> simply not enough extant documentation to support the use of sociological
> models. In the case of New Testament data the problem of historical distance is
> compounded by cultural difference and distance.[23]

This constraint is often voiced, but whereas it is sometimes a valid proviso, in
many instances there is more primary source material than often realised.[24]

---

[17] C. Geertz, 'Religion as a Cultural System', in ed. M. Banton, *Anthropological Approaches to
the Study of Religion* (London, 1966), 1-2.

[18] P.J. Richter, 'Recent Sociological Approaches to the Study of the New Testament', 78.

[19] Holmberg stresses the importance of historical research, but only carries it out himself in a
limited way. B. Holmberg, *Paul and Power*, 1, "no serious theological discussion can in the long
run do without the connection with reality that is mediated by historical investigation".

[20] E.A. Judge, 'The Social Identity of the First Christians, A Question of Method in Religious
History', *Journal of Religious History* 11 (1980), 210.

[21] Richter's term, 'proto-sociological' implies the priority of historical-descriptive work over the
later analytical study.

[22] C. Geertz, 'Religion as a Cultural System', 1.

[23] P.J. Richter, 'Recent Sociological Approaches to the Study of the New Testament', 85.

[24] Cf. E.A. Judge's comment in the published discussion of the colloquy, B.J. Malina, 'The
Gospel of John in Sociolinguistic Perspective', *Protocol of the Forty-Eighth Colloquy, Center for
Hermeneutical Studies in Hellenistic and Modern Culture* (11 March, 1984), 51. He suggests, "The

This study demonstrates that, at least with regard to secular leadership in Roman Corinth,[25] there is sufficient epigraphic, numismatic and literary source material to conduct the necessary historical research to place the Pauline material relating to the nature of leadership within its historical context.

d. *Social History as a Method*

Epstein, discussing Roman politics, argues that "Roman political behaviour ... can be understood only by examining the social background in which leaders responded to deeply embedded private motives."[26] Equally, it could be added that the nature of Christian leadership in Roman, as well as later, times cannot fully be understood without first examining both the social background and the 'deeply embedded' motives of those leaders. Similarly, Engels, in a discussion of Roman Corinth, argues that "the problems Paul encountered at Corinth were a reflection of the nature of the city's people", and that "This conflict between authority and individualism is ultimately a reflection of the Corinthian people themselves".[27] This important step of placing the Corinthian church within its historical socio-cultural setting is one that has been too rarely attempted.

The theoretical advantages of one sociological method over another have long been argued.[28] The value of adding to the discussion here is limited. Instead, in this study descriptive-historical work will be undertaken. A fresh look at the secular sources will demonstrate that an understanding of the Graeco-Roman background to leadership in Corinth considerably clarifies the discussion which Paul has with the church in 1 Corinthians 1-6. It will show that the conclusions which this study affords could not be reached without this social historical method and yet they remain consistent, not merely with occasional verses from the New Testament, but with Paul's consecutive argument throughout 1 Corinthians 1-6.[29]

In recent years the Corinthian community has received renewed attention from this social historical perspective. A number of studies have successfully employed similar historical research into Graeco-Roman Corinthian society and have valuably clarified the situation in the Pauline community at Corinth. In this category are A.D. Litfin's, *St. Paul's Theology of Proclamation: An Investigation of 1 Corinthians 1-4 in the Light of Greco-Roman Rhetoric,*[30]

---

great problem of the New Testament people ... is that they incestuously concentrate all the time on their few texts, when there is a magnificent array of contextual material all around their texts, increasing rapidly every year. Much of this material is very relevant to New Testament studies".

[25] Throughout this work the adjective 'secular' is used to describe those things which pertain to the world and society outside the church. In this sense it is contrasted with the adjective 'Christian', without implying a negative connotation.

[26] D.F. Epstein, *Personal Enmity in Roman Politics—218-43 BC* (London, 1987), 127

[27] D. Engels, *Roman Corinth, An Alternative Model for the Classical City* (Chicago, 1990), 110.

[28] See the literature cited in footnote 12 above.

[29] It will not, then, be argued that the model of leadership derived from the particular cultural society of Roman Corinth may validly be transposed to other situations in order to determine the nature of leadership in other Pauline churches situated in different cultures.

[30] Unpublished D.Phil dissertation (Oxford University, 1983).

T.B. Savage's, *Power through Weakness: An Historical and Exegetical Examination of Paul's Understanding of the Ministry in 2 Corinthians,*[31] Peter Marshall's volume, *Enmity in Corinth: Social Conventions in Paul's Relations with the Corinthians,*[32] and Bruce Winter's work, *Philo and Paul among the Sophists: A Hellenistic Jewish and a Christian Response.*[33] The present work adds to this developing picture by concentrating on matters of leadership in both secular and Christian Corinthian society.

John Barclay describes the difficulty of reconstructing "the attitudes and arguments of the other side" in New Testament exegesis as 'mirror-reading'.[34] The problem is clear and it is "an extremely difficult task, as prone to misinterpretation as the incidental overhearing of one end of a telephone conversation".[35] The problems inherent in mirror-reading the social situation, however, can be diluted by using the relevant and available evidence which can place, for example, 1 Corinthians within its social context. The information gleaned largely from "one end of a telephone conversation" can be carefully added to what is already known about the circumstances in order to reconstruct the other side of the conversation. The difficulties of mirror-reading are at their greatest using the first method described above which led to the consensus view. Social historical enquiry, however, would appear to be a better tool with which to make a safer reconstruction.

---

[31] Unpublished PhD dissertation (Cambridge University, 1986).

[32] (Tübingen, 1987).

[33] Unpublished PhD dissertation (Macquarie University, 1988).

[34] J.M.G. Barclay, 'Mirror-Reading a Polemical Letter: Galatians as a Test Case', *JSNT* 31 (1987), 73-93.

[35] M.D. Hooker, 'Were There False Teachers in Colossae?', in ed. M.D. Hooker, *From Adam to Christ* (Cambridge, 1990), 121.

CHAPTER TWO

EVIDENCE OF SECULAR LEADERS IN CORINTH

1. *Introduction*

In this chapter the available literary and non-literary sources will be assessed in order to describe the administration in first century Roman Corinth. Many commentaries on 1 and 2 Corinthians and other secondary works include short introductions to this colony. The aim here is to focus simply on that evidence useful for determining the structures of leadership in first century Corinth.[1]

First, some of the literary sources concerning the colonisation of the city will be examined. Secondly, the extent and nature of the non-literary source material will be assessed. Thirdly, the particular honorary posts in the Corinthian administration will be outlined. Finally, some notable instances from the epigraphic evidence of Corinthian leaders will be discussed.

2. *The Colonisation of Roman Corinth*

One of the primary distinctions of first century Corinth, which precludes drawing extensive parallels with many of its neighbouring cities, is that it had been refounded as a Roman colony in 44 BC. The significance of this historical datum is too readily ignored and a mistaken assumption is often that extensive parallels can readily be drawn between Roman Corinth and either the contemporary Greek cities or the earlier Greek city of Corinth.

Further to this it may be noted that Roman colonies themselves significantly differed from each other depending on when they were founded, by whom and for what purpose. Notably, they differed in terms of the exact definitions and distributions of leadership rôles within the city. It will be important, therefore, to concentrate on the extant information available from Corinth itself in the first and early second centuries in order to construct a picture of the administration and leadership of this important colony.[2]

The city of Corinth was refounded as a Roman colony by Julius Caesar after a 100 year period of desertion. There was no local infrastructure for the emperor to build on and the initial colonisation included freedmen.[3] In many

---

[1] W.A. Meeks, 'The Urban Environment of Pauline Christianity', *Seminar Papers: Society of Biblical Literature* (California, 1980), 119-20, rightly stresses the importance of placing Paul's communities within their particular civic background, whether it be Corinth, Philippi or Ephesus.

[2] See the extensive table of data compiled in Appendix A.

[3] Cf. Strabo, *Geography* 8.6.23.C, "Now after Corinth had remained deserted for a long time, it was restored again, because of its favourable position, by the deified Caesar, who colonised it with people who for the most part belonged to the freedman class". Cf. also Pausanias, *Description of*

ways Corinth may, therefore, be considered a new city, bound by few cultural traditions, other than those peculiar to a Roman colony and settled by people readily wanting to establish themselves. In this sense Corinth differs from many of its immediate neighbours in Greece.

Strabo, who passed through Corinth on his way to Rome in 44 BC, points out that Corinth—possibly the most celebrated of Caesar's colonies, *Colonia Laus Julia Corinthiensis*—was resettled for the most part with freedmen, for whom the Greek language would probably have been more familiar than the upper class Latin. Its site was almost certainly chosen for its mercantile potential.[4] These two factors—the predominantly freedman social character and the concern for economic trade—greatly affected the way in which this particular colony developed.

For many of the settlers the move to a new colony will have been in itself a step up the social ladder and the core of technical people, artisans, teachers, secretaries and financial investors, with which Corinth was initially populated created a climate which lent itself to social mobility. Many would have been on the look-out for further promotion in society and it is interesting that it was in Corinth that positions of city government were open to people of this socially mobile class of freedmen.

The policy of government was similar under both the Republic and the Empire—to maintain the ascendancy of the wealthier and higher classes. The importance of wealth and pomp within the city was correspondingly high. This may be seen principally in the buildings and festivals. It is clear from inscriptions on first century Corinthian buildings that new buildings were perpetually being erected or old ones reconstructed on an ever grander scale, compelled by the rising expectations of luxury.[5]

The wealth of this great city belonged to the élite leading figures of the administration. Salaries were a relatively low expense in local government and were paid to doctors and the lower grade employees of the city, if free men. Otherwise it was only small allowances which were given to the magistrates—almost all the costs being borne by the munificence of the rich few.

Grain supervisors were expected artificially to reduce the prices of this valuable commodity by underwriting the losses of selling low price grain. If the grain shortage cost the poor too dearly, then he would lose his popularity—something which the rich held on to at great cost. The *gymnasiarchs* would

---

Greece 2.1.2, "Corinth is no longer inhabited by any of the old Corinthians, but by colonists sent out by the Romans". See also E.D. Salmon, *Roman Colonization Under the Republic* (London, 1969), 135.

4   Corinth commands a strategic position on the isthmus between the Corinthian Gulf and the Saronic Gulf. The canal which now crosses the isthmus is much later. During Paul's time, however, ships and cargo were hauled overland at this point to avoid the much longer trip around the Peloponnese. See Strabo, *Geography* 8.6.20-23.

5   Cf. the catalogue in T.B. Savage, *Power through Weakness: An Historical and Exegetical Examination of Paul's Understanding of the Ministry in 2 Corinthians,* unpublished PhD dissertation (Cambridge University, 1986), 42.

supply oil free of charge at the games. The priests would provide victims for sacrifice at their own expense. The *agonothetes* would offer hospitality free of charge to the athletes during the games.[6] Such leaders were motivated at once by civic patriotism and personal ambition.[7] To the extent that such generosity was prompted by the desire for popularity it was also not a voluntary contribution. The plebeians could bring to play a considerable degree of public opinion against a leader, which went as far as to force his hand for him. Those in power had themselves to be rich enough to sustain their honorary post and their popularity.

A.H.M. Jones suggests that,

> From the beginning of the second century, if not earlier, there are signs that the governing classes of the cities were beginning to regard civic office as an irksome task rather than a coveted honour. The extravagant standard of living which the cities adopted and the emperors had failed effectively to curb threw a heavy burden on the civic officers, and the increasing demands of the central government ... laid a yet heavier financial responsibility on them.[8]

It was inevitable, therefore, that the demands of finance will have debarred many from accepting the offer of being in the curial class. Where curial rank was limited to the wealthiest of the citizens, it exaggerated all the more the differentiation between the rulers and the plebeians.

In Corinth, the city was divided for administrative purposes into tribes (*tribus,* φυλαί), of which the names of the following are known: Agrippia, Atia, Aurelia, Calpurnia, Claudia, Domitia, Hostilia, Livia, Maneia, Vatinia, Vinicia. Three social groupings divided the population: the non-citizens, the citizen voters, and the city council and annual magistrates.

3. *The Extant Non-Literary Evidence*

It is most important to gain as full a picture as possible of the leadership situation; for this it is necessary to inspect both the literary and non-literary evidence which is available. Barrow supports this approach, suggesting:

---

6   D.J. Geagan, 'Notes on the Agonistic Institutions of Roman Corinth', *Greek, Roman and Byzantine Studies* IV (1968), 69, suggests that out of all the liturgies in the *cursus honorum* at Corinth, it was the *agonothesia* which was the most burdensome. It was the *agonothetes* who subsidised the expense of the games and entertained the officials. In the Western Roman colonies, where the games were of lesser importance, it was the other magistrates who bore the expense of the festivals. This importance is seen in that the *agonothesia* could be placed either before or after the quinquennial duovirate in a person's *cursus honorum,* see footnote 44 below.

7   Cf. A.H.M. Jones, *The Greek City, From Alexander to Justinian* (Oxford, 1966), 249, "A man who wished to make a name for himself could no longer under the Roman peace lead his fellow citizens to victory in war, nor had he, as Plutarch remarks, much chance of suppressing tyrannies or winning fame as a wise legislator, when the constitution was fixed by the *lex provinciae.* If blessed with rhetorical gifts, he might cover himself with glory by persuading the emperor to make the city an assize town or a centre of the imperial cult, but once again the most obvious way of making himself prominent was to spend lavishly on the magistracies which he held and to give shows and feasts and distributions and buildings".

8   A.H.M. Jones, *The Greek City, From Alexander to Justinian,* 146.

The easiest way to give a picture of Greece would be to copy out the statements of Strabo, Dio Chrysostom and Pausanias, together with a few sentences from Plutarch himself. But it would be a picture inconsistent with the assessment which can be gathered from inscriptions and from incidental evidence in the literature.[9]

A considerable number of inscriptions covering the period 44 BC-AD 267 have been discovered.[10] Although many have been badly mutilated,[11] there are some 1500 texts dating from the Imperial period, including 1200 texts from the first and second centuries AD.[12] This epigraphic material is supplemented by a significant quantity of numismatic material from the site.[13] There is also a certain amount of literary material which is closely related to Corinth.[14] These data are valuable source material for the study of Corinthian leadership in the Roman period.

Whereas Plutarch, Dio Chrysostom and other writers of the period give a general understanding of leadership characteristics in the Graeco-Roman world, specific detailed prosopographical information about the honorary offices held by a considerable number of individuals is available from the epigraphic and numismatic data (see Appendix A).[15] Neither the literary nor non-literary sources for first century Corinthian life, although supportive, make the other redundant—they are both essential if as complete a picture as possible is to be established.[16]

---

[9] Cf. R.H. Barrow, *Plutarch and his Times* (London, 1967), 9.

[10] The American School of Classical Studies at Athens has produced extensive archaeological reports of inscriptions from Roman Corinth. Cf. especially, B.D. Meritt, *Corinth—Greek Inscriptions 1896-1927 Corinth: Results* viii, Part I (Cambridge, Massachusetts, 1931); and A.B. West, *Corinth—Latin Inscriptions 1896-1920 Corinth: Results* viii, Part II (Cambridge, Massachusetts, 1931); J.H. Kent, *Corinth—Inscriptions 1926-1950 Corinth: Results* viii, Part III (Princeton, 1966).

[11] Corinth was sacked by the Herulians in AD 267 and again by the Goths in AD 395, and this caused much of the damage. Other damage was probably the result of some of the many earthquakes which the city has suffered, including a particularly heavy earthquake in 1858 after which the old site was abandoned and New Corinth built a few miles to the North-East.

[12] There are still large residential and industrial areas which have not been completely excavated.

[13] Cf. especially, K.M. Edwards, *Corinth, Coins 1896-1929*, VI (Cambridge, Massachusetts, 1933); and M. Amandry, 'Le Monnayage des duovirs corinthiens', *Bulletin de Correspondance Hellénique, Supplément* XV (1988). Amandry has completed some excellent work on the coins of Corinth, and has consequently revised much of the dating reached by Edwards.

[14] There are no detailed works bearing on leadership in Corinth in particular. A small number of writers who were in some way connected with first century Corinth, however, do provide some material concerned more generally with leadership in Graeco-Roman society. The principal sources for the first and second centuries are Dio Chrysostom, Plutarch, Favorinus and Epictetus. J. Murphy O'Connor, *St Paul's Corinth—Texts and Archaeology* (Wilmington, 1983), 94, 98, argues that, within their own writings, both Plutarch and Dio Chrysostom betray first-hand knowledge of Roman Corinth.

[15] No study to date has sought to tabulate all the epigraphic and numismatic evidence for first and early second century Corinthian leadership.

[16] Cf. M.N. Tod, *Sidelights on Greek History, Three Lectures on the Light thrown by Greek Inscriptions on the Life and Thought of the Ancient World* (Oxford, 1932), 24, writes, "The illumination afforded by a literary record is often dim and diffused. A situation, a policy, a character, an age may be summed up in a phrase. We see the outlines only, the salient facts, but little or no detail.

It may be that epigraphic evidence gives only a limited view of the economic growth during the first two centuries, but it does offer a more complete and detailed picture of the local government institutions of a Roman colony in the first century (there were only two others in Achaea, *viz* Patrea and Delos).

There is an interesting development in the prevalence respectively of Latin and Greek in inscriptions over the first two centuries. The earlier inscriptions from the colony are predominantly written in Latin. This is to be expected since Latin was clearly the administrative language, but this does not mean that Latin was the most widely spoken language amongst the people. It may be seen from the numismatic evidence that Latin remained the official language until as late as AD 69.[17] During Hadrian's reign, however, there is a clear change which brings Greek to the forefront as the epigraphic language.

Nearly all the inscriptions which can reasonably be dated to the first century are official documents. These inscriptions "consist of dedications to divinities and the Emperors, texts that record gifts of buildings, copies of official rescripts, gravestones, and statues erected or honors bestowed by vote of the city council".[18] Kent notes that, "nothing has been found which makes a major contribution to the history of the province ... On the other hand, the inscriptions contain a great amount of miscellaneous information, both explicit and implicit, concerning local affairs of the Roman colony".[19]

Many of the inscriptions bear witness to the benefactions of some generous individuals—benefactions which include statues, pavements, small structures and whole buildings. As well as information regarding benefactions, it is also possible to construct a detailed picture of the local administrative institutions in Corinth.

4. *The Cursus Honorum*

Colonies differed in terms of the exact definitions and distributions of leadership rôles within the city.[20] Although much is the same throughout the Roman East, it is important that the general picture of civic administration is balanced with the specific details which can be obtained for Corinth itself in the first

---

Inscriptions rarely diffuse their light: they illuminate vividly, intensely, one small spot, leaving all around in darkness".

[17] D.J. Geagan, 'Notes on the Agonistic Institutions of Roman Corinth', 71, remarks, "Even at the time when Corinthian civic documents were written in Latin, Greek remained the official language at Isthmia. Thus it continued to be used for the lists of victors; even in Latin documents the Greek genitive plural was merely transliterated when the names of games were recorded". The change during Hadrian's reign was the result of the emperor's strong Greek influence as a devoted Hellenophile. AD 69 was the date at which Corinth stopped minting its own coins.

[18] Cf. J.H. Kent, *Corinth—Inscriptions,* 18.

[19] J.H. Kent, *Corinth—Inscriptions,* 20.

[20] Cf. however, F.F. Abbott & A.C. Johnson, *Municipal Administration in the Roman Empire* (New York, 1968), 79, "In the cities of the Orient the system of liturgies was one of their most characteristic features, and here it was developed to its fullest extent as a regular part of the civic administration".

century. For this reason an extensive table of leading figures from the colony at Corinth has been drawn up.[21]

The chief magistrates of a colony were *duoviri iure dicundo*. They were annually elected in pairs, serving as chief justices (since Roman colonies had no praetors), and executive officers of the council (*decurio*). Almost throughout the Roman colonies this was the highest judicial post that could be filled. From both inscriptions and coins in Corinth, it is possible to identify 58 *duoviri* and 11 others who were granted *ornamenta* of the *duoviri*.[22] It is clear that in Corinth the rôle was open to freedmen as well.[23] *Duoviri* had to fulfil specific 'qualifications' in order to be elected: they had to have integrity, be freeborn and be members of the community. It was further necessary to provide a down-payment on assuming the post, as an institutionalized election promise. This varied in amount from city to city and from candidate to candidate, but evidence suggests that it was by no means an inconsiderable sum.[24] One reason for this *Antrittsgeld* was to prove that a candidate for the post was financially capable of sustaining the job, for it was an unsalaried post, involving much outlay of capital.

The considerable financial outlay required of a magistrate can be seen from the *Lex Coloniæ Genetivæ Juliæ*. The *duovir* is obliged to arrange for the public a gladiatorial or dramatic show for a period of four days, financed to no less than the sum of 2,000 sesterces of his own money, and no more than the same sum of public money.[25]

Every fourth year there was the additional responsibility of taking the census and revising the membership of the city council or *ordo decurionum*, and in these years the title was that of *duovir quinquennalis*—a yet more highly prized post than that of *duovir*.[26] There are instances from Corinth

---

[21] See Appendix A.

[22] Occasionally the *ornamenta* of *duovir quinquennalis, duovir, praefectus, agonothetes, aedilis* and *decurio* are recorded. Such people did not actually serve in office but were awarded an honorary title in return for benefactions.

[23] This is particularly unusual. See Appendix A. 46, 92. J.W. Kubitschek in his article in *Pauly's Real-Encyclopädie* I (Stuttgart, 1894) on the aedile points out that a major election qualification for the post was to be free-born.

[24] P. Garnsey in 'Honorarium Decurionatus', *Historia* 20 (1971), 323, writes, "The levying of a fee on incoming magistrates was an obvious way of financing games and other events which were held to be essential to the life of the city". This was not so much the case for Corinth, because of the specific rôle of the agonothete. For the qualifications of the *duovir* cf. Liebenam's article on the office in *Pauly's Real-Encyclopädie* V (Stuttgart, 1905), although regarding *Ingenuität*, both in the West and in Corinth, freedmen were often not debarred from becoming *duoviri;* cf. E.G. Hardy, *Three Spanish Charters and other documents* (Oxford, 1912), 10.

[25] Aediles were expected to provide similar entertainments, but lasting only three days, using no more than 1,000 sesterces of public money and no less than 2,000 sesterces of their own money; E.G. Hardy, *Three Spanish Charters and other documents,* caps. LXX, LXXI.

[26] The Roman counting system was inclusive, and, therefore, it is every *fourth* year that the quinquennial duovir is elected.

where a *duovir quinquennalis* held the post more than once.[27] This suggests an exceptional honour, and also the possession of considerable wealth.

In the instance of a *duovir* being away for a period, a local *praefectus iure dicundo* was appointed by the *duovir* in his stead.[28]

Until the year AD 69 it was customary in Corinth for one or both of the *duoviri* to have their names and the title IIVIR or IIVIR QUIN impressed on the coinage of the colony during their term of office. Coins were not minted annually, however, but only when the need arose which means that there is not a complete list of *duoviri* for this period. Nonetheless the evidence which does exist considerably fills out the picture obtained from inscriptions alone. The specific dates of tenure of certain *duoviri* is not always clear from the coins. It becomes easier to construct a chronology, however, where the names on coins and inscriptions tally.[29]

The *duoviri* worked closely with two aediles who were also elected annually. Their responsibilities were the maintenance of public streets and buildings, managing the commercial *agorai*[30] and public revenue. They also served as judges in commercial and financial litigation.[31] In most colonies aediles also carried responsibility for the city games. In Corinth, however, this was taken care of by the *agonothetes* since the games at Corinth were considered internationally famous. It is clear that aedileship was an appointment requiring much financial outlay, and a prospective candidate for this post had necessarily to prove his financial capability. This was done, as for the *duoviri,* with an election down-payment, but also there is much evidence to show that a candidate would, for example, lay a pavement or finance part or all of a building as a benefaction. An important first century example of this is Erastus who laid a pavement in front of the Corinthian Theatre; Appendix A. 76,

---

[27] Cf. P Aebutius Sp f, Appendix A. 4, 92, 95, and C Julius Laconis Spartiaticus, Appendix A. 101.

[28] This might happen if some prominent non-Corinthian or the emperor were *duovir*, and, therefore, often absent from the city. There is evidence to show that in Corinth *praefecti iure dicundo* were occasionally appointed by the citizen body and by decree of the city council, cf. Appendix A. 92.

[29] Cf. M. Insteius Tectus and C. Heius Pamphilus in Appendix A. 92, 93.

[30] It is thus that they were called ἀγορανόμοι in Greek. D.J. Geagan, 'Notes on the Agonistic Institutions of Roman Corinth', 75, points out some interesting discoveries regarding this title in Corinth: "There is evidence for an *agoranomia* of the Isthmian festival. There is no certain instance of the title *agoranomos* being applied to a civic official or magistrate of Roman Corinth. Although the title *aedilis* is rendered *agoranomos* elsewhere, the only possible equivalent found at Corinth is *oikonomos* (Romans 16:23). Only three epigraphical references to the *agoranomia* or to an *agoranomos* are preserved from Roman Corinth: a dedication (SEG XI 50) indicated that 'Cn Pompeius Zenas dedicated to Dionysos a tenth part (?) when he was *agoranomos* of Zeus.' The *agoranomos* cited in Kent, # 308 clearly belongs to a religious organization, for which this stone contains a fragment of the statutes. The third (IG IV 203) relates the benefactions of P Licinius Priscus to the Isthmian sanctuary. Lines 23-27 indicate that 'the same man built the stoa next to the stadium with its vaulted chambers and adornments for the sake of the agoranomia'. It is only logical to conclude that such gifts to the Isthmian sanctuary would have been connected with an office and not the Roman aedileship".

[31] J.W. Kubitschek, s.v. 'Aedilis', 458-464, lists the tasks of the aedile under three headings, *cura annonae, cura urbis* and *cura ludorum*.

praenomen nomen ERASTUS.PRO.AEDILITatE S.P.STRAVIT. "Erastus in return for his aedileship laid (the pavement) at his own expense".[32]

Not only did the post of *aedilis* involve considerable financial outlay, it was also a very highly honoured position. Kubitschek lists the requirements of free birth,[33] no criminal record, and an honourable life. In addition, since the time of Augustus, aediles had to be at least 30 years old.[34] The honour placed upon this rôle can be seen in that the aedile was allowed to wear the highly sought after purple *toga praetexta.*

Kent suggests that in many colonies, but *not* Corinth, the combination of *duoviri* and *aediles* was collectively called the *quattuorviri.*[35] There is, however, in Appendix A. 33 the anonymous reference to a *quattuorvir.*

Decuriones, or members of the council (*ordo*), were elected every four years from among the *aediles* and *duoviri* during the quinquennial duovirate. They normally held the position for life. They also had to provide a down-payment on election to the council, thus proving that they were of sufficient financial means to carry the responsibilities. It is suggested by Fiebiger that there were normally 100 decurions, but frequently this number was considerably less.[36] Again this was seen as a highly honoured position; Fiebiger points out that "die D.-nen bildeten mit ihren Familien den *ordo splendidissimus* der Landstädte". Most of the principal responsibilities rested with this council. They had considerable influence on the executive *duoviri,* since many of the tasks of the *duoviri* had to be formally ratified by a vote of the *ordo.* It was in this body that the major concentration of power lay in any city. The *duovir* was limited in what he could do without the support of the decurions.

The *curator annonae* was appointed only during times of famine. His responsibility also involved considerable financial outlay.[37] This emergency post supplemented the normal work of the aediles and involved ensuring that there was not only sufficient bread in the city, but also that it was at an affordable price. Inevitably this meant that the *curator annonae* had artificially to reduce the price of grain either by finding cheaper sources or by subsidising the prices himself.[38] One particular instance regarding Corinth is the famine of

---

[32] See the later discussion of Erastus in Chapter Four below, 46-56.

[33] This was not necessarily always the case in Imperial Corinth.

[34] Evidence from Spain suggests that the age may more commonly have been 25 years; cf. E.G. Hardy, *Three Spanish Charters,* cap LVI. This changed after Augustus.

[35] Cf. J.H. Kent, *Corinth—Inscriptions,* 27.

[36] Fiebiger, 'Decurio' in *Pauly's Real-Encyclopädie* IV (Stuttgart, 1901).

[37] C.P. Jones, *The Roman World of Dio Chrysostom* (Cambridge, Mass. and London, 1978), 19, "In times of scarcity, when the regular machinery of the city became inadequate, generosity was essential. At this time there might be a call for a collective gift from the wealthy, a subscription (*epidosis*), or one of them might be induced to be the 'commissioner of the grain supply' (*epimeletes agoras, euthenias*). This was not a recurrent office (*arche*), but a position created in emergency and compulsory on the person elected, and thus a 'public service' or 'liturgy' (*leitourgia*)."

[38] Cf. Dio, *Orationes* 46.8, "Have I produced the most grain of all and then put it under lock and key, raising the price?"

AD 51 when the *curator annonae* was Ti. Claudius Dinippus.[39] If the grain shortage cost the poor too dearly, the *curator annonae* would risk serious civil dislocation and rioting.

It is unclear whether the *quaestor* or ταμίας, found only in a few Corinthian inscriptions, was a provincial or a municipal office. It is suggested that it was an annual post, and the lowest in the *cursus honorum*. There are also inscriptions referring to a chief engineer or *praefectus fabrorum*.[40] By the Imperial period this had become a military post of some seniority. Originally it had been an engineering staff officer.[41]

One further area of responsibility which carried especial prestige in Corinth was that of the organiser of the public games. There were normally both an *agonothetes* and a number of *hellenodikai*. The former was in charge of organising and financing the games and was assisted by sometimes ten *hellenodikai*. There is much specific evidence of these posts from the Corinthian epigraphic sources.[42] These games were of particular importance for Corinth since the colony hosted three major festivals: the biennial Isthmian games, the quadrennial Caesarean games, and the imperial contests. The most prestigious of the games was the Isthmian games, which ranked lower than the Panhellenic Olympic games, but above those of Delphi and Nemea. Wiseman points out that it was during the reign of Augustus that the Isthmian games was reinstituted and necessarily brought with it an immediate growth in the prosperity of the city.

The *agonothetes* contributed personally to the financing of the games, and therefore it is possible that these people were some of the most wealthy in the city.[43] This particular office was generally considered the highest honour in the *cursus honorum,* but there are a few exceptions to this.[44] Geagan divides the agonothetic inscriptions into four groups; those who had been *agonothetai* of the Isthmian and Caesarean as well as the imperial contests; those who had been *isagogeis* of the imperial contests and *agonothetai* of the Isthmian and Caesarean; those who were merely *agonothetai* of the Isthmian and Caesarean;

---

[39] Cf. Ti. Claudius Dinippus in Appendix A. 65. Cf. also B.W. Winter, 'Secular and Christian Responses to Corinthian Famines', *Tyndale Bulletin* 40 (1989), 86-106.

[40] Cf. anon., Appendix A. 18; Ti. Claudius Dinippus, Appendix A. 65; Aulus Arrius Proclus, Appendix A. 42; and Sextus Olius Secundus, Appendix A. 113.

[41] A. Bagdikian, *The Civic Officials of Roman Corinth,* unpublished MA dissertation (University of Vermont, 1953), 8.

[42] D.J. Geagan, 'Notes on the Agonistic Institutions of Roman Corinth', 74 points out, "There is evidence of multiple *agonothetai,* although there would seem to have been a single *agonothesia*". This may be since the cost of the games was so high that it was necessary to have multiple *agonothetai* in order to share the considerable costs. Cf. Appendix A. 64, 119, 152 and possibly also Appendix A. 129, 135.

[43] D.J. Geagan, 'Notes on the Agonistic Institutions of Roman Corinth', 69, suggests that it was the most burdensome of the liturgies in the *cursus honorum.*

[44] D.J. Geagan, 'Notes on the Agonistic Institutions of Roman Corinth', 28 notes that in Appendix A. 118, the agonothetic *ornamenta* occur between the duoviral and the quinquennial *ornamenta;* and in Appendix A. 157, 78 and perhaps Appendix A. 47 the agonothetic *ornamenta* are placed highest in the *cursus honorum.*

and the fourth group is those who were *isagogeis* of the imperial contests and never filled an *agonothesia*.[45]

5. *Leading Figures in Roman Corinth*

In the northeastern area of the agora a fragmented inscription is attributed to a certain Marcus Antonius Achaicus. He appears to have been an unusually prominent Corinthian and was elected to every one of the municipal offices in the city.[46] It is possible to determine that he was almost certainly a very wealthy man since he was voted *curator annonae,* and he dedicated at his own expense monuments in both Corinth and Argos to the imperial procurator of Achaea, Paetus.[47] It may well have been that these monuments were a repayment for some gift from Paetus, and they certainly show that Achaicus wanted it to be known that he had given so much from his wealth. There is the further information from an inscription in the southeastern area of the agora that Achaicus served as *agonothetes* in the Isthmian, the Nervanean Trajanean and the Caesarean games. This inscription shows something of the high respect in which this man was held, for it states that he was honoured after his death by decree of the city council with decurional honours.[48] It is probable that his public career spanned the period from AD 70-100, which was followed by up to two decades of semi-retirement. The importance of public esteem, titles and wealth is here shown to be great.

The second person who will be looked at provides a prime example of some of these leadership symbols. He can be dated with some certainty as a contemporary of Paul in Corinth. Tiberius Claudius Dinippus was honoured no less than 10 times with almost identical inscriptions dedicated to his name.[49] By comparing the inscriptions it is possible to make this reconstruction:

> TI. CLAUDIO.P.F.fab.
> DINIPPO.II.VIR.II.VIr.QUINQ.
> AUGURI. SACERDOTI.VICTORiae
> BRITANNIC.TRIBUNO.mILitum.LEG.VI
> HISPANENsis.PRAEF.FABRUM.
> III.ANNONAe.curATORI.AGONOTHETE.
> NERONEon.caesareon.et.ISTHmion
> et caeSAREon.tribules.tribus

---

[45] The *agonothetes* was assisted by an *isogogeus,* and there are a number of inscriptions of individuals who announced that they had been *isogogeis;* a further official was known as the *pyrophoros* who may have been the bearer of fire for the sacred altars, and, as D.J. Geagan, 'Notes on the Agonistic Institutions of Roman Corinth', 76, points out, this official could have been a child. There are a number of inscriptions celebrating this post.

[46] The inscription (Appendix A. 38) abbreviates much information concerning his public career—from aeD.PRAEF.I.D.CUR.ann.ii.vir.et.II VIR.quinq., it may be determined that Achaicus was *aedilis, praefectus iure dicundo, curator annonae, duovir* and *duovir quinquennalis.*

[47] Cf. Appendix A. 126.

[48] Appendix A. 38.

[49] Appendix A. 65.

This man was especially popular since he was elected *curator annonae* three times. This suggests that there were a series of famines in which the grain supply was severely hampered making it necessary for artificial manipulation of the market.[50] It is in this situation where a rich man would have been indispensable to the plebs by keeping the price of grain low. This was a very powerful way of gaining popularity. Dinippus not only fulfilled this post on three separate occasions, but he also was *duovir, duovir quinquennalis* and *agonothetes* of the Neronean, Caesarean and Isthmian games; furthermore he was priest of the Britannic victory, augur, military tribune of the Spanish 6th Legion and *praefectus fabrum*. This man was a good example of the characteristics which the Corinthian people, both plebs and council, admired, and as a direct result he gained great standing and popularity.

In addition to wealth and generosity, there were other grounds for gaining personal reputation in first century Corinth. There is evidence of a certain Marcus Valerius Taurinus who was honoured by vote of the city council for being a philosopher and a good orator, and having a fine character.[51]

$$\begin{array}{c}
\text{Μ. Βαλ[έριον] Μ. υ[ιον]} \\
\text{Ταυρε[ινο]ν, φ[ιλ-]} \\
\text{[όσο]φο[ν - - -]} \\
\text{[ρήτο]ρ[α ἀγαθόν].} \\
\text{ἡ [πόλις ἀρετῆς]} \\
\text{ἔνεκε[ν]} \\
\text{ψ(ηφίσματι) β(ουλῆς)}
\end{array}$$

Nothing more is known of this person, but it shows the high regard placed on wisdom, eloquence and good character in a leader.[52]

Spartiaticus, son of Laco, has a number of imperial and municipal offices listed, including procurator, military tribune, *duovir quinquennalis* and *agonothetes*. Notably, he is recorded in an inscription as having been granted equestrian rank under Claudius.[53] There was a great desire to move up the social ladder in imperial colonial cities, and from Corinth there are a number of examples where this has happened.[54]

---

50 Cf. B.W. Winter, 'Secular and Christian Responses to Corinthian Famines', 86-106, where he argues that some of the problems faced by the Corinthian Christian community and alluded to in 1 Cor 7.26 (the present ἀνάγκη) are the direct result of famine during the periods when Dinippus was curator of the grain supply.

51 Cf. Appendix A. 148.

52 Lucius Maecius Faustinus was also honoured by decree of the council for possessing similar qualities to those of Taurinus. Cf. Appendix A. 103.

53 Cf. Appendix A. 101.

54 Cornelius Pulcher also gained great honours *although* he was originally of freedman stock. J.H. Kent, *Corinth—Inscriptions*, says of him in inscription # 138, "Son of Tiberius Cornelius Pulcher of the tribe Fabia and perhaps a native of Epidauros where he served as agonothetes of the Asklepiaia, Gnaeus Cornelius Pulcher possibly made Corinth his home and certainly was a patron of the city. In Corinthian municipal affairs his earliest office seems to have been that of *praefectus iure dicundo;* he was later at various times *curator annonae, duovir quinquennalis,* and agonothetes of the festival Trajanea and of the festival Isthmia. In the Imperial service he was first a military tribune of Legion IV Scythia, later serving as procurator of Epirus and *iuridicus* of Egypt and Alexandria. In Greece he rose to high provincial office, being Helladarch of the Achaean League,

Lucius Castricius Regulus is described by Kent as one of the most prominent as well as one of the richest Corinthians of his time. He held a number of
municipal offices and was the first to preside over the Isthmian games of New
Corinth. Kent further notes from the inscription that,

> The first Corinthian agonothete in Roman times not only saw to it that buildings
> in the sanctuary were extensively repaired, but when the job was finished, he
> put on a gigantic feast to celebrate both the completion of the building program
> and the return of the games to Corinthian management. It is not improbable that
> he also made a large personal contribution to the cost of renovating the Isthmian
> sanctuary.[55]

It is also shown from the inscription that he expanded the programme of the
games to include an athletic contest for girls and a poetry or song competition.
This inscription was erected in accordance with the decree of the city council,
but the cost was sponsored by Regulus' son. It is certain that during the early
years of the century this man will have gained much political support and
friendships by these acts of generosity.

The final individual to be noted is Publius Aelius Sospinus. The inscription
dedicated to him reads,

> Because of his upright character and general excellence, the council and the
> citizens set up this monument to honour Publius Aelius Sospinus the orator
> (who is) the grandson of Antonius Sospis who was *agonothetes* three times (and
> who is the) son of Publius Aelius Apollodotus and Antonia Sosipatra, by vote of
> the city council.[56]

This orator was recognised both by the council and the citizens of Corinth for
his excellence. What is of particular interest is this man's connection with the
more well-known Plutarch. In the *Moralia,* Plutarch makes a number of references to this person when they meet in Corinth. This shows something of
Plutarch's links with Corinth, but it is also valuable to note the esteem in
which Plutarch holds this Corinthian man. In *Moralia* 723, Plutarch writes

> During the Isthmian games, the second time Sospis was exhibitor (agonothete),
> I avoided the other banquets, at which he entertained a great many foreign
> visitors at once, and several times entertained all the citizens. Once, however,
> when he entertained in his home his closest friends, all men of learning, I was
> present too.

In this gathering are Herodes, described as the professor of rhetoric, and
presented with special honour;[57] Protogenes, the professor of literature; and
Praxiles, a geographer. In a similar vein Sospis himself is described as a

---

and high priest of Greece; during the reign of Hadrian, he was appointed priest of Hadrian
Panhellenius and Panhellenic archon". (See Appendix A. 146).

[55] Cf. Appendix A. 59.

[56] Appendix A. 8, ['Η β]ουλὴ κ[αὶ ὁ δ]ῆμος [Π.] Αἴλιον Σώσπιν[ον] ῥήτορα, ἔκγονον Ἀν[τω]νίου
Σώσπιδος το[ῦ] τρὶς ἀγωνοθέτου, υἱὸν Π. Ἀιλίου Ἀπολλοδό[τ]ου καὶ Ἀντων[ί]ας Σωσιπάτρας, ἀνδρα-
γαθίας εἵνεκεν καὶ τῆς ἄλλης ἀρετῆς [ἀ]πάσης ἀνέστ[ησ]εν, Ψ(ηφίσματι) Β(ουλῆς). See also Appendix
A. 143.

[57] Herodes Atticus is celebrated in the Corinthian inscriptions. See Appendix A. 44.

teacher of rhetoric.[58] Clearly it is educated and eloquent men, such as Sospinus, who are admired and supported as leaders in Corinth, and it is such men that Plutarch particularly praises.

6. *Conclusions*

By using the available source material, it has been possible in this chapter to describe the administrative structures for leadership in first century Roman Corinth and the type of people who colonised the city. Some of the ways in which Corinth differed, not only from other Greek cities, but also other Roman colonies have also been outlined.

The specific instances of leading figures which were outlined show the importance of wealth in order to fulfil these honorary posts. The unusual position which freedmen enjoyed in the colony has also been clearly seen. Whilst this chapter has examined the available source material for leadership and its structures in Roman Corinth, the next chapter will focus on the dynamics of those leaders and how they exerted influence.

---

[58] Cf. Plutarch, *Moralia* 739.E.

CHAPTER THREE

PROFILE AND PRACTICES OF SECULAR LEADERS IN CORINTH

1. *Introduction*

Having described the evidence for leaders and the structures of leadership in first century Corinth, the aim of the present chapter is to illustrate those aspects of Graeco-Roman society which were characteristic of civic leadership. Discussion of the importance of status, relationships (both friends and enemies), and oratory will illustrate the nature of leadership in Roman Corinth.

2. *Status*

From Homeric days, Greek society had been founded on the praise and honouring of those described as ἀγαθοί or possessing ἀρετή.[1] No higher commendation could be given to a person, and the highest goal of many in society was to strengthen their claim to these terms.[2]

It is important to understand the background to such qualities in order to grasp why they were so highly prized. The reasons behind the value placed on the ἀγαθός may be seen in Homeric society. Regard was given to those things which society was most dependent on. Thus it was the brave warrior, who offered protection in war through his strength, speed and skill, who was most highly praised—to be ἀγαθός was to do something beneficial to society. To this extent ἀγαθός or καλός did not necessarily imply moral purity, but rather it suggested skill at achieving security and protection for one's dependants. Indeed, the apparently low value placed on the 'quieter moral' qualities, such as δικαιοσύνη, when compared to the ἀρετή of the ἀγαθός, often posed a problem in Greek society. To be 'good' was more important than to be 'just'; to be successful more important than to be righteous.[3]

---

[1] For a detailed discussion of the development of these terms see A.W.H. Adkins, *Merit and Responsibility, A Study in Greek Values* (Oxford, 1960).

[2] Cf. Dio, *Orationes* 69.1, "virtually all praise and refer to as 'divine' and 'auspicious' such things as valour and righteousness and wisdom and, in short, every virtue. Moreover, whomever they believe to be, or to have been, characterized by such virtues, or nearly so, him they admire and celebrate in song".

[3] Cf. A.W.H. Adkins, *Merit and Responsibility,* 56-7. Adkins looks at how both Plato and Aristotle tried to handle the problem of the disregard for the quieter moral qualities in contrast to the high regard for those qualities which apparently brought success. This ethical problem can be seen in Romans 5.7, where Paul points out the assumption that one might be prepared to die for an ἀγαθός person far more readily than for a δικαίος. A similar situation, but more directly linked with social class, is given by Dio Chrysostom in *Orationes* 32.50: "for whereas in the cause of δικαιοσύνη and ἀρετή and ancestral rights and laws for a good king, an ἀγαθός, one that does not

A further development of this situation was that a link between wealth and ἀρετή inevitably developed. In order to be a successful warrior, one had to possess effective armour. Such armour was expensive, and, necessarily therefore, only the rich could afford it. In consequence, it was the wealthy who were described as ἀγαθοί.[4] With this etymology, ἀρετή might best be translated *nobility* as it was a characteristic almost exclusively attached to the social élite.

On the reverse side of the coin, to be termed κακός was a considerable insult. Honour, by rights, belonged to those citizens who by their actions had proven themselves to be ἀγαθοί, and dishonour was due to those known as κακοί.[5]

As pressures on society changed, when strategic military defence was a less threatening problem, it became the mark of the ἀγαθός πολίτης that he was of great benefit to the political life of the city in which he lived. In order to gain esteem, a man should use his talents and his possessions to increase the political security and standing of his city.[6] It may also be noted that esteem was placed not simply on what a man did for his city, but also on the success that he brought to his household or friends—that is his φιλοί, those people or things which were dependent on him.[7] In general, wealth still remained one of the major characteristics of the ἀγαθός;[8] and, inevitably, ἀρετή continued to be linked with parentage and family background, wealth and inheritance.[9]

---

cling to life, will, if need be, suffer, and even die; yet if a man hangs himself for the sake of a chorus-girl, a low-born outcast, not fit to live, what depths of disgrace does that betoken!" See Appendix B, and the author's article, 'The Good and the Just in Romans 5:7', *Tyndale Bulletin* 41 (1990), 128-42.

[4] Cf. A.W.H. Adkins, *Merit and Responsibility,* 36. Cf. also A.W. Gomme, 'The Interpretation of ΚΑΛΟΙ ΚΑΓΑΘΟΙ in Thucydides 4.40.2', *Classical Quarterly* 47 ns 3 (1953), 65-8, who argues that the term καλοὶ κἀγαθοί is used by the wealthy of themselves, and carried the sense of well-born. Similar conclusions are drawn by G.E.M. de Ste. Croix in his excursus 'Additional note on KALOS, KALOKAGATHIA', *The Origins of the Peloponnesian War* (London, 1972)—property, wealth and a good education were all part of being καλοὶ κἀγαθοί.

[5] Cf. Dio, *Orationes* 39.2, "honour for the good citizens and dishonour for the base"; 66.1, "There are some who brand as dissolute and ill-starred such men as have a craving for money or for dainties or for wine or who are inflamed with lust for women or boys, and they regard each of these vices as the greatest disgrace, yet those who crave distinction and reputation, on the contrary, they applaud, thinking them illustrious"; see also 73.8 f.

[6] Cf. Dio, *Orationes* 34.29, speaking of his own times, writes, "For sometimes men without any ability to perceive what is needful, men who have never given heed to their own welfare in the past, incompetent to manage even a village as it should be managed, but recommended by wealth or family, undertake the task of government".

[7] Cf. Dio, *Orationes* 13.19, "But as to how you are to learn what is to your own advantage and that of your native city, and to live lawfully and justly and harmoniously in your social and political relations without wronging or plotting against one another, this you have never learned nor has this problem ever yet given you any concern ...".

[8] Cf. Dio, *Orationes* 12.10, "For indeed this alone I consider to be profitable—to know the men who are wise and able and omniscient. To such if you are willing to cleave, neglecting all other things—both parents and the land of your birth, the shrines of the gods, and the tombs of your forefathers—following wherever they lead, or remaining wherever they establish themselves ... giving them money or in some other way winning their favour, you will become happier than happiness itself. But if you are not willing to do this yourselves, mistrusting your own natural ability, or pleading poverty or age or lack of physical strength, you will at least not begrudge your sons this

When it was no longer necessarily the landed aristocrats who possessed wealth, a tension arose regarding the distinction within society based on whether one was ἀγαθός or possessed ἀρετή. Social mobility made it possible for some of those of the 'lower' classes to become 'successful'. These *nouveaux riches* could in turn display their prosperity, and thus also, by rights, their ἀρετή.[10]

The picture which emerges is that the well-being of one's dependants was of much greater value than the well-being of any one other individual. Wealth was of supreme value, the rich were of far greater importance than the poor and esteem far more highly sought than justice alone. Society as a whole was strongly biased in favour of those who were already privileged. Social progression was inevitably the goal of most, especially in the urban culture.

These expectations which stemmed from Homeric days formed the structural basis to much of later Greek society, and the same picture may be seen in the empire of the first century AD. The Roman empire was through and through an 'estate' society with legal definitions of social rank. Understanding this is of foundational importance to grasping the leadership dynamics in the Roman colony of Corinth.[11] This is directly linked with the fact that wealth and property remained the basis of the society's structure and social advancement.

A primary aim of those who sought personal advancement was the pursuit of esteem and praise, φιλοτιμία.[12] This love of honour could also be the downfall of leaders in the first century. Plutarch writes: "in public life one

---

boon nor deprive them of the greatest blessings, but you will persuade them or compel them by any and all means, to the end that your sons, having been properly educated and having grown wise, may thenceforth be renowned among all Greeks and barbarians, being pre-eminent in virtue and reputation and wealth and in almost every kind of power. For not only do virtue and renown attend upon wealth, as we are told, but wealth likewise and of necessity accompanies virtue".

9   Cf. Dio, *Orationes* 15.29, "The case is the same with those known as γενναῖος and εὐγενής. For those who originally applied these names applied them to persons who were εὐγενής in respect to virtue or excellence, not bothering to inquire who their parents were. Then afterwards the descendants of families of ancient wealth and high repute were called εὐγενής by a certain class"; 29.2, regarding Melancomas, Dio writes, "In the first place, he had the good fortune to be truly εὐγενής. For it is not because he chanced to have forebears who were πλούσιος ... that this man was καλός γεννητός. That term applies to those who have come from good parents, as this man did". Dio tries to counter this direct link between ἀρετή and family by suggesting that virtue should be attributed to those who are virtuous, and not simply those who are well-born, *Orationes* 15.31.

10   Clear examples of this may be seen in the city of Corinth in the first century where the freedman class are given much opportunity to establish their social standing by the strategic use of their new-found wealth.

11   Cf. K. Hopkins, 'Élite Mobility in the Roman Empire', in ed. M.I. Finley, *Studies in Ancient Society, Past and Present Series* (London, 1974), 103.

12   One of the principal places where this can be seen is in the epigraphic evidence of first century cities. Corinth itself provides many suitable examples of inscriptions where honour is displayed either by the benefactor himself, or by a dependent friend on his behalf. Such inscriptions, often accompanied by statues, would be erected in the most prominent parts of the city in order to have the greatest effect. In Corinth such inscriptions are found in the public places; around the agora, in front of the Theatre, and along the main streets, for example the Lechaion Road. Kent gives a list of many benefactions mentioned in the inscriptions in *Corinth—Inscriptions 1926-1950 Corinth: Results,* viii, Part III (Princeton, 1966), 21.

must escape, not from one tyrant, the love of boys or women, but from many loves which are more insane than that: love of contention, love of fame, the desire to be first and greatest, which is a disease most prolific of envy, jealousy, and discord"; "the public activity of old men is not only in speech but also in actions, free from ostentation and desire for popularity".[13]

a. Class Distinctions

There are three overlapping ways in which the various social rankings in the empire have been classified: the *honestiores/humiliores* distinction, the freeborn/slave, and the citizen/alien categorisation.[14] In its crudest form, society was divided into two classes, but it is important to bear in mind that depending on which particular categorisation was being used, a person may find himself sometimes in the upper and sometimes in the lower division.[15] Part of this complication is the distinction which existed between rank and status.[16] That is, for example, some *humiliores* possessed citizenship whilst other *honestiores* did not.[17] A person's apparent status within society did not always match the actual rank which he held.

This class structure was firmly endorsed in many ways and ran deeply throughout daily life. Those who were well-born were proud to display their nobility;[18] those who had moved up the social ladder were keen to forget their social past; and those who could not move, tried to hide their true estate. Social prejudice was firmly established.[19] To be well-born made a considerable difference to a person's fortune. Plutarch goes as far as to recommend that if a man should want his children to have such an advantage in life, he should avoid cohabitation with women of lesser standing because honourable birth is a καλὸς θησαυρός.[20] He lists three of the major advantages which one could possess: εὐγένεια καλή, πλοῦτος and reputation or honour.[21] Social prejudice was such that it was considered out of place for a man of established reputation to be found discoursing with a *humilior*.[22]

---

[13] Plutarch, *Moralia* 788.E; 791.B.

[14] Cf. P. Garnsey, 'Legal Privilege in the Roman Empire', in ed. M.I. Finley, *Studies in Ancient Society, Past and Present Series* (London, 1974), 159.

[15] A free-born man may be a citizen or an alien; a *humilior* could be either free-born or slave.

[16] Cf. E.A. Judge, *Rank and Status in the World of the Caesars and St. Paul* (Christchurch, New Zealand, 1982), 9, "'Rank' is meant to denote any formally defined position in society, while 'status' refers to positions of influence that may not correspond to the official pattern of the social order. Status tends to convert itself into rank, and rank is the fossilised status of the past, defending itself against the aspirations of those who have only status, often newly acquired".

[17] P. Garnsey and R. Saller, *The Early Principate, Augustus to Trajan* (Oxford, 1982), 23 ff.

[18] Cf. Dio, *Orationes* 39.1.

[19] Cf. for example Dio, *Orationes* 74.9, "Nobody trusts slaves when they make an agreement, for the reason that they are not their own masters".

[20] Cf. Plutarch, *Moralia* 1.A-B.

[21] Cf. Plutarch, *Moralia* 5.C-D.

[22] Cf. Dio, *Orationes* 4.1-3, where Alexander is noted for his readiness to converse with a poor man; cf. also *Orationes* 9.7-8.

In the class of *honestiores* were the senators, equestrians, decurions and veteran soldiers. The qualifications for these ranks were set out very clearly. During the first, second and third centuries there were about 600 members of the Imperial Senate, which comprised the aristocratic élite. These senators possessed a minimum financial capital of 1,000,000 sesterces; the equestrian orders had a minimum property requirement of 400,000 sesterces; and the decurions were generally the top 100 members of a city, with 100,000 sesterces as a minimum capital wealth.[23]

Membership of the order of decurions was dependent on membership of a respectable Roman family, and a history of good character with no criminal record.[24] In many cities it was also necessary to have been free-born.[25] The final requirement was the payment of sureties and securities to sustain the demands which would be made upon the office;[26] it was also essential that the decurion resided in a house of suitable opulence within the city.[27]

Decurions, along with senators and equestrians, were entitled to special legal privileges as *honestiores*. This legal privilege is said to be directly dependent on one's character, birth and wealth.[28] One of the aspects of this legal privilege for the decurions is that they could be exempt from the punishment normally due to capital crimes, and instead could be exiled as their sentence.[29] Part of this legal privilege lay in that a judge was expected, in a court case, to speak in favour of the man of higher rank. This bias could even be as severe as to prevent a man of low rank even being able to bring a case against his social superiors.[30]

The *humiliores* class included all slaves and those freedmen who had not risen by virtue of finance to the rank of *honestior*.

Freedmen were on a distinctly lower social plane than the free-born. The stigma of having once been a slave was one which could not easily be removed. This stigma was attached to the distinctively servile *cognomen* (typically Greek) of the freedman, while the *nomen* always showed the connection with his former master.

---

[23] Cf. K. Hopkins, 'Élite Mobility in the Roman Empire', 103.

[24] Cf. the discussion of decurions in Chapter Two, 16.

[25] This was not necessarily the case in Corinth, which had been founded by Julius Caesar and initially populated with many freedmen.

[26] The rank of decurion in the city was unsalaried and yet made many financial demands on the man, thus making it necessary to have considerable financial capital.

[27] Cf. P. Garnsey, *Social Status and Legal Privilege in the Roman Empire* (Oxford, 1970), 243 f. Cf. also P. Garnsey, 'Aspects of the Decline of the Urban Aristocracy in the Roman Empire', *ANRW* II.1 (Berlin, 1974), 241, where he points out that most decurions would have been benefactors, if only at a modest level.

[28] Cf. P. Garnsey, *Social Status and Legal Privilege*, 234.

[29] Cf. P. Garnsey, *Social Status and Legal Privilege*, 242.

[30] See the relevant discussion in Chapter Five, 62-66. Cf. also P. Garnsey, 'Legal Privilege in the Roman Empire', 146.

The status of a freedman could be seen in his name; in the fact that he had
to wear the close-fitting cap, the *pilleus*;[31] the fact that his marriage contracted
as a slave carried no mandatory legal validation;[32] he was not exempt from
torture, as opposed to Roman citizens;[33] if he could join the army at all, some
of the most prestigious regiments were barred to him;[34] and he could not be a
priest to a Roman deity in an official capacity.[35]

One of the areas in which the freedman could gain honour, however, was in
the *Augustales seviri*. This was an office in the Imperial cult only open to
freedmen.[36] Such a freedman, by generous benefaction, might significantly
enhance his own status, and consequently that of his sons also.[37]

Despite the stigma of having once been a slave, there were considerable
opportunities for freedmen in the Empire. In many instances they amassed
considerable wealth for themselves and enjoyed the accompanying respect and
honour. One of the larger monuments in Corinth was erected by the freedman
Gnaeus Babbius Philinus—illustrative of the fact that this man had risen from
his background to great heights in Corinthian society.[38]

It appears also to be the case that there were more opportunities for freedmen in the imperial service than there were for free-born. This could well have
been because they offered a lesser political threat to the emperor because of
their greater dependence upon him for patronage.

The son of a freedman was not bound by all the disadvantages of his father,
and was considered a free-born man. If his father had been granted citizenship
on manumission, what is more, the son of the freedman automatically
inherited the status of Roman citizen also.

Prejudice was so strong against the slave that it was the goal of most in
slavery to win their freedom. Dio Chrysostom describes it as the most shameful and wretched of states (αἴσχιστος καὶ δυστυέστατος).[39] Slavery was characterized by a total lack of freedom. It is the free who have use of wisdom and

---

[31] The *pilleus* was worn at manumission, and not necessarily elsewhere. Dio, *Orationes* 14.24,
suggests that the *pilleus* ought to be more widely worn in order to distinguish the free man from the
slave.

[32] An astute freedman would regularize his cohabitation and manumit those children who had
been born to him whilst a slave.

[33] Cf. A.M. Duff, *Freedmen in the Early Roman Empire* (Cambridge, 1958), 63.

[34] Cf. A.M. Duff, *Freedmen in the Early Roman Empire,* 66.

[35] But he could assist a priest of a Roman deity, or be a priest to a non-Roman deity. Cf. A.M.
Duff, *Freedmen in the Early Roman Empire,* 66.

[36] Cf. J. Reynolds, 'Cities', in ed. D. Braund, *The Administration of the Roman Empire 241 BC-
AD 193* (Exeter, 1988), 49. See Appendix A. 12, 22, 47, 108.

[37] A. Bagdikian, *The Civic Officials of Roman Corinth,* unpublished MA dissertation
(University of Vermont, 1953), 21 f., "The purpose of this group was to do honor to Augustus, and
it was non-political in character. Also by creating this group Augustus made available for local use
this class's resources ...".

[38] The circular Babbius Monument is between the expansive agora and the West Shops, and
alongside some of the smaller Corinthian temples. His name has been found on four Corinthian
buildings, and he is honoured in inscriptions more frequently than any other benefactor in Corinth.
He was elected *duovir* in about AD 9-11. For more information see Appendix A. 46.

[39] Dio, *Orationes* 14.1.

free-will; slaves are only there to obey without question, and are thus considered ignorant beings.[40] By definition, a slave is one who has no rights, and is likened by Dio Chrysostom to no more than a possession, another of the master's goods.[41]

This understanding of the social situation must replace the popular concept of a crude 'two layer' view of Graeco-Roman society; all the more in the case of the advanced city of Corinth. Along these lines Vanderbroeck explains,

> The socio-political stratification of the Roman urban plebs, which became manifest in the participation in collective behavior, had the following appearance: The slaves, whose influence from a political point of view was slightest, were at the bottom. Above them were the free citizens who still found themselves in a position of dependence on the élite. The upper stratum of the urban plebs was formed by the public clientele, or the Forum crowd, or the plebs contionalis, for the major part composed of freedmen, artisans and shopkeepers. Socially and economically, and consequently politically, these persons took up an independent position.[42]

b. *Status Symbols*

It was a conscious and openly expressed desire to be glorified above one's competitors. Dio writes,

> the clearest mark of a true king: he is one whom all good men can praise without compunction not only during his life but even afterwards. And yet, even so, he does not himself covet the praise of the vulgar and the loungers about the market-place, but only that of the free-born and noble, men who would prefer to die rather than be guilty of falsehood;[43]
>
> it should be explained that Alexander was by common report the most ambitious of men and the greatest lover of glory. He was anxious to leave his name the greatest among all the Greeks and barbarians and longed to be honoured, not only—as one might put it—by mankind the world over, but, if it were at all possible, by the birds of the air and the beasts of the mountains. Moreover he looked down on all other men and thought that no one was a dangerous rival in this matter.[44]

but Dio notes that such aspirations are not always easy to live by:

> the spirit who presides over men who love glory is always aspiring and never touches the earth or anything lowly; no, he is high and lifted up as long as he enjoys a calm and clear sky or a gently blowing zephyr, feeling ever happier and happier and mounting to the very heavens, but often he is enwrapped in a dark cloud when accompanied by some unpopularity or censure from the many people whom he courts and honours and has appointed to the mastery over his own happiness.[45]

---

[40] Cf. Dio, *Orationes* 14.15, 17.

[41] Dio, *Orationes* 15.24.

[42] P.J.J. Vanderbroeck, *Popular Leadership and Collective Behavior in the Late Roman Republic (Ca. 80-50 BC)* (Amsterdam, 1987), 92. Vanderbroeck's work more specifically is an analysis of leadership in Rome of the late Republic; there are certain analogies, however, which may be drawn with the first century situation in Roman Corinth.

[43] Dio, *Orationes* 1.33.

[44] Dio, *Orationes* 4.4-5.

[45] Dio, *Orationes* 4.118-9.

The high value placed upon status and the widespread love of honour, φιλοτιμία, was such that it became important to display one's status in an ostentatious manner. The privileges attached to certain social grades were rigorously pursued and paraded. Both Dio Chrysostom and Plutarch are at times caustic in their criticism of the extents to which people will go in order to advertise their social status, either real or preferred. Plutarch writes:

> So of all kinds of love that which is engendered in states and peoples for an individual because of his virtue is at once the strongest and the most divine; but those falsely named and falsely attested honours which are derived from giving theatrical performances, making distributions of money, or offering gladiatorial shows, are like harlots' flatteries, since the masses always smile upon him who gives to them and does them favours, granting him an ephemeral and uncertain reputation.[46]

Plutarch's high regard for personal reputation and its rôle in career advancement may be noted. He writes: "not all men expect that the power derived from πλοῦτος, λόγος, or σοφία will accrue to them but no one who takes part in public life is without hope of attaining the reverence and repute to which old age leads"; "and deeming every public office to be something great and sacred, we must also pay the highest τιμή to one who holds an office".[47]

Status symbols were of vital importance to the social climbers in the ruling class. Vanderbroeck lists some of these symbols and their value,

> The cursus honorum, the military assignments, and the provincial governorship of a popular leader were not only advantageous to the individual himself, but also a condition for good image and thereby successful leadership and subsequent career opportunities. In this way a leader could prove that he was worthy of his function as a leader. Politicians also could demonstrate their abilities as advocates in trials.[48]

Military successes were especially rewarded with wide acclaim. During the first century AD in the provinces, however, this was a less common option open to leaders.

Those of the *ordo* of decurions were permitted to sit in special seats at the public entertainments.[49] These seats were in the front row of the theatre in full view of the whole gathering. Those who were to sit there would be seen by all as they processed to the front of the Theatre.[50] Plutarch notes a practice where

---

[46] Plutarch, *Moralia* 821.F.

[47] Cf. Plutarch, *Moralia* 787.D; 816.A; cf. also 821.C.

[48] P.J.J. Vanderbroeck, *Popular Leadership and Collective Behavior in the Late Roman Republic,* 133.

[49] Cf. Dio, *Orationes* 31.108; 66.2; 75.7, "furthermore, most beautiful are the rewards which it has established for their benefactions, having devised crowns and public proclamations and seats of honour, things which for those who supply them entail no expense, but which for those who win them have come to be worth everything".

[50] Such seats may be seen at Sicyon, west of Corinth, the site where the Isthmian games were held prior to their return to Isthmia itself. They were high backed seats of a greater comfort. Unfortunately it is not possible to see remains of such seats at the Isthmian Sanctuary, or in either the Odeon of Herodes Atticus or the Theatre at Corinth. In the case of the large Theatre at Epidaurus, however, it is most plain that the seats of honour were actually carved from a different

some people would install themselves in the front seats, not because they were entitled through honour to them, but because, in full view of the whole Theatre, they could give up their seats in flattery of the rich when they were to appear.[51] The decurions were also recognized because they wore the distinctive purple *toga prætexta*.[52] The colour purple was considered to be a colour of great honour.

One of the strongest pressures upon the man who wanted to increase the esteem in which he was held, was to enter the competitive round of ostentatious expenditure in benefactions for friends and the city. Some such people would get into serious debt through having tried to maintain appearances of generosity.[53] The giving of benefactions could be widely advertised. The administrative structure of the city was such that it was highly dependent on the private gift of money, or a building. To have one's name inscribed above the door of some important, new, public building, or to erect a statue to oneself with a fulsome inscription was a powerful status symbol.[54]

A further expression of one's status was to have a large following of adherents with you through the day as you pursued business, in the agora or in the courts, and a large clientèle who attended your house at the outset of the day waiting to receive the daily dole of money (*sportulæ*).

3. *Patronage and Friendship*

The expectations of relationships in the first century were very different from the dynamics of relationships which are seen today. It is for this reason that any attempt to appreciate leadership within the Graeco-Roman world is limited without first understanding the obligations and limitations of social relationships within that society. There were, for example, two clearly defined types

---

colour marble (a red-pink colour, where those of the rest of the Theatre are a grey-white), in order to distinguish them all the more clearly.

[51] Cf. Plutarch, *Moralia* 58.C.

[52] Cf. Dio, *Orationes* 34.29, "And what is more serious is that these men, not for the sake of what is truly best and in the interest of their country itself, but for the sake of reputation and honours and the possession of greater power than their neighbours, in the pursuit of crowns and precedence and purple robes, fixing their gaze upon these things and staking all upon their attainment, do and say such things as will enhance their own reputations". See also *Orationes* 47.25; 49.11.

[53] Cf. Dio, *Orationes* 17.18; Plutarch, *Moralia* 822.D, "But if your property is moderate and in relation to your needs strictly circumscribed 'as by centre and radius', it is neither ignoble nor humiliating at all to confess your poverty and to withdraw from among those who have the means for public expenditures, instead of borrowing money and making yourself at once a pitiful and a ridiculous object in the matter of your public contributions; for men are plainly seen to lack resources when they keep annoying their friends or truckling to money-lenders so that it is not reputation or power, but rather shame and contempt, which they acquire by such expenditures"; see also *Moralia* 822.F.

[54] Cf. Dio, *Orationes* 31.108. See also Plutarch, *Moralia* 820.D, "For if it is not easy to reject some favour or some kindly sentiment of the people, when it is so inclined, for men engaged in a political struggle for which the prize is not money or gifts, but which is a truly sacred contest worthy of a crown, a mere inscription suffices, a tablet, a decree, or a green branch ...". See the benefactions celebrated in Corinthian inscriptions.

of relationship—those between equals and those between unequals. The former were also strictly defined into those between friends and between enemies.

Marshall's recently published study, which looks in detail at the conventions of friendship and enmity within the Graeco-Roman world, uses this background as a starting point for a study of the dynamics of relationship between Paul and the Christians at Corinth. He suggests that the expectations of both friendly and hostile relationships were clearly drawn up, and there was a sharp distinction made between friend and enemy. There were clearly established social expectations of how to act towards each other within this simple framework of friends and enemies.[55]

Closely linked with the conventional distinctions between classes is the awareness of the equality or inequality in relationship between two people, which was defined on the grounds of rank and status. There was a highly-developed protocol of the expected ways in which such relationships were to be conducted based on a series of mutual obligations.

The principal dynamic which is to be studied is that of patronage—a convention which was widely prevalent in the Republic, but seemed to change very little during the Principate.[56] This practice did much to reinforce the already firmly established views about social distinction. The basis behind this institution is the power behind the giving and receiving of gifts. Those who exploited this power recognised that others could be placed in their debt when given some benefaction; the debtor could, therefore, be held to owe the benefactor both honour and gratitude. The recipient of a *beneficium* was expected to publicize the generosity of his patron.[57] It is clear, therefore, that what was in theory a voluntary practice, was in reality a convention bound by extensive obligations and debts; and what was apparently an act of great generosity, in fact was in many ways self-regarding in motivation. As long as both parties recognised that they were receiving some benefit from the 'friendship', however, then the basis of the relationship was considered firm.

First century Graeco-Roman society was a society where success at many levels depended on status, reputation and public estimation, which in turn depended entirely on friendships. Such friendships were maintained through a continuous flow of generosity in two directions. It may therefore be seen that success was dependent at root on wealth, even considerable wealth.

---

[55] Cf. P. Marshall, *Enmity in Corinth: Social Conventions in Paul's Relations with the Corinthians* (Tübingen, 1987), 38.

[56] Cf. R.P. Saller, *Personal Patronage under the Early Empire* (Cambridge, 1982), 12, 30, 205. Cf. *idem*, 3, where Saller points out the view of G.E.M. de Ste. Croix that the collapse of the Republic even brought about a growth in patronage.

[57] S.C. Mott suggests in 'The Power of Giving and Receiving: Reciprocity in Hellenistic Benevolence', in ed. G.F. Hawthorne, *Current Issues in Biblical and Patristic Interpretation* (Grand Rapids, 1975), 60, that the obligation of rendering honour and gratitude was both a motivation and a control over "personal, political and diplomatic conduct". The power lay in that it offered the opportunity to the receiver of a gift to place the original benefactor in obligation to him, *idem*, 65. Cf. also R.P. Saller, *Personal Patronage under the Early Empire*, 20, 126.

This relationship between unequals, the upper strata and the lower strata of society, is mostly classed as a patron/client relationship—legal and economic support given in return for political services.[58] The dependence between these groupings is bi-directional, however; not only do the lower classes need the financial support of the rich, but the wealthy are as much in need of the loyal support of the poor.

The foundation of this institution was the giving of a gift to a friend. Its intended design was to increase the status of the donor, thus winning him public recognition. Furthermore, the obligation does not rest there; the recipient is under social pressure to respond by returning the favour with a show of yet greater generosity—indeed this is the only way by which he may avoid losing face.[59] If he fails to outdo the original donor in munificence, then the relationship is one of dependence rather than friendship.[60] It is clear, furthermore, that this is a practice which remained essentially unchanged from Homeric days until the first century AD.

The strength of the obligation was so great that failure to return a gift was considered an injustice (*iniuria*) and reasonable grounds for enmity.[61] In this way the relationship could turn from one of friendship to one of hostility; and to incur hostility was often more costly in terms of loss of status than the trouble of maintaining the friendship.[62] One of the principal aims of having

---

[58] Cf. P.J.J. Vanderbroeck, *Popular Leadership and Collective Behavior in the Late Roman Republic,* 52; cf. also 163 f., "In pursuing a career at the top, it does not seem at first sight purposeful to mobilize the group of artisans and shopkeepers, because their rôle hardly counted in the centuriate assembly which elected the highest magistrates. Yet support of the *plebs contionalis* was necessary: to reach the top one first had to be elected to the lower offices by the tribal assembly. Popular support was necessary in competing with other members of the élite, for the people had the power to assign provinces and other commands whereby money and prestige could be accumulated; both were absolutely necessary to hold a position of power at the top of Roman society. Popular support was further important in the many public trials ... for prestige was a significant factor in Roman social and political culture. In general, considering the organization of the Roman polity, popular support was indispensable to exert a decisive influence on the legislative process". 163 f., "The foremost reason for a politician to seek support among the lower citizenry was that it was the only *legitimate* alternative to work his will if agreement among the élite proved impossible. The Roman city-state institutions offered ample opportunity for action, even if it was accompanied by violence. Another, but illegitimate alternative was the military".

[59] Cf. Seneca, *Moral Essays* 1.4.3; 2.18.5.

[60] Cf. A.R. Hands, *Charities and Social Aid in Greece and Rome* (London, 1968), 26. Cf. P. Marshall, *Enmity in Corinth,* 1-3. "Pliny calls it the code of friendship; according to it 'the one who takes the initiative puts the other in his debt and owes him no more until he is repaid,' 'Neque enim obligandus sed remunerandus est in amoris officio qui prior coepit,'" *Letters* 7.31.7, P. Marshall, *idem,* 10 f.; "this continued agonistic attitude was only possible between those equals or near equals within the upper strata of society ... ", *idem,* 12. See also Seneca, *Moral Essays* 1.1.3.

[61] Cf. Plutarch, *Moralia* 90.F, "For it is not so καλός to do a good turn to a friend as it is αἰσχρός not to do it when he is in need". Dio describes it as an obligation in *Orationes* 40.3, "For there is nothing more weighty, no debt bearing higher interest, than a favour promised. Moreover, this is the kind of loan, when, as one might say, because of tardy payment the favour turns into an obligation, an obligation the settlement of which those who keep silent demand altogether more sternly than those who cry aloud. For nothing has such power to remind those who owe you such obligations as your having utterly forgotten them". Seneca goes as far as to suggest that even a delay in returning a benefaction is a sign of enmity, *Moral Essays* 2.1.2; 3.22.3.

[62] Cf. P. Marshall, *Enmity in Corinth,* 17 f., A.R. Hands, *Charities and Social Aid in Greece and Rome,* 26.

wealth was to make a good number of friends or dependants, and so increase one's own status.[63] This wealth was traded for things which in the end money could not directly buy.[64]

The giving of benefactions was in itself an action which attracted a great deal of honour. The city itself was so dependent on the generosity of its benefactors that such people were honoured often out of all proportion to their benefaction.[65] Such disproportionate honour was deliberate in that it encouraged the benefactor, and others, to continue to dedicate benefactions, and gain for themselves yet more prestige.[66] It is clear, therefore, that wealth was essential to progress in society, since without it one could never buy friends.[67]

Friendship was considered one of the most important of the relationships a man might have, and something to be protected at great cost.[68] The necessity of close and numerous friends is endorsed by Dio Chrysostom:

> Friendship, moreover, the good king holds to be the fairest and most sacred of his possessions, believing that the lack of means is not so shameful or perilous for a king as the lack of friends, and that he maintains his happy state, not so much by means of revenues and armies and his other sources of strength, as by the loyalty of his friends.[69]

It was often that the whole of a man's career depended on the number and type of friends that he might have. A great number of friends suggested both popularity and honour,[70] and well-chosen friends could be of particular value in an unforeseen situation of crisis, whether financial, legal or political.[71]

---

[63] Cf. Plutarch, *Moralia* 778.D. Seneca, *Moral Essays* 5.43.1.

[64] Cf. A.R. Hands, *Charities and Social Aid in Greece and Rome,* 32 f., such benefits which could not be bought included legal support, banking and insurance.

[65] Cf. S.C. Mott, 'The Power of Giving and Receiving: Reciprocity in Hellenistic Benevolence', 69, the honour and power attributed to the benefactor was valuable enough to be displayed in a legal situation. The man on trial would display the extent to which the city was in debt to him on account of his many benefactions, and the jurors would be under obligation to look favourably upon him. Plutarch in *Moralia* 817.D includes the phrase, "... to be held in high esteem because they are benefactors of the community". The benefactions could take many different forms which might benefit the city: the construction of a public building; the provision of grain during famine; the giving of banquets; financial assistance during the city games; Plutarch, *Moralia* 823.D. Dio, *Orationes* 31.43, "For all men know how much more permanent a benefaction is than power, for there is no strength which time does not destroy, but it destroys no benefaction"; the benefaction carries more weight in the city than power itself.

[66] Cf. B.W. Winter, 'The Public Honouring of Christian Benefactors, Romans 13:3-4 and 1 Peter 2:14-15', *JSNT* 34 (1988), 89-92.

[67] Cf. Plutarch, *Moralia* 93.E, "It is impossible to acquire either many slaves or many friends with little coin. What then is the coin of friendship?"; 527.F, "Such is the felicity of wealth—a felicity of spectators and witnesses or else a thing of naught".

[68] Cf. Dio, *Orationes* 1.30, "τοῦ καλλίστου καὶ ὠφελιμωτάτου κτήματος, φιλίας"; see also *idem,* 3.86.

[69] Dio, *Orationes* 3.86.

[70] Cf. Plutarch, *Moralia* 94.B, "In the houses of rich men and rulers, the people see a noisy throng of visitors offering their greetings and shaking hands and playing the part of armed retainers, and they think that those who have so many friends must be happy".

[71] Plutarch also mentions that the excessive craving for large numbers of friends often appeared unpleasant, and sometimes meant that previous friendships were neglected, Plutarch, *Moralia* 93.C. He also mentions the different services a friend might offer: company on a journey to foreign parts, defence in a legal suit, help in judging a case, support in a wedding celebration, or at a funeral. For

One of the common ways that a man might progress in his political career was through the support of a patron. He might attach himself to someone already established in the city and benefit from his superior's reputation.[72] The support of an influential friend could be invaluable. Plutarch suggests that, by careful calculation, friends might assist one's cause in the assembly considerably. Initially they should dissent from his viewpoint, but gradually and deliberately appear to be swayed by his careful argument and change their position as if by conviction. Clearly this cannot be done too frequently, but may be used to great advantage in the more important cases. At lesser instances the friends, or at least some of them, should agree to differ lest it appear that the support is always prearranged.[73]

The key words in the patron/client relationship are *patronus, cliens, amicus, beneficium, meritum* and *gratia*. More often only the last four words are found, since *patronus* and *cliens* carried an implication of social inferiority and therefore would normally be tactfully avoided in inscriptions.[74] Regardless of the social class differences in a patron/client relationship, both parties would be called *amici*.[75]

The particular *beneficia* which were given would differ depending on the needs and status of the recipient. Towards a slave, a patron might offer manumission; to his freedman, he might offer the daily *sportulæ;*[76] the emperor might offer offices, statuses, privileges, immunities, and money as *beneficia*.[77] In return the manumitted slave may be under obligation to promise to continue to serve his master either in his house, or in his business; the freedman might attend his master throughout the day, thus adding to his entourage and apparent status;[78] and the emperor might be shown *gratia* by either having a statue dedicated to him, by being named in the recipient's will, or even by being given religious *vota*.[79]

Marshall closes his chapter on 'The Relationship of Friendship' by noting that the chief end of wealth was to acquire friends. The importance of ἀρετή

---

these reasons to have many friends is useful, but the drawback is that equally you have more people to call on you for assistance; *idem,* 95.C, E, 808.B-C.

72 Cf. Plutarch, *Moralia* 805.E-F; 806.C; 814.C.

73 Cf. Plutarch, *Moralia* 813.B.

74 Such 'benefaction' terminology is evident in the Corinthian inscriptions themselves, both in Greek and in their Latin equivalents. See the following instances in J.H. Kent, *Corinth—Inscriptions 1926-1950 Corinth: Results,* viii, Part III (Princeton, 1966): ἀνδραγαθίας εἵνεκεν, 226; ἀρετή, 128, 226, 265, 267, 268, 300; εὐεργεσία, 124; εὐεργέτης, 102, 503; εὔνοια, 267; καλοκαγαθία, 264; πίστις, 265; τιμή, 300, 308; φίλος, 136, 146, 265, 305, 361; *amicus,* [125], 134?, 135, 137, 224, 357; *bene merito,* 165, 222; *felicissimus,* 506; *fides,* 310; *honorare,* [166], 167, 168, [173], 176, 177, [180], [184], [185], 192, [219].

75 Cf. R.P. Saller, *Personal Patronage under the Early Empire,* 8 f., 12. *Cliens* does appear in inscriptions but very rarely, and *patronus* occurs a little more frequently.

76 Cf. Plutarch, *Moralia* 795.A.

77 Cf. R.P. Saller, *Personal Patronage under the Early Empire,* 24, 55.

78 Cf. R.P. Saller, *Personal Patronage under the Early Empire,* 205; A.R. Hands, *Charities and Social Aid in Greece and Rome,* 26, the size of a man's clientèle was a sign of his status, wealth and power. Cf. also A.M. Duff, *Freedmen in the Early Roman Empire,* 94.

79 Cf. R.P. Saller, *Personal Patronage under the Early Empire,* 71.

and ἀνδραγαθία as qualities, the foundational importance of the patronage relationship, the strictly defined differences in social status, and the extent to which people displayed their status and the reliance which the city had on benefactions, all reflect the fact that wealth and φιλοτιμία formed the basis of Graeco-Roman society.

4. *Enmity*

With regard to hostile relationships, it should be pointed out that invective was a widely-used form of attack; its purpose is twofold. First, "to show by contrast how much more favoured in every way the ridiculer is than his enemy (such self-commendation may be direct or, as is more often the case, implied by the unfavourable comparison made with the enemy)", and secondly, "to ensure the public humiliation and disgrace of the enemy".[80] In contrast to invective, friendship was maintained, not only by munificence, but also by a custom of recommendation.[81]

Epstein, in an important work on enmity in the Republican period, writes, "The pursuit of *inimicitiae* and the destruction of one's enemies were firmly entrenched among those virtues Romans thought necessary for the acquisition of *dignitas, virtus,* status and nobility—qualities the Roman aristocracy pursued from birth".[82] Epstein describes enmity as one of the most powerful influences in Roman history[83] and a significant aspect of political, legal and civic life. The subject of enmity will be discussed in greater detail in Chapter Five below as an important aspect of litigation.

5. *Oratory*

In the world in which Dio Chrysostom lived and worked, the importance of rhetoric should not be underestimated. C.P. Jones remarks, "The spoken word

---

[80] P. Marshall, *Enmity in Corinth,* 52. *Idem,* 59, says of such invective, "In spite of this long familiarity, the conventional nature of invective, the reluctance to enter into hostile relations, and the responsibility and acceptance of invective as a rhetorical device, there remained much that could not be passed off lightly. Personal abuse, injury to a man's status or dignity, an unjust legal decision, prosecuting or testifying against a man on charges involving his *caput* and *existimatio* would almost certainly create a relationship of enmity". Invective, while it contained elements of truth, commonly involved exaggeration (see *idem,* 280).

[81] P. Marshall, *Enmity in Corinth,* 96. Cf. also *idem,* 123 f. where Marshall writes, "While praise is not essential to letters of recommendation, it is an important element in the relationship between the recommended and the recommender and between the recommended and the recipient. Where praise of character is clearly unnecessary, it is still given unabashedly. In a similar vein, where it appears that no written recommendation is necessary—existing friendships, subsequent recommendations, ancient traditions, a character which commends itself,—letters are still sought and given. These considerations illustrate the importance with which written recommendations were regarded by all parties in forming a relationship and the fundamental importance of friendship in its wide range of intimacy and services to this practice".

[82] D.F. Epstein, *Personal Enmity in Roman Politics—218-43 BC* (London, 1987), 28.

[83] D.F. Epstein, *Personal Enmity in Roman Politics,* 128.

was paramount: without oratory a Greek could not enter civic life, where he had to persuade his colleagues in the council or his inferiors in the assembly, to plead courts of law, and to represent his city before governors and emperors".[84] For Dio Chrysostom, eloquence without wisdom, however, was not a thing to be proud of. Much in his *Orationes* on Kingship touches on this aspect.[85]

Oratory was important even in peace time;

> Nowadays, then, when the affairs of the cities no longer include leadership in wars, nor the overthrow of tyrannies, nor acts of alliances, what opening for a conspicuous and brilliant public career could a young man find? There remain the public lawsuits and embassies to the Emperor, which demand a man of ardent temperament and one who possesses both courage and intellect.[86]

One of the principal tools of statesmanship was seen to be the power to persuade by speech.[87] Plutarch writes: "How, then, is it possible that a private person of ordinary costume and mien who wishes to lead a State may gain power and rule the multitude unless he possesses persuasion and attractive speech?"[88] and,

> The wolf, they say, cannot be held by the ears; but one must lead a people or a State chiefly by the ears, not, as some do who have no practice in speaking and seek uncultured and inartistic holds upon the people, pulling them by the belly by means of banquets or gifts of money or arranging ballet-dances or gladiatorial shows, by which they lead the common people or rather curry favour with them. For leadership of a people is leadership of those who are persuaded by speech.[89]

Since leadership largely belonged to those who had the power of persuasion, it followed that oratory was a most highly prized ability. Dio Chrysostom praises a man who sacrifices much in order to become proficient in public speaking:

> Although I had often praised your character as that of a good man who is worthy to be first among the best, yet I never admired it before as I do now. For that a man in the very prime of life and second to no one in influence, who

---

[84] C.P. Jones, *The Roman World of Dio Chrysostom* (Cambridge, Mass. and London, 1978), 9.

[85] Cf. Dio, *Orationes* 1.8, "it is only the spoken word of the wise and prudent, such as were most men of earlier times, that can prove a competent and perfect guide and helper of a man endowed with a tractable and virtuous nature, and can lead it toward all excellence by fitting encouragement and direction"; *Orationes* 4.1-3, "many give no less admiration and credit to Alexander than to Diogenes because, although he was ruler over so many people and had greater power than any other man of his day, he did not disdain to converse with a poor man who had intelligence and the power of endurance. For all men without exception are naturally delighted when they see wisdom honoured by the greatest power and might; hence they not only relate the facts in such cases but add extravagant embellishments of their own; nay more, they strip their wise men of all else, such as wealth, honours, and physical strength, so that the high regard in which they are held may appear to be due to their intelligence alone".

[86] Plutarch, *Moralia* 805.A-B.

[87] Plutarch, *Moralia* 792.D, "but the mental habit of public men—deliberation, wisdom, and justice, and, besides these, experience, which hits upon the proper moments and words and is the power that creates persuasion—is maintained by constantly speaking, acting, reasoning, and judging".

[88] Plutarch, *Moralia* 801.E.

[89] Plutarch, *Moralia* 802.E.

possesses great wealth and has every opportunity to live in luxury by day and night, should in spite of all this reach out for education also and be eager to acquire training in eloquent speaking, and should display no hesitation even if it should cost toil, seems to me to give proof of an extraordinary noble soul and one not only ambitious, but in very truth devoted to wisdom.[90]

The pursuit of skill in public-speaking was prompted by various quite different motivations. Dio Chrysostom lists three common desires for eloquence:

Take oratory, for instance. There are many well-born men and, in public estimation, ambitious, who are whole-heartedly interested in it, some that they may plead in courts of law or address the people in the assembly in order to have greater influence than their rivals and have things their own way in politics, while the aim of others is the glory to be won thereby, that they may enjoy the reputation of eloquence; but there are men who say they desire the mere skill derived from experience, some of these being indeed speakers, but others only writers, of whom a certain man of former times said they occupied the borderland between philosophy and politics.[91]

The search for status and recognition was also the motivation for many ill-equipped figures to pursue public speaking. Plutarch describes such oratory in the strongest of terms: "So this is what we must understand concerning statesmanship also: that foolish men, even when they are generals or secretaries or public orators, do not act as statesmen, but court the mob, deliver harangues, arouse factions, or under compulsion perform public services".[92] The public speaking of a true statesman is not characterised by theatrical gestures and flowery words.[93] Dio Chrysostom has a similar analysis: "Such a man, ever turning and revolving, a flatterer of peoples and crowds, whether in public assemblies or lecture halls, or in his so-called friendship with tyrants or kings and his courting of them—who would not feel pity for his character and manner of living?"[94] Dio Chrysostom also describes such orators as deceitful people who accept praise for themselves which is rightly due to another.[95]

Oratory was thus used as a powerful status symbol (most especially by the sophists). It was the grounds for considerable public display, and therefore provided the opportunity to gain both reputation and public honour.

---

[90] Dio, *Orationes* 18.1. Dio continues, *Orationes* 18.2, "And you, as it seems to me, are altogether wise in believing that a statesman needs experience and training in public speaking and in eloquence. For it is true that this will prove of very great help toward making him beloved and influential and esteemed instead of being looked down upon".

[91] Dio, *Orationes* 24.3.

[92] Plutarch, *Moralia* 796.E.

[93] Plutarch, *Moralia* 802.E.

[94] Dio, *Orationes* 4.124.

[95] Dio, *Orationes* 18.3, "Time and again, at any rate, there may be seen in our cities one group of men spending, handing out largess, adorning their city with dedications, but the orators who support these measures getting the applause, as though they and not the others had brought these things about"; 34.31, "Accordingly men come forward to address you who are both empty-headed and notoriety-hunters to boot, and it is with mouth agape for the clamour of the crowd, and not at all from sound judgement or understanding, that they speak, but just as if walking in the dark they are always swept along according to the clapping and the shouting".

Characteristic of Graeco-Roman leadership was the pursuit of persuasive eloquence.

6. *Conclusions*

It has become apparent that leadership in the Graeco-Roman world was extremely expensive and therefore also élitist—the tall order expected of such leaders could only be fulfilled by a narrowly defined group. In order to be involved in high positions of responsibility, it was a necessary pre-requisite to be among the wise, well-born and powerful. Leadership, and even prospective leadership, was very much on show and had to prove itself (principally in financial terms). Leaders had to make an impact on those they led in order to be elected by them, and this could only be done by making a good impact, often through benefactions.

One of the major reasons for pursuing leadership in the city was the inevitable accompanying honour and esteem that would be received. This would lead to increased status and grounds for more praise. It is this picture of leadership in the Roman empire which is prevalent in the extant literature. A leader is one who is respected, who has standing and honour, who is eloquent in the assembly, who has a number of influential friends. He recognises and affirms the social barriers of class and status, and has financial means. It is against this background of secular leadership described in these two chapters that the situation in the church of Corinth will be assessed.

CHAPTER FOUR

CHRISTIAN LEADERS IN SECULAR CORINTH

1. *Introduction*

Having discussed the nature of Graeco-Roman leadership in the preceding chapters, it cannot be assumed *ipso facto* that this same background applies to the Pauline material regarding leadership in the epistle. In this chapter evidence from the Christian community will be brought together which demonstrates that this is the appropriate background. It will be shown that there were in the Corinthian community some who were also significant figures in the surrounding secular society, and who would, therefore, have been familiar with leadership practices and attitudes in that society.

2. *The Wise, the Powerful and the Well-born*

1 Corinthians 1.26 proves very significant in any discussion of the social status of those in the Pauline churches. The enigmatic character of the verse is observed by noting that it has been used both by those wishing to defend the argument that Paul appealed only to the socially depressed, and by those wishing to demonstrate that Paul's churches included some from the social élite of the city.[1]

Until relatively recently, the majority of interpreters stressed that the Pauline churches appealed to the lower classes. This argument, first made by Celsus, was largely adopted by others, and reinforced by Deissmann in this century.[2] Deissmann's conclusions are based on assumptions of social class

---

[1]   C.F.D. Moule, *The Birth of the New Testament* (London, 1962), 157, "In the first place, the passage in 1 Cor 1 would probably never have been written had there not been educated Christians in that congregation who were contemptuous about the crudities of others. To some extent, then, it bears witness to the very reverse of the conditions it is often used to illustrate". Cf. also E.A. Judge, *The Social Pattern of the Christian Groups in the First Century: Some Prolegomena to the Study of New Testament Ideas of Social Obligation* (London, 1960), 59, "Far from suggesting anything else, the overworked exclamation 'not many wise ..., not many mighty, not many noble, are called' (1 Cor i. 26) plainly admits this situation. Taking the words at their face value, they merely imply that the group did not contain many intellectuals, politicians, or persons of gentle birth. But this would suggest that the group did at least draw upon this minority to some extent". K. Schreiner, 'Zur biblischen Legitimation des Adels: Auslegungsgeschichtliche Studien zu 1. Kor. 1,26-29', *Zeitschrift für Kirchengeschichte* 85 (1974), 317-57, gives a history of interpretation from the early church fathers to the present, and demonstrates how interpretation of this verse has changed.

[2]   Cf. Celsus' comment, quoted by Origen in *Contra Celsum* 3.44: "Their injunctions are like this, 'Let no one educated, no one wise, no one sensible draw near. For these abilities are thought by us to be evils. But as for anyone ignorant, anyone stupid, anyone uneducated, anyone who is a child, let him come boldly.' By the fact that they themselves admit that these people are worthy of their God, they show that they want and are able to convince only the foolish, dishonourable and stupid,

derived from *koiné* papyrological finds, as distinct from the purely literary
sources. He concludes that Paul's social status lies "below the literary upper
classes and above the purely proletarian lowest classes".[3]

It is clear from the verse in question, Βλέπετε γὰρ τὴν κλῆσιν ὑμῶν, ἀδελφοί,
ὅτι οὐ πολλοὶ σοφοὶ κατὰ σάρκα, οὐ πολλοὶ δυνατοί, οὐ πολλοὶ εὐγενεῖς, that
these two perspectives are not mutually exclusive. Paul's statement that there
are not many wise in human terms, not many powerful and not many of noble
birth demonstrates that there were, at the least, some who fitted these
categories; equally, however, there were some who could not be classed as
wise, influential or well-born. The Corinthian church, it seems clear, contained
a social mix.[4]

A further question which has dominated interpretation of this verse has
been the background to the key terms σοφός, δυνατός and εὐγενής. Much of
this section of 1 Corinthians 1.10–3.23 is a carefully drawn contrast between
the wisdom of the world and that of God.[5] It is in the light of this broader
context that the meaning of σοφός, δυνατός and εὐγενής must be seen.

Munck firmly demonstrates the widely-accepted assumption that wisdom,
power, and noble birth were qualities highly lauded by the sophists.[6] Since his
contribution, this view has received much broader acceptance.[7]

---

and only slaves, women, and children". See also A. Deissmann, *Paul: A Study in Social and
Religious History* (ET: ed 2: London, 1926), esp. 29-51.

[3]   A. Deissmann, *Paul: A Study in Social and Religious History,* 51. He does point out, 50-51,
however, the difficulty and sometimes inconsistent results which this study produces.

[4]   W. Wüllner lists four of the common interpretations of the triad in 1 Corinthians 1.26, in
'Ursprung und Verwendung der σοφός-, δυνατός-, εὐγενής-Formel in 1 Kor 1, 26', in edd. E.
Bammel, C.K. Barrett, W.D. Davies, *Donum Gentilicium — New Testament Studies in Honour of
David Daube* (Oxford, 1978), 165-6: "Der formelhafte Charakter dieser triadischen Bezeichnung
der Korinther hat bisher vier verschiedene Interpretationen hervorgebracht: (1) die älteste und
dominierende Interpretation sieht in der triadischen Formel soziale, ökonomische Hinweise. (2) Man
hat versucht, die triadische Formel rein rhetorisch oder stilistisch zu erklären. (3) Ein anderer
neuerer Versuch, die Herkunft der drei genannten Eigenschaften zu erleutern, bezieht sich haupt-
sächlich auf den kynischen anti-εὐγενής topos, der in der Polemik gegen die Sophisten seinen Sitz
haben mag. (4) Schließlich hat man die eigenartige Komposition der drei genannten Eigenschaften
aus einem bestimmten Teil der nachbiblischen liturgischen Tradition zur Erinnerung des Tages der
Zerstörung des Tempels zu erklären versucht".

[5]   See the discussion on pages 101-2of Chapter Seven below.

[6]   J. Munck, *Paul and the Salvation of Mankind* (London, 1959), 162-3, n. 2. Munck lists many
instances where sophists chose to display their influence and high birth, and, indeed, demonstrates
that this was seen as the assumed social background to any sophist. Cf. also G.W. Bowersock,
Greek Sophists in the Roman Empire (Oxford, 1969), 17, 21, " ... a sophist's family was generally
not obscure, at least locally. The career required journeys and public benefactions, not to mention
the fees for instruction by great teachers, fees which were possible only for the wealthy; and the
wealthy were the local aristocrats. With the aid of Philostratus and certain ample inscriptions, it is
possible to be precise about the social background of the sophists"; 22, "... the evidence is
overwhelming that sophists almost always emerged from the notable and wealthy families of their
cities"; 26, "With his money, his intellect, and his influence a sophist was in a particularly
favourable position to aid his city, whether it were his native city, his adoptive, or both"; 28, "The
social eminence of the sophists in their cities and provinces brought their families swiftly and
inevitably into the Roman upper class"; see also E.L. Bowie, 'The Importance of Sophists', *Yale
Classical Studies* 27 (1982).

[7]   G. Theissen, *The Social Setting of Pauline Christianity: essays on Corinth* (Edinburgh, 1982),
70-3. B.A. Pearson, *The Pneumatikos-Psychikos Terminology in 1 Corinthians. A Study in the
Theology of the Corinthian Opponents of Paul and its Relation to Gnosticism* (Montana, 1973), 40,

Dio Chrysostom, in his second oration on slavery and freedom, explains how it is wrongly, but commonly, held that nobility of character is used to describe those of noble birth.[8] Plutarch equally notes the link between wisdom on the one hand, and wealth, noble birth and influence on the other.[9] Aristotle describes Fortune in terms of noble birth, riches and power.[10] Sänger particularly refers to Josephus, demonstrating that δυνατός refers to those who had wealth.[11] He concludes,

> Als Fazit läßt sich festhalten: Die drei Adjektive, mit denen der Apostel in 1 Kor 1.26 b die Adressaten des Briefes—genauer: einen Teil von ihnen—anspricht und charakterisiert, benennen jeweils die konkreten Gründe ihrer Zugehörigkeit zur sozialen Oberschicht. Paulus wendet sich an eine Gemeinde, in der es, wenngleich zahlenmäßig nicht sehr ins Gewicht fallend, Christen gab, die antike Bildung (σοφοί), Reichtum (δυνατοί) und vornehme Herkunft (εὐγενεῖς) repräsentieren.[12]

Philo devotes his treatise, *De Virtutibus,* to this subject of noble birth.[13] He argues, in a similar vein to Dio Chrysostom, that nobility of character should be regarded as a quality distinct from nobility of parentage. He opens the debate by noting,

> This shows also that those who hymn nobility of birth (εὐγένεια) as the greatest of good gifts and the source too of other great gifts deserve no moderate censure, because in the first place they think that those who have many generations of wealth and distinction behind them are noble, though neither did the

---

who adds further, arguing from Philo's *De Virtutibus,* that εὐγενής refers also to spiritual high birth. R.A. Horsley, 'Pneumatikos vs. Psychikos: Distinctions of Spiritual Status among the Corinthians', *HTR* 69 (1976), 269-88, esp., 282-3, adopts a similar stance. See also J.A. Davis, *Wisdom and Spirit: An Investigation of 1 Corinthians 1.18-3.20 Against the Background of Jewish Sapiential Traditions in the Greco-Roman Period* (Lanham, 1984), 191 n. 42.

[8] Cf. Dio, *Orationes* 15.29, "For of those who are called slaves we will, I presume, admit that many have the spirit of free men, and that among free men there are many who are altogether servile. The case is the same with those known as γενναῖοι and εὐγενεῖς, for those who originally applied these names applied them to persons who were well-born in respect to virtue or excellence, not bothering to inquire who their parents were. Then afterwards the descendants of families of ancient wealth and high repute were called εὐγενεῖς by a certain class"; 31, "'But,' you will object, 'it is impossible for anyone to be γενναῖος without being εὐγενής at the same time, or for one who is εὐγενής not to be free; hence we are absolutely obliged to conclude that it is the man of ignoble birth who is a slave". Cf. also *idem,* 31.74, "One person is more prominent than another owing to his εὐγένεια or his ἀρετή, and it may also be on account of his πλοῦτος or for other good reasons".

[9] Plutarch, *Moralia* 58.E, "Again, some people will not even listen to the Stoics, when they call the wise man at the same time rich, handsome, well-born, and a king; but flatterers declare of the rich man that he is at the same time an orator and a poet, and, if he will, a painter and a musician, and swift of foot and strong of body; and they allow themselves to be thrown in wrestling and outdistanced in running ..."

[10] Aristotle, *The art of Rhetoric* 2.12.2, τύχην δὲ λέγω εὐγένειαν καὶ πλοῦτον καὶ δυνάμεις καὶ τἀναντία τούτοις καὶ ὅλως εὐτυχίαν καὶ δυστυχίαν.

[11] D. Sänger, 'Die dynatoi in 1 Kor 1.26', *ZNW* 76 (1985), 289, n. 30.

[12] D. Sänger, 'Die dynatoi in 1 Kor 1.26', 290-1. Cf. also *idem,* 287, "Die σοφοί sind Angehörige gebildeter Kreise, die der sozialen Oberschicht angehören. Daß σοφός in diesem Sinn zu deuten ist, legt u. a. εὐγενής nahe"; 290, "Paulus hat 1 Kor 1.26 diese ökonomische Valenz im Blick, wenn er einige Christen in Korinth als δυνατοί anredet", where he refers especially to Josephus.

[13] See esp. Philo, *De Virtutibus* 187-227.

ancestors from whom they boast descent find happiness in the superabundance of their possessions.[14]

In support of his argument, Philo cites on the one hand the instances of ignoble sons being born to the most noble of parents, Adam and Noah; and on the other hand the noble Abraham being the product of an ignoble Chaldean astrologer.[15]

Those characteristics which were widely sought in first century Graeco-Roman society are here denounced by the Jewish philosopher:

> For silver and gold and honour and offices and good condition of body and beauty (ἄργυρος γὰρ καὶ χρυσὸς τιμαί τε καὶ ἀρχαὶ καὶ σώματος εὐεξία μετ' εὐμορφίας) are like men set in command for ordinary purposes compared with service to queenly virtue and have never seen the light in its full radiance.[16]

Philo concludes *De Virtutibus* by advising, "Must we not then absolutely reject the claims of those who assume as their own precious possession the nobility (εὐγένεια) which belongs to others, who, different from those just mentioned, might well be considered enemies of the Jewish nation and of every person in every place?"[17]

Referring to a further section from Philo (*Det.* 33-4), Winter writes,

> Furthermore, the sophists describe themselves in synonymous categories in an actual debate (συζήτησις) in the first century and developed an argument strikingly similar to that of Paul's in 1 Cor. 1.26-31. In an extant verbatim report of a sophists' debate they boasted about their status, cataloguing the external evidence of their success which was a μάρτυς.[18]

Wüllner has written extensively on the source and implications of the triad in 1 Corinthians 1.26.[19] Significantly, he notes that this particular triadic formula is unprecedented, but suggests that the themes involved are widely employed in a broad selection of literature:[20] the themes appear in the Old Testament in judgment prophecies to foreign kings, prophecies about the eschatological king of Israel, the Royal Psalms (especially enthronement psalms), and the Wisdom poetry; in the Apocryphal writings in Sirach, in 2 Enoch, The Psalms

---

[14] Philo, *De Virtutibus* 187.

[15] Philo, *De Virtutibus* 199-2, 211-9. Cf. also 206, "These examples may serve as landmarks common to all mankind to remind them that those who have no true excellence of character should not pride themselves on the greatness of their race".

[16] Philo, *De Virtutibus* 188.

[17] Philo, *De Virtutibus* 226.

[18] B.W. Winter, *Philo and Paul among the Sophists: A Hellenistic Jewish and a Christian Response,* unpublished PhD dissertation (Macquarie University, 1988), 200.

[19] W. Wüllner, 'The Sociological Implications of 1 Corinthians 1.26-28 Reconsidered', in ed. E.A. Livingstone, *Studia Evangelica* VI (Berlin, 1973), 666-72; *idem,* 'Ursprung und Verwendung der σοφός-, δυνατός-, εὐγενής- Formel in 1 Kor 1,26', 165-184; *idem,* 'Tradition and Interpretation of the "Wise - Powerful - Noble" Triad in 1 Cor 1,26', ed. E.A. Livingstone, *Studia Evangelica* VII (Berlin, 1982), 557-62.

[20] The *Thesaurus Linguae Graecae* CD ROM, which contains some 80% of the *Thesaurus Linguae Graecae* corpus, indicates that the triad σοφός, δυνατός, εὐγενής occurs in Greek literature, other than in 1 Corinthians 1.26, only in later Christian writers—Basil, Eusebius, Gregory Nyssa, John Chrysostom, Macarius and Origen. In most of these instances it is as a direct quotation from 1 Corinthians 1.26.

of Solomon, Wisdom of Solomon; in the Rabbinic literature; in the Jewish Hellenistic literature; in the Classical and Hellenistic Greek literature; and in the New Testament.[21] The value of this work lies in the conclusion which can be drawn: Paul's terminology can be assumed to be conventional with traditional meanings.[22]

Winter, discussing 1 Corinthians 1.26, argues correctly that

> There can be no doubt that these descriptive terms used in 1 Cor. 1.26 refer to the ruling class from which rhetors and sophists came ... The epigraphic evidence from that city clearly shows that rhetors contributed to the political life of Corinth and would have been regarded as among the δυνατοί, εὐγενεῖς, and the σοφοί.[23]

Thus, Paul's use of these significant terms in 1 Corinthians 1.26 clearly implies that there were in the congregation some from the ruling class of society.[24] Meeks, in his *The First Urban Christians,* is therefore wrong to conclude that the Corinthian community, whilst consisting of a reasonable cross-section of society, lacked representation from the upper and lower echelons.[25]

In 1 Corinthians 3.18, Paul is clearly aware that there were within the Corinthian community those who certainly counted themselves amongst the established in society. He urges those who consider themselves to be wise in the eyes of society (σοφὸς ἐν τῷ αἰῶνι τούτῳ) rather to become fools.[26]

---

[21] W. Wüllner, 'Ursprung und Verwendung der σοφός-, δυνατός-, εὐγενής- Formel in 1 Kor 1,26', 168-9.

[22] Wüllner rightly draws the conclusion from the triadic formula in 'The Sociological Implications of 1 Corinthians 1.26-28 Reconsidered', 672, that "inferences drawn from archaeological sources notwithstanding, the Corinthian Christians came by and large from fairly well-to-do bourgeois circles with a fair percentage also from upper class people as well as the very poor. But to use 1 Corinthians 1.26-28 as the most important text in the whole New Testament for allegations of Christianity's proletarian origins is indefensible and no longer tenable simply and chiefly on grammatical grounds". Also *idem,* 672, "Neither in verse 26, nor in verses 27-28 is there even a trace of any evidence that the Corinthians belonged to proletarian circles".

[23] B.W. Winter, *Philo and Paul among the Sophists,* 200.

[24] G. Theissen, *The Social Setting of Pauline Christianity,* 71-3; R. Jewett, *The Thessalonian Correspondence: Pauline Rhetoric and Millenarian Piety* (Philadelphia, 1986), 120; A.J. Malherbe, *Social Aspects of Early Christianity* (ed 2: Philadelphia, 1983), 30; D. Sänger, 'Die δυνατοί in 1. Kor. 1,26', 287.

[25] W.A. Meeks, *The First Urban Christians—The Social World of the Apostle Paul* (New Haven and London, 1983), 72-3, "It is a picture in which people of several social levels are brought together. The extreme top and bottom of the Greco-Roman social scale are missing from the picture. It is hardly surprising that we meet no landed aristocrats, no senators, *equites,* nor (unless Erastus might qualify) decurions. But there is also no specific evidence of people who are destitute—such as the hired menials and dependent handworkers; the poorest of the poor, peasants, agricultural slaves, and hired agricultural day laborers, are absent because of the urban setting of the Pauline groups. There may well have been members of the Pauline communities who lived at the subsistence level, but we hear nothing of them".

[26] See the further discussion of 'wisdom of this age' in Chapter Seven below, 101-2.

3. *Evidence of Leading Figures in the Church*

Theissen undertakes an analysis of the social standing of some named individuals within the Corinthian congregation drawing the conclusion that a number from the community were socially high class.[27]

Crispus, mentioned in Acts 18.8 as a synagogue ruler, is singled out by Paul as one of the few that he has baptized (1 Cor 1.14). Theissen argues that the post of synagogue ruler, with its responsibility for the synagogue buildings, was probably entrusted to a wealthy man who would be in a position to supplement the synagogue funds from his own pocket.[28] With such a background, Crispus would certainly count amongst the influential and wealthy in Corinthian society.

Gaius is another of the members of the church who is singled out for specific mention. Paul, writing to the Romans, remarks that Gaius showed hospitality to the whole church in his own house.[29] Stephanus is also mentioned by Paul as a householder.[30] Theissen observes that information about householders proves valuable in determining private circumstances.[31] These named individuals, Crispus, Gaius and Stephanus, are certainly amongst the influential, and may therefore be included in Paul's statement in 1 Corinthians 1.26.[32] Barrett refers to such as these from Corinth, arguing that their social position may well have caused them to "gravitate into positions of leadership" in the Corinthian community and be included amongst the few "wise, powerful and nobly born".[33]

4. *Erastus*

Erastus is a figure from the New Testament who will prove to be one of the most important links with the secular leadership of Roman Corinth.[34]

The discovery of an inscription dedicated by an Erastus in Roman Corinth has prompted much speculative discussion as to the likelihood of there being a

---

[27] G. Theissen, *The Social Setting of Pauline Christianity*, 73-96. Cf. also M. Hengel, *Property and Riches in the Early Church: Aspects of a Social History of Early Christianity* (London, 1974), 38.

[28] G. Theissen, *The Social Setting of Pauline Christianity*, 74, cites inscriptional evidence in support of this.

[29] Rom 16.23.

[30] 1 Cor 1.16; 16.15 ff.

[31] G. Theissen, *The Social Setting of Pauline Christianity*, 83.

[32] B. Fiore, "'Covert Allusion' in 1 Corinthians 1-4', *The Catholic Biblical Quarterly* 47 (1985), 95, with regard to this influential group, concurs with Theissen and Judge: "Theissen's analysis of the social stratification within the Corinthian community (even discounting certain exaggerations in his claims) suggests the importance of the small but influential group of upper class Christians for the organization and continuation of the community's life in faith. Judge's description of the early Christians as 'scholastic community' suggests the interest of at least the Christian patrons to resemble those of other groups around sophists and professional rhetoricians".

[33] C.K. Barrett, *Church, Ministry, and Sacraments in the New Testament* (Exeter, 1985), 36-7.

[34] Rom 16.23.

common identity between the Erasti mentioned in the New Testament and the Erastus of the Corinthian pavement. The information which can be gleaned from this inscription will first be determined, before considering any link between the epigraphic Erastus and that of the New Testament.

a. *The Corinthian Inscription*

The inscription may be found on two paving slabs forming part of a larger pavement prominently placed east of the stage building of the Roman theatre. The whole area of pavement may have been 19 x 19 m.[35] The original inscription consisted of three slabs 0.66 m. high,[36] 0.15 m. thick with letters of height 0.18 m.[37] The total length of the three slabs may have been 5.57 m.[38] The slabs were cut from grey Acrocorinthian limestone, and the letters were probably originally made of bronze (apart from some lead in two of the punctuation marks, it is only the cuttings for the letters which can now be seen). The central and much of the right hand slabs have been found. The central slab, found *in situ* in April 1929, reads:

ERASTUS·PRO·AED
S·P·STRAVIT

Two portions of the right hand slab were found in March 1928 and August 1947,[39] thus allowing the more complete reading:

ERASTUS·PRO·AEDILITatE
S·P·STRAVIT

praenomen nomen Erastus in return for his aedileship
laid (the pavement) at his own expense[40]

The left hand slab, yet to be found, would probably provide the praenomen and nomen of this Erastus. Kent calculates, on the assumption that the second line is complete and was placed symmetrically below line 1, that Erastus' nomen consisted of five or six letters, and that there was no space for either a

---

[35] Cf. T.L. Shear, 'Excavations in the Theatre District and Tombs of Corinth in 1929', *American Journal of Archaeology* 33 (1929), 525; D.W.J. Gill, 'Erastus the Aedile', *Tyndale Bulletin* 40 (1989), 294.

[36] The fragments from the right hand slab are both 0.64 m. high, but would allow the possibility of an original height of 0.66 m.

[37] The height of this lettering is unusual amongst the Corinthian inscriptions and suggests a benefactor of considerable wealth.

[38] Thus J.H. Kent, *Corinth—Inscriptions 1926-1950 Corinth: Results,* viii, Part III (Princeton, 1966), # 232, where the central slab is 2.27 m. and the right and left hand slabs are supposed to be 1.65 m. (the fragments from the right hand slab allow a reconstruction to a probable original width of 1.65 m). *Contra* D.W.J. Gill, 'Erastus the Aedile', 2.

[39] One part was found in the East Parodos of the Theatre, and the other in the basement of a late vaulted building southwest of the Theatre.

[40] S·P is a standard abbreviation for *sua pecunia*, 'with his own money' (see J.H. Kent, *Corinth—Inscriptions,* # 231 for a similar inscription celebrating a benefaction given *sua pecunia*).

patronymic or tribal abbreviation. He then concluded that this Erastus was a freedman.[41]

It was first considered that the central slab formed the complete inscription.[42] The earliest assessments of the inscription, based only on this central slab, drew the conclusion that PRO·AED signified that this Erastus had been both procurator and aedile.[43] It was on the basis that procurator might reasonably be translated οἰκονόμος that it was originally held that the Erastus of the inscription might be the same as that of Romans 16.23.[44] By 29th November 1930, de Waele had become convinced, however, that the 1929 inscription was incomplete.[45] After the initial confidence that Erastus had been both procurator and aedile and that he had been the friend of Paul,[46] Roos, Van de Weerd, Cadbury and de Waele all posed the correct suggestion that PRO·AED stood for *pro aedilitate* (or some similar phrase meaning "in return for aedileship"). They each came to express reservation that the Erastus of the Corinthian pavement was the same Erastus of Romans 16.23.[47]

Harrison's argument, although published in 1964, takes no account of the right hand slab of the inscription.[48] His supposition is that PRO·AED stands

---

[41] Cf. J.H. Kent, *Corinth—Inscriptions,* # 232. He suggests, "Erastus was probably a Corinthian freedman who had acquired considerable wealth in commercial activities". H.J. Cadbury, 'Erastus of Corinth', *JBL* 50 (1931), 52, is incorrect, however, to draw the conclusion that Erastus must have been a slave on the grounds that "the old Corinthian Greek stock was completely exterminated or reduced to slavery by Mummius". There is the clear example of the wealthy Spartan Euryclid family holding prominent positions in the Corinthian colony. This was pointed out to me by D.W.J. Gill. Cf. P. Cartledge & A. Spawforth, *Hellenistic and Roman Sparta* (London, 1989), 104, 110-1. See also J.H. Kent, *Corinth—Inscriptions,* # 314.

[42] So H.J. Cadbury, 'Erastus of Corinth', 52, n. 35; T.L. Shear, 'Excavations in the Theatre District and Tombs of Corinth in 1929', 525.

[43] T.L. Shear, 'Excavations in the Theatre District and Tombs of Corinth in 1929', 525; F.J. de Waele, 'Erastus, oikonoom van Korinthe en vriend van St. Paulus', *Mededeelingen van het Nederlandsch historisch Instituut te Rome* 9 (1929), 44; A.M. Woodward, 'Archaeology in Greece, 1928-1929', *Journal of Hellenic Studies* 49 (1929), 221. Each of these draws a parallel between the Erastus of the inscription and the Erastus of Romans 16.23.

[44] T.L. Shear, 'Excavations in the Theatre District and Tombs of Corinth in 1929', 525; F.J. de Waele, 'Erastus, oikonoom van Korinthe en vriend van St. Paulus', 44.

[45] Cf. H.J. Cadbury, 'Erastus of Corinth', 52, n. 35. H. Van de Weerd also suggested this in 'Een Nieuw Opschrift van Korinthe', *Revue Belge de Philologie et d'Histoire* 10 (1931), 88. A.G. Roos notes the incompleteness of the inscription in 'De Titulo quodam latino Corinthi nuper reperto', *Mnemosyne* 58 (1930), 160-1.

[46] Cf. T.L. Shear, 'Discoveries at "The Wealthy City of the Double Sea"', *The Illustrated London News* (August 17, 1929), 286, "All the available evidence indicates that this pavement existed in the first century AD, and there is no reason to doubt that the Erastus mentioned was the friend of St. Paul".

[47] A.G. Roos, 'De Titulo quodam latino Corinthi nuper reperto', 162-3; H. Van de Weerd, 'Een Nieuw Opschrift van Korinthe', 92, 94-5; H.J. Cadbury, 'Erastus of Corinth', 53-4, 58; and F.J. de Waele, 'Die Korinthischen Ausgrabungen 1928-29', *Gnomon* 6 (1930), 226.

[48] P.N. Harrison, *Paulines and Pastorals* (London, 1964), 100-105. R. Stillwell, *The Theatre, Corinth* ii, American School of Classical Studies at Athens (Princeton, 1952), 4 and plate II, appears to be the first citation of the fuller inscription. He gives reference to its forthcoming publication in J.H. Kent, *Corinth—Inscriptions.* C.E.B. Cranfield, *The Epistle to the Romans* II (Edinburgh, 1979), and F.F. Bruce, *The Letter of Paul to the Romans* (ed 2: Leicester, 1989) *ad loc.* overlook the same evidence.

for *pro aedile* or *pro aedilis* (that is deputy aedile).[49] The crucial piece of evidence in the right hand slab clearly demonstrates the incorrectness of his assumption: the noun is *aedilitas,* not *aedilis,* and thus the translation is "in return for aedileship", and not "deputy aedile".

PRO·AEDILITATE·S·P·STRAVIT ("laid this with his money in return for aedileship"), signifies that the pavement was laid by an Erastus as part of an election promise. There is a similar election promise, but of an unknown building, by another first century aedile from Corinth, named Hicesius.[50] Such election promises were described by the term *pollicitatio.*[51]

The present information clearly leads to the assumption that an Erastus, possibly a freedman, laid a pavement in the square, east of the stage building of the Theatre at Corinth, at his own expense and in return for being appointed to the position of aedile.

The inscription itself is brief, yet is full enough to admit a clear meaning; nonetheless it has prompted considerable debate. The major question surrounding this inscription is whether the Erastus mentioned in the inscription can be identified with the Erastus mentioned in Romans 16.23.[52] The chief matters of discussion are first, the date of the inscription; secondly, the relationship between Paul's word οἰκονόμος and the title on the inscription; and thirdly, the relative rarity of the name Erastus.[53] The dating of the inscription to the middle of the first century AD is not widely disputed.[54] Discussion must, therefore, centre on the equivalence or otherwise of the terms aedile and οἰκονόμος and the relative commonness of the name Erastus. Only after this discussion will it be assessed whether these Erasti may be identified.

b. *Aedile and Οἰκονόμος*

The principal problem which has dominated the debate over Erastus rests with determining the synonymity or otherwise of aedile and οἰκονόμος. Romans 16.23 reads, ὁ οἰκονόμος τῆς πόλεως, whereas the Latin of the inscription is clearly *aedile.* As has been pointed out, it was the initial assumption that the inscription described Erastus as procurator which raised the possibility that procurator and οἰκονόμος might have been equivalent expressions. Kent, after demonstrating that the inscription unequivocally reads *pro aedilitate,* does not,

---

[49] P.N. Harrison, *Paulines and Pastorals,* 103-4. Harrison does point out that the abbreviation PRO·AED occurs nowhere else. He also works on the incorrect assumption that the office of aedile was a permanent appointment, 105. It was in fact an annually elected post, and there is no evidence of anyone in Corinth holding the position for more than one year, or being reappointed to the post at a later date.

[50] Cf. J.H. Kent, *Corinth—Inscriptions,* # 231: "Hicesius the aedile built this [building] at his own expense, with the official permission of the city council". Cf. also P. Licinius Priscus Juventianus, in *IG* 4.203.

[51] Cf. P. Garnsey, '*Taxatio* and *pollicitatio* in Roman Africa', *JRS* 61 (1971), 116-29.

[52] Rom 16.23, ἀσπάζεται ὑμᾶς Γάιος ὁ ξένος μου καὶ ὅλης τῆς ἐκκλησίας. ἀσπάζεται ὑμᾶς Ἔραστος ὁ οἰκονόμος τῆς πόλεως καὶ Κούαρτος ὁ ἀδελφός.

[53] Cf. J.H. Kent, *Corinth—Inscriptions,* # 232.

[54] Kent, confidently dates the inscription from its lettering to the Neronian period.

however, reject the identification of the two Erasti, although it now clearly has to be argued on the basis of assuming Erastus the οἰκονόμος to be aedile and not procurator. Key aspects of this lengthy debate, as it has developed, will be described.

The usual Greek equivalent for aedile is ἀγορανόμος or ἀστυνόμος and scholars have questioned why Paul, if it is the same Erastus, does not use one of these more usual terms.[55] It needs to be noticed also, however, that the term ἀγορανόμος first appears in the Corinthian inscriptions in the second century (170 AD).[56] During the first century AD, the inscriptions suggest that Latin was the official language of administration in the colony. In the time of Paul it may well, therefore, have been the case that ἀγορανόμος was not widely used in Roman Corinth.[57]

It should also be pointed out that H.J. Mason in his *Greek terms for Roman Institutions—A Lexicon and Analysis,* gives epigraphic examples from Hierapolis, Philadelphia and Smyrna which provide evidence that ἀγορανόμος and οἰκονόμος are equivalent expressions in a Roman *municipium* or colony.[58] Οἰκονόμος could describe a number of positions—*actor, dispensator, vilicus* or *aedilis coloniae.*[59] From Hierapolis, Philadelphia and Smyrna, Mason gives instances of οἰκονόμοι τῆς πόλεως who were aediles.[60] If this is the case in Corinth also, then there is no reason from the titles why aedile and οἰκονόμος could not be considered identical.[61]

Cadbury points out, however, that the thorough work of Landvogt on the inscriptional evidence for οἰκονόμος has been "all but completely ignored in New Testament commentaries and dictionaries".[62] This thorough study of the development of the term οἰκονόμος offers valuable insight on the present discussion.[63] Landvogt demonstrates that οἰκονόμος could refer to a number of

---

[55] H.J. Mason, 'Greek Terms for Roman Institutions—A Lexicon and Analysis', *American Studies in Papyrology* XIII (Toronto, 1974), 175. D. Magie, *De Romanorum iuris publici sacrique vocabulis sollemnibus in Graecum sermonem conversis* I (Halle, 1904), 11. Magie also notes, however, some instances where unusual Greek translations of Latin offices have been made, 25.

[56] P. Licinius Priscus Juventianus fulfils an election promise, not dissimilar to that of Erastus, in return for his aedileship, ὑπὲρ ἀγορανομίας. J.H. Kent, *Corinth—Inscriptions,* # 306.

[57] Thus, G. Theissen, *The Social Setting of Pauline Christianity,* 80.

[58] Cf. H.J. Mason, 'Greek Terms for Roman Institutions—A Lexicon and Analysis', 71, 175 f. *IG.Rom.* 4.813; 4.1630; 1435. D. Magie, *De Romanorum iuris publici sacrique vocabulis sollemnibus in Graecum sermonem conversis* I, does not note any parallel between these two terms.

[59] H.J. Mason, 'Greek Terms for Roman Institutions—A Lexicon and Analysis', 71.

[60] *Inscriptiones Graecae ad res Romanas pertinentes* 4.813; 1435; 1630. The last of these is an inscription recording honours held by a sophist of Philadelphia. One of the honours was specifically that he had been ὁ τῆς πόλεως οἰκονόμος.

[61] G. Theissen, *The Social Setting of Pauline Christianity,* 78.

[62] H.J. Cadbury, 'Erastus of Corinth', 47. P. Landvogt, *Epigraphische Untersuchungen über den OIKONOMOS: ein Beitrag zum hellenistischen Beamtenwesen,* Dissertation (Strassburg, 1908).

[63] For a later work looking at financial offices see D. Magie, *Roman Rule in Asia Minor to the end of the Third Century after Christ* (Princeton, 1950), vol I, 61; vol II, 850-1.

different posts, and consequently, at different times and places, might refer to an office of considerable prestige or a menial, servile rôle.[64]

He describes the responsibilities of the οἰκονόμος showing great overlap with the colonial aedile:

> Die Hauptkompetenzen des οἰκονόμος in diesen Freistaaten bestehen in der Sorge für Aufschrift und Aufstellung von Psephismen und Statuen, in Bestreitung der Kosten für jene Besorgungen sowie für Kränze und Gastgeschenke. ... Kurz, das Chararakeristische für die ganze Amtstätigkeit des οἰκονόμος ... in dieser Periode ist, daß er lediglich als Kassen- oder Finanzbeamter fungiert.[65]

Landvogt reaches the further conclusion that the οἰκονόμος and the ταμίας, although distinct offices, had considerable overlap in their responsibilities.[66] This assessment of the inscriptions clearly suggests that the οἰκονόμος was an eminent post.[67] If the Erastus of Romans 16.23 fits this definition of οἰκονόμος (from the free cities of Asia Minor, before the Roman period), he is, as Cadbury points out, "a man of some position. For it was indeed an office of honor".[68]

The Pauline context, however, is Corinthian and dating from the reign of Nero or Claudius. Cadbury suggests that in such a context the office would probably have been more lowly: a financial assistant of servile origin.[69] He then considers that the Vulgate's translation of *arcarius civitatis* may be the most appropriate. However, this is too dogmatic an inference. The weakness of such a suggestion is that it finds support from the Vulgate's translation of the term *arcarius civitatis* meaning a low-level financial bureaucrat.[70] Cadbury

---

64 P. Landvogt, *Epigraphische Untersuchungen über den* OIKONOMOS, 16, "Nach der historischen Entwickelung ergeben sich für uns folgende Gesichtspunkte: Der οἰκονόμος tritt auf: A. als öffentlicher Beamter in Freistaaten und zwar: 1. als Beamter der πόλις selbst; 2. als Beamter eines politischen Teiles des Staates; 3. als Beamter politischer Körperschaften. B. als Privatbeamter und zwar als Beamter: 1. in der Monarchie der hellenistischen Zeit; 2. der kaiserlichen Haushalte in römischer Zeit; 3. von Privatvereinen; 4. von einzelnen Privatpersonen". Cf. also Liddell/Scott/Jones: "οἰκονόμος, 2b, title of a subordinate state official, *IG* 5(2),389,15 (4-3 BC) ; also of a high financial officer, *Inscr. Prien.* 6.30 (4 BC) *B Mus Inscr.* 448.7 (Eph. 4 BC)".

65 P. Landvogt, *Epigraphische Untersuchungen über den* OIKONOMOS, 17.

66 P. Landvogt, *Epigraphische Untersuchungen über den* OIKONOMOS, 19-21.

67 G. Theissen, *The Social Setting of Pauline Christianity,* 77, "In these instances the term οἰκονόμος (τῆς πόλεως) refers to a high position. It is held by officials who deal with financial matters, erect columns, but have different responsibilities in different cities. These are not simply treasurers, but alongside them will frequently be found the ταμίας".

68 H.J. Cadbury, 'Erastus of Corinth', 49. F.F. Bruce, *The Letter of Paul to the Romans,* 266 suggests that Erastus held the more minor position of *arcarius,* but may have later been promoted to that of aedile. For further evidence of the senior rank of οἰκονόμος, cf. R.S. Bagnall, *The Administration of Ptolemaic possessions outside Egypt* (Leiden, 1976), 220, 224-8.

69 Cf. also A.G. Roos, 'De Titulo quodam latino Corinthi nuper reperto', 164. R. Lane Fox, *Pagans and Christians* (Harmondsworth, 1988), 293, suggests that to be 'steward of the city' was an eminent post of a public slave. He concludes, "it is quite uncertain whether this man could be the Erastus whom a recent inscription in Corinth's theatre revealed as a freeborn magistrate, the aedile of the colony". The argument rests partly on whether the genitive of οἰκονόμος τῆς πόλεως is a possessive genitive, 'the city's official'. See G. Theissen, *The Social Setting of Pauline Christianity,* 76.

70 See for example J.H. Moulton & G. Milligan, *The Vocabulary of the Greek Testament; Illustrated from the Papyri and other Non-Literary Sources* (Grand Rapids, 1980), 442-3; οἰκονόμος,

doubts the two Erasti are identical on the basis of the unlikelihood that a public slave, *arcarius,* might later rise to the coveted position of aedile.[71]

Horsley draws parallels between the οἰκονόμος of Romans 16.23 and οἰκονόμοι in a number of inscriptions from Nikaia in the imperial period.[72] He points out that the οἰκονόμος could be either a slave or a patron of some influence. The parallels are not close, however, since the examples appear to refer to private stewards, rather than a city official; furthermore, Nikaia was not a Roman colony. No clear parallel can be drawn with Corinth unless recognition is given that the city was a colony, with a different administrative organisation than other Greek cities.[73]

In addition to the distinction between colonial and non-colonial offices, Corinth also was unusual in the tasks which it gave to its aediles.[74] Normally, aediles would be given responsibility for the management of the public streets, market places and buildings. Much of their work involved the city's revenues, and they could often also act as judges in financial litigation. In addition, they would take charge of the public games. In Corinth, however, the administration of the games was considered a more prestigious post because of the prominence of the city in the national and international games. These games were funded at enormous expense largely by their president, thus requiring that whoever filled this honorary post had to be of substantial means and give financial guarantees of his wealth. In Corinth, because of its extraordinary games, this responsibility was given to an *agonothetes.*[75] On these grounds it has been suggested that the usual Greek equivalent for aedile may have been considered inappropriate by Paul whilst writing to a Corinthian readership.[76] It may have been for this reason that Paul referred to Erastus as an οἰκονόμος τῆς πόλεως instead of the more usual aedile.

Theissen's conclusion is that the two Erasti are probably the same person, but at different stages in his public career. He considers the Pauline descrip-

---

"The meaning 'treasurer' which is given to the word in Romans 16.23 is common both in Ptolemaic and in Roman times, though latterly the position sank much in importance: see *P.Tebt* 1.5 1. 159 (118 BC), *P.Tebt* 2.296 1. 12 (AD 123)". See also W.A. McDonald, 'Archaeology and St. Paul's Journeys in Greek lands, part III—Corinth', *Biblical Archaeologist* 5 (1942), 46, n. 2, "The argument that oikonomos is translated arcarius in the Vulgate and that the arcarius in Roman cities was usually of servile origin, while the aedile was of higher social standing, loses its point when we take into account the fact that oikonomos to an easterner like Paul might denote a very similar position to a Roman aedile". Cf. G. Theissen, *The Social Setting of Pauline Christianity,* 76. Cf. also L. Mitteis, and U. Wilcken, *Grundzüge und Chrestomathie der Papyruskunde* I (Leipzig and Berlin, 1912), 158-9, for the view that οἰκονόμος was an imperial financial slave.

[71] Cadbury, 'Erastus of Corinth', 56.

[72] G.H.R. Horsley, 'οἰκονόμος', *New Documents Illustrating Early Christianity* 4 (1987), 160-1.

[73] Cf. G. Theissen, *The Social Setting of Pauline Christianity,* 78.

[74] J.H. Kent, *Corinth—Inscriptions,* # 27.

[75] In a brief discussion of Erastus, J. Stambaugh and D. Balch, *The Social World of the First Christians* (London, 1986), 160, draw their conclusion, based wrongly on the assumption that the aedile was responsible for the games, that "Erastus therefore belonged to the municipal aristocracy, and this wealthy official may well be the same as the Christian mentioned by Paul".

[76] G. Theissen finds this unconvincing on the grounds that separate officials for games are attested elsewhere as well, *Studien zur Soziologie des Urchristentums* (Tübingen, 1979), 243.

tion, οἰκονόμος, to be the equivalent of the Latin *quaestor* rather than a menial slave, and that only later did Erastus become the aedile of the pavement.[77] However, just as there is no evidence for the Greek term ἀγορανόμος in this period, so also there is no evidence for the Greek equivalent for quaestor (ταμίας) in this period.[78]

One further problem is raised in an article by A.G. Roos. He advances one reason for considering why the Erastus referred to in Romans 16 could not have been that of the Corinthian aedile.[79] The duovir, aedile and quaestor were compelled, on embarking on an office, to make an oath *"per Iovem et divos imperatores et genium principis deosque Penates"*.[80] In his view, it was incompatible with the New Testament faith for a Christian to make such an oath to the Roman Emperor and gods. Roos draws attention to the reference made by Pliny the Younger to the emperor Trajan regarding how to treat Christians who refused to swear an oath of allegiance to the emperor.[81] According to Pliny, the method he chose to adopt was to demand that a person accused of being a Christian should invoke the Roman gods, offer adoration to an image of the emperor and curse Christ, "none of which acts, it is said, those who are really Christians can be forced into performing". It may be noted, however, that B. Winter has found strong evidence from Romans 13.3 and

---

[77] Cf. G. Theissen, *The Social Setting of Pauline Christianity,* 81-83. See also V.P. Furnish, 'Corinth in Paul's time. What can Archaeology tell us?', *Biblical Archaeology Review* 15 (1988), 20, "Although an *aedile* was not a city treasurer, but more like a commissioner of public works, one did not attain an aedileship without having first served the city in other important capacities. In the case of Erastus the *aedile*, we may suppose, one of these earlier offices was that of *quaestor,* or municipal financial officer". Cf. also J. Murphy O'Connor, 'The Corinth that Paul saw', *Biblical Archaeologist* 47 (1984), 155, who offers the suggestion, "Since the pavement antedates the middle of the first century AD, this person is identified with the Erastus who became one of Paul's converts. ... It is not impossible that Paul met Erastus in the latter's official capacity—that is, when paying rent or taxes on his workspace, which would explain why he calls Erastus 'the treasurer of the city'". F.A. Philippi in *Commentary on St Paul's Epistle to the Romans* (ET: Edinburgh, 1878), offers a similar suggestion of Erastus as a *quaestor.*

[78] G. Theissen, *The Social Setting of Pauline Christianity,* 82. D. Magie, *De Romanorum iuris publici sacrique vocabulis sollemnibus in Graecum sermonem conversis* I, 11.

[79] Cadbury also points out the difficulty of a Christian assuming such a post, although he does not spell out the reasons which are given in A.G. Roos, 'De Titulo quodam latino Corinthi nuper reperto', 160-165.

[80] Roos refers to T. Mommsen, *Gesammelte Schriften* I, 320-1 and Leg. Salpens, 26, who states that within five days of entering upon magistracy, in front of a congregation of decuriones or *conscripti,* the magistrates take a public oath by Jupiter, by divine Augustus, divine Claudius, divine Vespasianus Augustus, and by divine Titius Augustus and by the genius of the *imperator* Domitianus Augustus and by the *dei Penates* "that they will rightly perform whatsoever they believe to be in accordance with this law and to the common interests of the citizens of the municipium Flavium Salpensanum, and that they will not, knowingly and of wrongful intent, do ought contrary to this law or to the common interest of the citizens of the said municipium, and that they will neither prevent others from so doing as far as they are able; and that they will neither hold nor allow a meeting of the decuriones, nor express any opinion except such as in their judgment is consistent with this law and the common interest of the citizens of the said municipium". The additional clause is given, however, that: "Any person failing to take such oath shall be condemned to pay to the citizens of the said municipium 10,000 sesterces and in respect to the said money, the right to take legal action, to sue and to prosecute, shall belong at will to every citizen of the said municipium, and to any other person specified by this law".

[81] Pliny, *Epistulae* 10.96.

1 Peter 2.14 to suggest that Christians were actually strongly encouraged to be involved in matters of the local city, especially in giving benefactions to the local civic community.[82]

The outcome of this extensive debate is that, over a period, the title οἰκονόμος covered a wide range of rôles and in some circumstances οἰκονόμος could be linked with aedile. This does not mean, however, that a link can as yet be drawn between the two Erasti. It merely allows the possibility.

c. *The name 'Erastus'*

The relative rarity of the cognomen Erastus is also significant in the discussion. The name is mentioned three times in the New Testament, and it is agreed amongst those who discuss the problem in relation to the archaeological evidence that there is just this one inscription, the Erastus pavement, which draws attention to an Erastus in Corinth. It is important, therefore, not only to weigh up the New Testament evidence for identity between these three occurrences, but also to outline some of the extra-Biblical evidence for other Erasti.[83]

The name Erastus is mentioned three times in the New Testament, and in each instance it is as a friend of Paul's.[84] It is possible to see a connection with both Corinth and Ephesus in each of these references, as Cadbury has pointed out.[85] Redlich affirms the common identity between these Erasti.[86] Hemer states, however, regarding the New Testament references to Erastus, "There is no sufficient reason to affirm either of these identifications, and the illustrative value of the case is rather that Paul's helper(s) associated with Ephesus and Corinth bear a name otherwise attested among prominent persons in those cities". Hemer tends to agree with Cadbury that identification is doubtful.[87]

Hemer has pointed out that the name is perhaps less common than often appreciated;[88] however, he does indicate epigraphic instances of Erasti from Ephesus.[89] A number of other instances of Erasti have been found covering a

---

[82] Cf. B.W. Winter, 'The Public Honouring of Christian Benefactors: Romans 13.3-4 and 1 Peter 2.14-15', *JSNT* 34 (1988), 87-103.

[83] See the brief discussion in W. Ollrog, *Paulus und seine Mitarbeiter: Untersuchungen zu Theorie und Praxis der paulinischen Mission* (Neukirchen-Vluyn, 1979), 50-3.

[84] Acts 19.22; Rom 16.23; and 2 Tim 4.20.

[85] H.J. Cadbury, 'Erastus of Corinth', 45.

[86] E.B. Redlich, *S. Paul and his Companions* (London, 1913), 231-2.

[87] C.J. Hemer, *The Book of Acts in the Setting of Hellenistic History* (Tübingen, 1989), 235.

[88] C.J. Hemer, *The Book of Acts in the Setting of Hellenistic History*, 235. C.E.B. Cranfield, *The Epistle to the Romans,* and H.A.W. Meyer, *Critical and Exegetical Handbook to the Epistle to the Romans* (ET: Edinburgh, 1879), *ad loc.* suggest the name was common.

[89] C.J. Hemer, *The Book of Acts in the Setting of Hellenistic History,* 235, "The best example is the Ti. Claudius Erastus from a Curetes list dated to AD 54-59, referring to the son of the *prytanis* named at the head of the list (*I. Eph.* 1008.8). The example in MM (*SIG*3 838, cited by them from *SIG*2 388) is also a leading Ephesian, but is later (= *I. Eph.* 1487, Ephesus, AD 128-29)". Cf., however, V.P. Furnish, 'Corinth in Paul's time. What can Archaeology tell us?', 20, "No other person of this name is known to have been an official in Corinth, and since the name itself is not common, it would appear that this Erastus is the same one whom Paul and the author of 2 Timothy mention".

broad geographical area and time period.[90] It remains the case that the name Erastus is relatively uncommon, although little can be argued from this statistic.

The assumption that, apart from the pavement inscription and the New Testament, the name Erastus is not otherwise found in Corinth, has widely been made.[91] One further instance of a reference to a Corinthian Erastus has come to light, however, although it has not as yet been noticed by those commentating on the Erastus problem. In 1960, a white marble dedication, mentioning an Erastus was found at Skoutéla in Corinth which dates from the second century AD. This was published much later by D.I. Pallas and S.P. Dantes and is not referred to by the American School of Classical Studies at Corinth:[92]

[Οἱ]·Βιτέλλιοι	[The] Vitellii
[Φρο]ντεῖνος	[Fro]ntinus
[καὶ·Ἔ]ραστος	[and E]rastus
[τῷ· - -]	(dedicate this) [to] -
[- - -]ι	[- - -]

A more detailed discussion of this inscription is given in the author's recent article on Erastus.[93] This second inscription to a Corinthian Erastus can neither be linked with the earlier inscription, nor with the Erasti mentioned in the New Testament. The grounds for confident rejection of this second inscription are clear: it has a second century dating and it is a pagan dedication. It is important, however, to note that such sure grounds for rejection do not apply to the first century Erastus inscription. It must be conceded that the grounds for rejecting an identification between Erastus, the aedile of the first century inscription, and Erastus, the οἰκονόμος τῆς πόλεως, are more slender.

d. *Are the Two Erasti to be Identified?*

It has been seen that New Testament commentators are generally doubtful as to the possibility of one and the same man being referred to in each of these New Testament references.[94] It has been conceded here that the present information does not allow us to make a certain identification between the Erastus of Romans 16.23 and that of the first century Corinthian inscription. Οἰκονόμος in some contexts clearly refers to a domestic slave.[95] It must be

---

[90] *SEG* 11, 622 (Laconia), and 994 (Messenia); *SEG* 24, 194 (Attica); *SEG* 25, 194 (Attica); *SEG* 28, 1010 (Bithynia); *CIG* 269; 1241 (Sparta); 1249 (Sparta); 6378. These cover the broad span from the third century BC to the third century AD. I am grateful to D.W.J. Gill for drawing my attention to some of these instances.

[91] Cf. J.H. Kent, *Corinth—Inscriptions*, # 232.

[92] D.I. Pallas, S.P. Dantes, Ἐπιγραφες ἀπο την Κορινθω, *Archaiologike Ephemeris* 1977 (1979), 75-76. Cf. also *SEG* 29 (1979), no. 301.

[93] A.D. Clarke, 'Another Corinthian Erastus Inscription', *Tyndale Bulletin* 42 (1991), 146-151.

[94] Those against the identification include, Dunn, Cranfield, Michel, Murray, Leenhardt, Meyer, Philippi, Wilckens.

[95] See Paul's use of the term in 1 Cor 4.1.

seen, however, that the possibility certainly remains that an οἰκονόμος τῆς πόλεως within the first century colony was a Greek equivalent for aedile, and that in the same year in which Erastus the aedile laid his pavement in fulfilment of an election promise, Paul wrote to the church in Rome sending greetings from the aedile, termed οἰκονόμος τῆς πόλεως.[96]

Crucially, however, it must be contended that attempts to solve the question of the status of the Erastus of Romans 16.23 simply through its relation to the Erastus of the pavement are misguided. Even if this identification is rejected, there are further grounds to assess the status of the Erastus of the Corinthian church.

Theissen raises some provocative questions regarding the status of Erastus in Romans 16.23.[97] He notices that only in this one passage does Paul highlight the secular rank of a member of one of his churches. It is unlikely that this would have been done if Erastus had been no more than a slave. It is suggested that such an exceptional case indicates relatively high status.[98]

Regardless of any direct connection between these Erasti, there is the firm probability that in the Erastus of Romans 16.23, there is a figure who was one of the established people of Corinth, and was in a position to offer hospitality to the whole church of Corinth.

It can be concluded that there is the interesting occurrence of some biographical detail describing one of the more important members of the Christian community at Corinth, and one of Paul's travelling companions. It is reasonable to argue back from the circumstances suggested in Romans 16.23 that this particular οἰκονόμος τῆς πόλεως was a position not of a public slave, but one of considerable honour.[99] Here is one figure who certainly belonged to the οὐ πολλοὶ δυνατοί of 1 Corinthians 1.26.[100]

---

[96] Cf. G. Theissen, *The Social Setting of Pauline Christianity*, 81.

[97] G. Theissen, *The Social Setting of Pauline Christianity*, 75.

[98] G. Theissen, *The Social Setting of Pauline Christianity*, 76. Cf. also O. Broneer, 'Corinth, Center of St Paul's missionary work in Greece', *Biblical Archaeologist* 14 (1951), 94, "He was probably the same Erastus who became a co-worker of St. Paul (Acts 19:22; Rom 16:23; where he is called *oikonomos*, 'chamberlain' of the city), a notable exception to the Apostles' characterization of the early Christians: 'Not many wise men after the flesh, not many mighty, not many noble are called' (I Cor 1:26)".

[99] J.D.G. Dunn reaches a slightly less confident conclusion in his commentary, *Romans 9-16* (Waco, 1988), 911; "Though οἰκονόμος could denote a high financial officer within the local government of Corinth, it is not clear how high the rank was within the administrative hierarchy. οἰκονόμος could denote a high financial officer, but also a role fulfilled by slaves and freedmen ... Be that as it may, the possibility remains (we can put it no more strongly) that Erastus was a Roman citizen ... of some wealth and notable social status". C.E.B. Cranfield, in *The Epistle to the Romans, ad loc.*, draws a similar conclusion as to the high responsibility of this city official who was also in the Christian community. Cf. also W. Sanday & A.C. Headlam, *A Critical and Exegetical Commentary on The Epistle to the Romans* (Edinburgh, 1920); F.A. Philippi, *Commentary on St. Paul's Epistle to the Romans, ad loc.*; W.A. Meeks, *The First Urban Christians*, 59.

[100] G. Theissen, *The Social Setting of Pauline Christianity*, 83; O. Broneer, 'Corinth, Center of St Paul's missionary work in Greece', 94; J.D.G. Dunn, *Romans 1-8*, 43.

5. *Conclusions*

It has been shown that, in 1 Corinthians, Paul specifically addresses some in the congregation who were from the higher classes of Graeco-Roman society.

In 1 Corinthians 1.26, Paul expressly uses terminology which was commonly used by other writers of the period to describe those who were influential, and therefore among the wise and well-born. He comments that some, although not many, from this social band were in the church. It was further seen that Paul continued in 1 Corinthians 1-6 to use terminology of this kind—for example, wisdom and wealth. However small this group may have been in the church, their influence is sufficiently significant for Paul to devote much of the opening sections of the letter to their situation.

In addition to the general references which Paul makes, it has also been seen that Paul more specifically refers to some individuals from the Corinthian church who were from these established classes. The clearest reference is to the leading figure, Erastus, for which there may also be extra-biblical evidence.

In Chapters Five and Six, further cumulative evidence will be given from the Corinthian community demonstrating that there were members of the church who were among the influential in society.

CHAPTER FIVE

SECULAR PRACTICES OF CHRISTIAN LEADERS:
I. GOING TO COURT

1. *Introduction*

In Chapters Two and Three the nature of Graeco-Roman leadership in the first century colony of Corinth was portrayed, indicating the structures of authority and the dynamics of leadership in that society. It has been shown in Chapter Four that Paul specifically addresses some Christians in Corinth who belonged to those élite ranks of society, and therefore that the Corinthian church included some from the higher classes in Hellenistic society. Further evidence supporting this contention will be given in Chapters Five and Six. It will also be demonstrated in these two chapters that some of the secular practices normally pursued by leaders in Corinthian society were also being practised by Christians in the Pauline community.

The Roman legal system in Corinth will first be considered, demonstrating the ways in which secular leaders used it to their own advantage. The instance raised by Paul of leading figures in the church taking each other to the secular courts will then be discussed in the light of the Roman legal background. It will be argued that the Christian brothers involved in litigation were of senior status, that they had turned to the lawcourts to settle their disputes in much the same way that secular leaders did and that they resorted to litigation in order to advance their own social standing. It will also be shown that Paul prefers private arbitration and considers that even those of low social standing in the church are qualified to handle such disputes.

Paul describes a situation in 1 Corinthians 6 where some in the community were taking legal disputes before the secular authorities in Corinth (cf. verses 1, 6, and 7).[1] Winter is probably correct in arguing that Paul refers in this instance to civil rather than criminal disputes.[2] This may be deduced from the description in 1 Corinthians 6.2 of "a trivial case", κριτήριον ἐλάχιστον. It may

---

[1] B.W. Winter, 'Civil Litigation in Secular Corinth and the Church, The Forensic Background to 1 Corinthians 6.1-8', *NTS* 37 (1991), 559-572, is especially informative on this question and I am grateful to him for allowing me to refer to an early copy of his article. See also L. Vischer, *Die Auslegungsgeschichte von 1. Kor. 6,1-11* (Tübingen, 1955), and R.H. Fuller, 'First Corinthians 6:1-11: An Exegetical Paper', *Ex Auditu* 2 (1986), 96-104.

[2] So also W.H. Mare, 221, who argues more specifically for non-criminal property cases; and *contra* J.H. Bernard, 'The Connexion Between the Fifth and Sixth Chapters of 1 Corinthians', *The Expositor,* Series 7, Vol 3 (1907), 433-443, and P. Richardson, 'Judgment in Sexual Matters in 1 Corinthians 6:1-11', *Novum Testamentum* 25 (1983), 37-58, who both argue that the legal disputes concern the sexual offence of 1 Cor 5. Both W.H. Mare, 221, and B.W. Winter, 'Civil Litigation in Secular Corinth and the Church', 561, distinguish this instance from the case of criminal courts in Romans 13.3, 4.

be added by way of further support that the references in 1 Corinthians 6.7 and 8 to 'being wronged' and 'cheated' also suggest the sort of offence which would have come under the umbrella of civil jurisdiction—claims of possession, breach of contract, damage, fraud, and injury.[3] It is the civil legal process, therefore, which provides the correct background to Paul's discussion in 1 Corinthians 6.

2. The Civil Legal Process in Roman Corinth

A number of historical problems prevent definite conclusions from being drawn regarding the nature of the legal system in mid-first century Corinth. The Roman legal system had developed considerably during the late Republic and early Principate, and it was not until the 'classical period' of Roman law (the second and early third centuries AD) that some degree of stability was attained.[4] This makes it difficult to determine at what stage of the development to place the situation described in 1 Corinthians. Furthermore, it is necessary to distinguish between the prevailing system in Rome and the practices in the colonies and provinces. It has been suggested that, in the provinces especially, the governors had a degree of freedom regarding the handling of the law; this further limits the possibility of arriving at 'assured results' regarding the Corinthian situation in the Pauline community.

It must be said, however, that there is sufficient evidence to shed some light on the situation described by Paul in 1 Corinthians. It is widely accepted, for example, that by the early Empire, the majority of civil cases were handled by the governor and sometimes also before a single judge.[5] The jury-system, which had been more commonly used in the criminal jurisdiction of the Republican period, is unlikely to have been the process alluded to in 1 Corinthians 6.1.[6]

---

[3]   Cf. the important work on this subject, P. Garnsey, *Social Status and Legal Privilege in the Roman Empire* (Oxford, 1970), 181, n. 1

[4]   H.F. Jolowicz & B. Nicholas, *Historical Introduction to the Study of Roman Law* (ed 3: Cambridge, 1972), 5 f.

[5]   P. Garnsey, *Social Status and Legal Privilege,* 181, argues that during the Republic and early Empire the majority of civil cases were handled by a *formula,* which gave considerable powers to the praetor. It is this process which will be described. It appears from Garnsey, *contra* Winter, that juries were only involved in *quaestiones,* or criminal cases, during the Republican period. The formulary procedure for civil private cases was handled by praetor and judge. The *cognitio* procedure was adopted during the later Principate, and such courts could handle either criminal or civil cases. P. Garnsey, *op. cit.,* 172, suggests that it only 'began to make inroads into the civil law' in the latter part of the first century. Thus, the private judge and the *cognitio* judge are to be differentiated. "*Cognitio* was parasitic on the jury-court system; it also proved more attractive, especially to weaker plaintiffs, than the formulary system in civil law, administered by praetor and private judge. In time, *cognitio* was applicable in the trial of all offences, as the distinction between public crime and private delict slowly declined in importance", *op. cit.,* 5.

[6]   J.A. Crook, *Law and Life of Rome* (London, 1967), 85, "Jurisdiction other than that before the praetors at Rome was on an entirely different footing. The governor of a province, as fount of all procedural law, was entitled simply to *cognoscere,* try a case, which (as opposed to the *ius dicere* of the praetors) meant to try it completely before himself with any procedure he saw fit—summon the

The formulary system was a two-stage process: *actio in iure* and *actio apud iudicem*. A plaintiff initiated proceedings by approaching the magistrate and requesting a suit (*actio in iure*). If the magistrate were satisfied with the case, the plaintiff would then issue a private summons for the defendant to appear before the magistrate in order to answer a charge (*in ius vocatio*). The next stage would be dependent on the action being accepted by the defendant. Once the plaintiff had declared the nature of the case before the magistrate and defendant, the magistrate could then suggest a *formula* (instruction containing the factual details of the case) which would be debated and agreed upon by both parties. A judge acceptable to both parties would then be appointed. The magistrate passed on to the judge the details of the case. The case would then be heard before the judge (*actio apud iudicem*) and a sentence passed.[7] Thereafter it was the responsibility of the plaintiff to ensure that the judgment was carried out by the defendant. It may thus be seen that at a number of stages, the process could at the least be held up by the defendant, and at most the procedure could be aborted.

In the colony of Corinth, it was the two *duoviri iure dicundo,* as their name suggests, who were the chief justices.[8] There were no praetors in Roman colonies and therefore it is these magistrates who filled the highest judicial posts.[9] The governors of the provinces would leave many of the minor cases to the local *duoviri*. It may therefore be assumed that it is one of these officials, together with the appointed judge, who are referred to in 1 Corinthians 6.1 and

---

parties, determine the issue, hear the evidence, pronounce the judgment, and see to its execution. ... but if there was more work than he wished to cope with directly he was equally entitled to 'give a judge'. In theory this was very different from the formulary system; there was no question of choice of judge by the parties nor of *formula*—the instruction of the judge could be in any form". Cf. also W. Kunkel, *An Introduction to Roman legal and constitutional History* (ET: ed 2: Oxford, 1973), 86, "The overwhelming majority of civil actions in the later Republic took place, however, not before the *centumviri* but as a rule before single judges (*sub uno iudice*); though in certain special cases they were also held before small colleges of arbitrators (*arbitri*) or so-called 'recoverers' (*recuperatores*), who all functioned without being presided over by a magistrate. Here the only function of the magistrate was to carry out a preliminary proceeding in which he had to decide on the admissibility of the plaintiff's claim and to appoint the judge or judges by whom the case would be heard".

7   Cf. P. Garnsey, *Social Status and Legal Privilege,* 181, 187. For the process as a whole during the Principate in Rome see also J.A. Crook, *Law and Life of Rome,* 73-83. Crook points out that most commonly it is a single judge who is brought to hear the case (*op. cit.,* 78). However it is recognised that sometimes a jury was used (*op. cit.,* 79).

8   Cf. J. Wiseman, 'Corinth and Rome I: 228 BC-AD 267', *ANRW* II.7.1 (Berlin, 1979), 498. The founding charter for another colony points out the legal jurisdiction of the *duoviri; Lex Coloniae Genetivae Juliae,* XCIV, "No person in this colony shall adjudicate or have jurisdiction, save the duoviri, or a praefectus left in charge by a duovir, or an aedile, as provided for in this law".

9   H.F. Jolowicz & B. Nicholas, *Historical Introduction to the Study of Roman Law,* 349, "The *II viri iure dicundo* presided over the *decuriones,* but as the name implies, their chief duties were judicial. They, or courts under their presidency, had exercised criminal jurisdiction of some importance in republican times, but this was taken from them under the principate and transferred to imperial authorities, the municipal magistrates being left with no more than minor powers of police. Their civil jurisdiction was more important, though limited to cases involving small sums, and further by the principle that the municipal magistrates could not exercise rights, such as that of *missio in bona* or *in integrum restitutio,* which depended on *imperium*".

6 as οἱ ἄδικοι and οἱ ἄπιστοι.[10] The validity of Paul's criticism that the judges were unjust is shown by reference to the general practice of legal officials and judges in the first century.[11]

3. *Legal Privilege*

In Graeco-Roman times it was widely assumed that there was no equal standing before the law. Exercising legal privilege was a normal fact of the Roman judicial system. Respect for status was all-pervasive in Imperial society, and it did not seem remarkable that legal privilege should be directly linked with the honour in which an individual was held. There were accepted ways, therefore, by which litigants could enhance their own chances of success in the courts. Three aspects of that privilege will be discussed in order to demonstrate that only those of senior status would have undertaken public litigation: the importance of status; ways of obstructing the legal process; and the use of *vituperatio.*

a. *The Importance of Status in the Legal Process*

At the heart of the issue of legal privilege was the widespread Graeco-Roman preoccupation with personal standing and reputation. It is clear that this was the case in the political sphere.[12] It was no less the case, however, in the realm of litigation—both civil and criminal—during the first century.[13] All parties involved in litigation had to be aware of their own status in relation to that of the other parties.

The prosecution had to assess to what extent it had an advantage in social standing over its opponents before embarking upon legal proceedings.

The defendant needed to weigh up the possible cost of losing his public reputation if he lost the case; whether he had an ally or enemy in the judge; or even whether an out-of-court cash settlement might ensure saving face.

The judge had to bear in mind, not only the promotion of his own career, but also how not to compromise the good name of the upper classes. It was his

---

[10] *Contra* B.W. Winter, 'Civil Litigation in Secular Corinth and the Church', 561-63, the plural does not refer to judge and jury, since it was not normal for juries to be involved in local cases of civil jurisdiction. Winter argues that we are dealing with both judge and juries in 1 Corinthians 6 partly on the grounds that ἄδικοι (1 Cor 6.1) and ἄπιστοι (1 Cor 6.6) are both plural. It may be, however, that Paul is referring to the equivalent of the praetor and the judge (both of whom, Garnsey suggests, could be accused of injustice). Winter instances in n. 10 an edict from Augustus, but this simply shows that what is normal for civil cases of this period was that judges, as opposed to simply the praetors themselves, were brought into the proceedings (cited in J.A. Crook, *Law and Life of Rome,* 86).

[11] This is convincingly argued by B.W. Winter, 'Civil Litigation in Secular Corinth and the Church', 562-64, with reference to epigraphic and papyrological evidence of the injustices perpetrated by judges and juries.

[12] See the discussion in Chapter Three above.

[13] Important works on this topic include J.M. Kelly, *Roman Litigation* (Oxford, 1966); J.M. Kelly, *Studies in Civil Judicature* (Oxford, 1976); and the thorough research of P. Garnsey, *Social Status and Legal Privilege.*

responsibility, therefore, to decide whom it would be most advantageous to favour.

Thus it was understood that all parties would do everything in their power to extend their own reputation, something which could normally only be achieved at the cost of another's. The conscious and unconscious prejudices of both judge and jury were, therefore, very significant in any legal dispute. A jury would certainly take into consideration the family background, wealth and social position of each party in reaching their verdict.[14]

The possession of *honor* and *dignitas* were pre-requisites for legal privilege.[15] For these fortunate people with *honor* and *dignitas* there were a number of widely-used means of influence. Cicero described three of the most powerful as *gratia, potentia* and *pecunia,* all of which, in his view, ought to have no part in the pure working of the law.[16]

Pecunia refers to the overt use of bribery.[17] It may be added, however, that merely the possession of wealth and property, without necessarily bargaining with it, was in itself influential. The rich man, simply by virtue of his riches, had an advantage over the poor man.[18]

Potentia and *gratia* were influences less frowned upon by society, and to a much greater extent it was assumed that those with such standing would use them to their own ends. This was taken so much for granted that merely the possession of high status by the defendant could deter a plaintiff from taking his superior to court; likewise, high status on the part of the prosecutor could give him increased confidence in undertaking legal proceedings. *Potentia* in Cicero's words was "the possession of resources sufficient for preserving one's own interests and weakening those of another".[19]

Moreover, someone with status in society, and therefore good standing before the law, might avoid either initiating legal proceedings or being taken to court in order not to risk damaging that reputation. This meant that out-of-court cash settlements would often be preferred to being subject to public scrutiny.[20]

---

[14] P. Garnsey, *Social Status and Legal Privilege,* 4.

[15] P. Garnsey, *Social Status and Legal Privilege,* 234, 258.

[16] Cicero, *Pro Caecina* 73, "What is the civil law (*ius civile*)? That which can be neither perverted by favour (*gratia*) nor violated by influence (*potentia*) nor falsified by money (*pecunia*)", cited by P. Garnsey, *Social Status and Legal Privilege,* 207; J.M. Kelly, *Roman Litigation,* 33; and B.W. Winter, 'Civil Litigation in Secular Corinth and the Church', 566. J.M. Kelly, *op. cit.,* 51, suggests, with reference to the works of Tacitus and Suetonius, that *gratia* and *pecunia* were no less used to influence during the Principate than in the Republic.

[17] The use of bribery was most common in criminal cases during the Republic, and in civil cases during the Empire, by frequency of textual evidence, J.M. Kelly, *Roman Litigation,* 37. Kelly wants to point out (*op. cit.,* 41), however, that it was by no means a praised act. It was recognised as wrong and a perversion of justice. Bribery was not only offered to the judge, but also to witnesses, and even in some cases to the opponents' supporters, cf. J.M. Kelly, *op. cit.,* 41.

[18] Cf. P. Garnsey, *Social Status and Legal Privilege,* 207.

[19] Cicero, *De Inventione Rhetorica* 2.56.169; cited by P. Garnsey, *Social Status and Legal Privilege,* 208.

[20] Cf. J.M. Kelly, *Studies in Civil Judicature,* 96, 98, 100.

There are a number of instances where Cicero tries to persuade a friend to "do the right thing" by showing understanding and leniency to some other friend.[21] Kelly draws this analysis:

> The same elements always recur; a statement of how closely bound the person recommended is to Cicero; a hint that litigation of some kind is on the way; a request, usually softened by some stock phrase (*quoad tua fides dignitasque patietur*) that the magistrate will see the claim of Cicero's client satisfied; an assurance that a favour will give Cicero the greatest pleasure. We never find in so many words the request that justice and the rules of law should be side-stepped or partially applied; only a request for favours so far as justice will permit.[22]

One further instance where legal privilege was exercised lies in the area of punishment. It was widely accepted that harsher punishments would be meted out to those litigants of a lower social status.[23]

Kelly helpfully summarizes the situation thus:

> the administration of justice, civil as well as criminal, tended both in the pre-classical, classical, and post-classical periods of jurisprudence to be subject to the influence of powerful men; sometimes that influence found expression in the outright bribery of judges, advocates, or witnesses; more often it operated by fear, by favour, and by personal connexions. The theory of an equal and objective justice was perfectly familiar, but no one reckoned on finding it applied in practice.[24]

This suggests that only those of senior status would have undertaken public litigation.

b. *The Obstacles to Prosecution*

In addition to those aspects of legal privilege listed above, there are a number of points along the route to prosecution where a plaintiff's cause could be hindered.[25]

First, it is to be understood that the law insisted that certain people were protected from having a summons brought against them. These included the plaintiff's parents or patron, or the city's magistrates or priests.[26] The reason was in order to protect *existimatio* thus preventing a man of low status damag-

---

[21] See for example Cicero's letters *Ad Familiares* 13.53, 13.55, 13.58, 13.59, 13.65.

[22] J.M. Kelly, *Roman Litigation,* 58. The "stock phrase" may be found in *Ad Fam.* 13.53 l. 1.

[23] P. Garnsey, *Social Status and Legal Privilege,* notes this point in 99 f., 121, 178, 199 f.

[24] J.M. Kelly, *Roman Litigation,* 61.

[25] Cf. P. Garnsey, *Social Status and Legal Privilege,* 218, 277.

[26] Cf. P. Garnsey, *Social Status and Legal Privilege,* 181. Cf. also *Digest* 4.3.11.1 (cited by P. Garnsey, *op. cit.,* 182), "An action will not be given to certain persons, for example, to sons or freedmen proceeding against parents or patrons, since it carries *infamia*. Nor, however, should it be given to a man of low status against someone pre-eminent in status—for example, to a commoner against a consular of assured prestige, or to a man of wanton and wasteful life, or someone worthless in some other way, against a man of faultless life. Labeo says this". Cf. also *Digest* 37.15.2; 44.4.4.16. P. Garnsey, *op. cit.,* 187, suggests that his case might be refused merely on the grounds that a prosecutor was of a lower social status than his opponent.

ing seriously the career of, for example, a respected politician by taking him to court.[27]

It is clear, secondly, that the magistrate was in a position to refuse a private summons if it appeared unreasonable or unsuitable.[28] Garnsey points out that a private summons could consequently be a tool of discrimination in the hands of the magistrate. He might choose to prevent the 'good' name of his friend, the defendant, being brought into question in the courts.[29] It was certainly also possible for the magistrate to curry favour with the rich and powerful in the city by refusing their opponents a legal hearing. Furthermore, an inferior plaintiff could be refused a hearing simply because his opponent's superior status was in danger of being brought into disrepute by the legal case. For this reason law-suits initiated by men of humble origin were probably not frequent.[30]

A third difficulty in bringing a man to justice could be the reluctance of the defendant to obey a summons.[31] If the defendant chose to ignore the summons, then only persuasion or force were left to the plaintiff if the case were to continue.[32] The magistrate was not required to assist the plaintiff in bringing his opponent before the law. (Garnsey points out, however, that the weaker plaintiff might be helped by a more senior patron; furthermore, the Roman sense of what is right might put pressure on the defendant not to flout the law).[33]

Fourthly, it was the magistrate who controlled the details of the *formula,* or parameters, within which the case was to be heard and defended before the judge. For this reason it was not unusual for personal loyalties to be exercised.

Finally, the state did not compel the defendant to carry out his sentence. It was up to the plaintiff to exact his full reward.

A dramatic instance of the handicap which the socially inferior man had in the face of his betters is seen in Seneca's *Controversiae* 10.1. A rich man is depicted taunting a poor man in the secure knowledge that it is improbable that he will be taken to court even though he has murdered the poor man's father. The poor man is all too aware that he is unlikely to be able to bring a case against his superior, and even should he succeed in bringing his opponent

---

[27] Cf. P. Garnsey, *Social Status and Legal Privilege,* 184, 186.

[28] Cf. P. Garnsey, *Social Status and Legal Privilege,* 187; J.M. Kelly, *Roman Litigation,* 28 f.

[29] Cf. P. Garnsey, *Social Status and Legal Privilege,* 194.

[30] Cf. P. Garnsey, *Social Status and Legal Privilege,* 217.

[31] Cf. J.M. Kelly, *Roman Litigation,* 14, "Roman litigation in the republican and classical periods was devoid of the sanction of state power ... and ... the only physical sanction of Roman litigation in these periods consisted in such force as the plaintiff was able to muster in order to overbear the actual or possible resistance of a weaker defendant". Kelly rightly points out that under these circumstances only the strong plaintiff is likely to bring proceedings, and only the weaker defendant will submit to litigation. Cf. also P. Garnsey, *Social Status and Legal Privilege,* 189.

[32] R. Taubenschlag, *The Law of Greco-Roman Egypt in the Light of the Papyri, 332 BC-640 AD* (ed 2: Warsaw, 1955), 501, gives evidence from Egypt where, if a defendant failed to appear, he was summoned three times. If these failed, a judgment by default was passed.

[33] P. Garnsey, *Social Status and Legal Privilege,* 189.

before a magistrate, it is improbable that he would ever be successful. All that the plaintiff's father had done was to try and bring litigation against the rich man. In such a situation, the only weapon that the poor man might have is to convince the people that his superior is a murderer and thereby make him lose his reputation and maybe, in the end, his political career as well.[34]

Garnsey describes this inequality in the legal system thus:

> It remains a fact that the law itself provided no mechanism for redressing the balance between two parties of unequal strength. The praetor played no active part in enforcing either the judgement of a court or his own edicts. If a stubborn defendant was brought to accept the judgement of a court, this was achieved by the combination of social pressures and the intervention of such private supporters as the plaintiff was fortunate to possess.[35]

c. *Vituperatio*

In a society where social status and personal prestige were valued so highly, and the rôles of friendships and patronage were considered of great importance, it is not surprising also to find that personal reputation was pursued at considerable cost. Great lengths were taken to defend one's reputation if put at any risk. In such a climate, enmity was as costly as friendship was beneficial.[36]

In the process of litigation, the action of a prosecutor could so seriously damage his opponent's political esteem that the defendant would be expected to defame the character of the plaintiff in public. By so doing, he would assert his own uprightness over that of his opponent.[37] Hostility, expressed in personal insult, could be an extremely powerful weapon in the court room, and was unashamedly used.[38] It must be understood that, in first century litigation,

---

[34] Cited by P. Garnsey, *Social Status and Legal Privilege,* 216 f.; J.M. Kelly, *Roman Litigation,* 49-50, D. Daube, '"Ne quid infamandi causa fiat": The Roman law of defamation', *Atti del Congresso Internazionale di Diritto Romano e di Storia del Diritto, Verona 1948* (Milan, 1951), 433; and B.W. Winter, 'Civil Litigation in Secular Corinth and the Church', 565.

[35] P. Garnsey, *Social Status and Legal Privilege,* 205.

[36] D.F. Epstein, *Personal Enmity in Roman Politics—218-43 BC* (London, 1987), 128, "The distinctive Roman constitution and the value set by Roman society on political success were the second major reason for the predominant influence of *inimicitiae.* A Roman politician built power and influence through a network of friends, relatives and clients united by the bonds of trust. Any violation or interference with these bonds had the potential for destroying careers and therefore sparked *inimicitiae.* The Roman constitution reinforced *inimicitiae* among the Roman politician's priorities: the Roman ruling class was not accountable to the governed in the modern democratic sense, and this insulation gave the leaders even more freedom to devote their energies to the destruction of their enemies. Rather than being guided by any public accountability, the *nobiles,* who respected no ambition outside of the *cursus honorum,* competed viciously for the tiny number of curule offices. Losers received no consolation prizes. They faced social extinction uncomforted and unbuoyed by ideological conviction and resolve. Envy against the successful and fortunate was the inevitable by-product".

[37] It was the extraordinary damage that conviction could bring which meant that a prosecutor was viewed as nothing less than an *inimicus,* cf. D.F. Epstein, *Personal Enmity in Roman Politics,* 90 f.

[38] D.F. Epstein, *Personal Enmity in Roman Politics,* 90, "The Roman prosecutor and the men who supported him by contributing hostile speeches or damaging evidence generally could expect to evoke far more personal resentment than the modern prosecutor, insulated by the more impersonal traditions of the modern criminal justice system. The convicted Roman found it almost impossible

such *inimicitiae* were not only socially acceptable but also virtually inevitable. Any citizen engaging in either criminal or civil litigation was likely to be subject to such treatment.[39] Kelly argues:

> The advocate in a Roman action was permitted to use the most unbridled language about his client's adversary, or even his friends or relations or witnesses; and this was so even where the expressions used were quite irrelevant to the issue at trial; indeed, the less relevant the attack, the more extreme the comments might be. What the Romans called *reprehensio vitae* or *vituperatio*—a personal attack on the character of one's opponent—was taken as absolutely normal; and rhetoric manuals dealt in great detail with the most effective way to construct a *vituperatio*.[40]

It may thus be seen that *vituperatio* was a key weapon in the armoury of the first century Graeco-Roman politician.[41]

A number of conclusions may be drawn from this survey. First, the Graeco-Roman world of legal suits was a world where the socially inferior were severely disadvantaged. They were prejudiced against both in legal procedure and legal privilege.

Secondly, the law courts provided a forum where the successful litigant could greatly enhance his own reputation, whilst at the same time injuring that of his opponent.

Thirdly, the aspiration to support friends and denigrate enemies was in many cases more important than to speak the truth or see justice done.

Fourthly, it may be assumed that plaintiffs were almost entirely people of high social status. The requirements of reputation and influence in order to be

---

to view his prosecutor as a mere agent of an unbiased judicial system, motivated solely by his duty to the public to ferret out alleged wrongs. The reasons for this difference are clear enough. In Rome the prosecutor was not a public servant who chose his target disinterestedly, but a private citizen who competed for the privilege, interested more often in personal objectives than the common weal. Rivalry and ambition to secure a reputation for public speaking often induced young men to display their talents by prosecuting distinguished public figures for whom they had no personal feeling, positive or negative. Other successful prosecutors might attain far more tangible rewards ranging from money to seniority rights in the Senate. It was difficult for a prosecutor to avoid giving the impression that he was hunting glory and profit in the wreckage of his victim's career. Not only the victims themselves, but also Roman society at large pictured Roman prosecutors as vultures who disgraced the family name".

[39] D.F. Epstein, *Personal Enmity in Roman Politics*, 97, "The Roman courts provided the most convenient outlet for conducting private warfare. Roman judicial tradition generally encouraged this practice by considering *inimicitiae* a socially acceptable basis of prosecution"; also *op. cit.*, 91 f., "This lack of restraint helps to explain why prosecutor and defendant could so rarely avoid *inimicitiae*: it was a very rare Roman whose *auctoritas* could survive unscathed the public airing and slandering characteristic of the law courts"; also *op. cit.*, 129, "The criminal trial was a particularly important manifestation of *inimicitiae*. Prosecution invariably led to *inimicitiae* because of the highly personal nature of the Roman adversary system. Roman prosecutors more often took cases for personal reasons than as impersonal agents asserting the judicial interests of the state".

[40] Cf. J.M. Kelly, *Studies in Civil Judicature*, 98 f., and Cicero, *Pro Murena* 11 where *reprehensio vitae* is regarded as normal judicial formality.

[41] D.F. Epstein, *Personal Enmity in Roman Politics*, 127 f., "A reputation for successfully pursuing *inimicitiae* was a vital asset to a Roman politician seeking to establish and maintain an influential voice within Roman governing circles because there was so much admiration and respect for men who battled and destroyed their foes".

successful in litigation precluded many of those from the lower classes ever initiating legal proceedings.

4. *Paul and Litigation*

This survey of the civil legal process in the Corinthian colony during the first century AD has a number of implications for the situation described in the Pauline community. These implications will be discussed under two headings: first, what does 1 Corinthians 6.1-8 demonstrate regarding these leading figures in the community; and secondly, what can be determined about the structure which Paul is advocating for dealing with internal legal disputes?

a. *Leading Figures in the Community*

The following conclusions may be drawn regarding those leading figures of the community who were entering into litigation with each other. First, the system of civil claims was so clearly a system in favour of those with established status that it is reasonable to assume that the disputes discussed by Paul in 1 Corinthians 6 were initiated by those from the higher echelons in the society of the colony—leading figures within the Pauline community.[42] To have overcome all the obstacles to litigation listed above, it must be concluded that these brothers were of senior status. This further supports the thesis argued in Chapter Four that the community included some from the higher social classes.

Secondly, it may reasonably be assumed that in the secular law courts, with its unbelieving judges, the Christian litigants were at least exposed to the same injustices that were prevalent in the judicial system, and at most were party to them as well. That is, they exercised whatever powers they possessed to enhance their own chances of success, be it *vituperatio, pecunia, potentia* or *gratia*. Evidence for the use of *vituperatio* may well be found in Paul's comments in 1 Corinthians 6.7-8, διὰ τί οὐχὶ μᾶλλον ἀδικεῖσθε; διὰ τί οὐχὶ μᾶλλον ἀποστερεῖσθε; ἀλλὰ ὑμεῖς ἀδικεῖτε καὶ ἀποστερεῖτε, καὶ τοῦτο ἀδελφούς.

A third conclusion is the strong likelihood that these legal proceedings were being used by members of the Christian community to establish their own standing and reputation at the cost of another's. It has been shown that this practice was widespread within the secular courts, and Paul's comments in 1 Corinthians 6.7 and 8 suggest that similar animosity existed between these two brothers. This superiority established in secular litigation may well have been used for greater personal influence in the Christian community. Such

---

[42] Cf. G.D. Fee, 229, who argues that these brothers are among those in the community who have property, and draws the inference that they may also be some of the leaders within the church. This adds to the evidence discussed in Chapter Four above that there were those in the Pauline community who were from the higher classes of Corinthian society.

enmity would increase one's advantage in the divisions over personalities discussed by Paul in 1 Corinthians 1.12 and 3.21.

b. How Should Christians Handle Internal Legal Disputes?

Paul clearly disagrees with the practice which is happening in the Corinthian church where brothers are taking each other to the secular law courts. His language in 1 Corinthians 6.1 is particularly strong where he opens the section with τολμᾷ, and refers to the magistrates as οἱ ἄδικοι. In 1 Corinthians 6.6 he further describes the secular legal authorities as ἄπιστοι.

i. The Case for Private Arbitration

Paul does, however, suggest an alternative to going to the colonial magistrates. It would appear from 1 Corinthians 6.1 and 5 that, for Paul, the option of handling the case internally is certainly permissible, and preferable to taking the dispute before the unjust judges (οἱ ἄδικοι). 1 Corinthians 6.2 further implies that Paul expects the saints to handle the small affairs between themselves.

The case for arbitration is not affected by the identity of the 'despised' in 1 Corinthians 6.4, who may be interpreted as either the secular authorities, or those within the church who were of low social status.[43] In either eventuality Paul would be advocating private arbitration. Either he prefers that some from the church are appointed, be they even the 'despised'; or, alternatively, he asks why, given their ability to handle such issues, they should still go to the secular Corinthian courts.

1 Corinthians 6.5 further suggests that Paul prefers private arbitration. He asks, with some irony, that surely there is someone in the church qualified, 'wise enough', to adjudicate over such issues between brothers. Those in the church who have appealed to their own wisdom, as Paul suggests in 1 Corinthians 3.18, would have been embarrassed by his irony that they had not been able to find anyone sufficiently 'wise' in the church to handle such matters and had, therefore, resorted to external adjudication.

ii. The Identity of the 'Despised'

The question of the identity of οἱ ἐξουθενημένοι should be discussed in greater detail. Robertson, in his Grammar, noting the ambiguity in the form of the imperative, lists καθίζετε in 1 Corinthians 6.4 as one of the instances where only the context can decide. There are three possibilities to be discussed. Either the sentence is an indicative statement, or it is an indicative interrogative, or it may be an imperative.

The particular mood is significant to the identity of οἱ ἐξουθενημένοι. If the sentence is a question, as in Nestle-Aland xxvi, then the identity of the 'despised' may be determined thus, "Therefore if you have disputes about such

---

[43] It is the mood of καθίζετε which determines who should be interpreted as 'the despised'. This problem will be addressed below.

matters, *do you appoint* as judges men of little account (the unbelieving judges) in the church?"[44] Equally, if the sentence is taken as an indicative statement, Paul may be interpreted to be referring to the situation outlined in 1 Corinthians 6.1—they have been taking their disputes to the secular authorities.[45] The third possibility, a present imperative, changes the sense considerably: "Therefore, if you have disputes about such matters, *appoint* as judges even men of little account in the church!"[46] If Paul is not going to contradict what he declared in 1 Corinthians 6.1, then 'the despised' must in this sense refer to some of the members within the community.

In the one instance Paul, in 1 Corinthians 6.1, is disgusted at those who are taking internal disputes to those who are not themselves believers. This disgust is then reiterated in 1 Corinthians 6.4. In the other instance, Paul's disgust at their actions is countered by a solution which he himself offers, that is, to take the matter to people within the community. He deems that even the 'despised' members of the church are qualified to handle such matters.

If the former solution is adopted, then 'despised' is a reference to Paul's belief that whatever status a man might have in the world, that status is of no avail within the Kingdom of God—disputes are being taken to those who have no standing when it comes to matters of the church and therefore may be considered 'despised'. In the latter instance 'despised' is an ironical comment referring to people who, by virtue of their eschatological rôle as judges, are especially qualified to handle βιωτικά, and yet in the world's eyes they *may* have no such qualification or accompanying status. It is from the secular perspective—and this is Paul's irony—that they might be termed οἱ ἐξουθενημένοι.

In support of an imperative in 1 Corinthians 6.4, three other statements within the immediate context may be noted. In 1 Corinthians 6.1, Paul clearly advocates taking law-suits before the saints (καὶ οὐχὶ ἐπὶ τῶν ἁγίων). In 1 Corinthians 6.2 he asks whether those in the community see themselves as competent enough to judge minor cases (ἀνάξιοί ἐστε κριτηρίων ἐλαχίστων). Furthermore, 1 Corinthians 6.5 suggests that Paul might expect to find someone in the group who might be wise enough to judge such disputes (οὕτως οὐκ ἔνι ἐν ὑμῖν οὐδεὶς σοφὸς ὃς δυνήσεται διακρῖναι ἀνὰ μέσον τοῦ ἀδελφοῦ αὐτοῦ?). These three statements suggest that Paul is prepared to allow such disputes to be handled internally. It would be consistent with this understanding to interpret καθίζετε as an imperative. Paul prefers such actions to be handled within the community and so in 1 Corinthians 6.4 he expressly instructs that such arbitration should be arranged. This then raises parallels

---

[44] Thus, H. Conzelmann, 105; G.D. Fee, 236; C.K. Barrett, 137; W. Schrage, 412; B.W. Winter, 'Civil Litigation in Secular Corinth and the Church', 559.

[45] Thus, H.A.W. Meyer, *Critical and Exegetical Handbook to the Epistles to the Corinthians* I (ET: Edinburgh, 1892), 168. It would be possible, although unlikely, to interpret ἐν τῇ ἐκκλησίᾳ as the secular city council (cf. Acts 19.32).

[46] Thus, J.B. Lightfoot, *Notes on epistles of St. Paul from unpublished Commentaries* (London, 1904), 211; C.J. Ellicott, 96; W.H. Mare, 222; F. Godet, 290.

from the Old Testament and later Jewish, notably Qumran, practice.[47] The Romans certainly gave both Jews and non-Jews the right to settle their own disputes, without resort to the Roman legal courts.[48] Bammel notes this right accorded to the Jews by the Romans and suggests that Paul, although no longer eligible to resort to the Jewish courts, nonetheless proposes that the Christians adopt a similar practice of handling their affairs internally.[49]

The interpretation should be adopted which understands καθίζετε to be imperative, Paul's comment to be ironical, and the 'despised' to refer to those in the church who might not be of high status in the eyes of Corinthian society. In this way, Paul opposes those in the community of high social status who have resorted to the secular law courts to protect their interests and reputations. Instead he points out that even those looked-down upon by that secular society, 'the despised', are qualified to handle the minor disputes of their fellow brothers.

An important qualification to this practice of private arbitration supported by Paul is found in 1 Corinthians 6.7-8, where he would prefer that none went as far as to have lawsuits with his brother, instead he should turn the other cheek. Paul would rather that this situation had never arisen. It would have been better if the brothers could accept being wronged, rather than let the dispute escalate into a legal case.

5. *Conclusions*

It has been argued that an understanding of the Roman legal background sheds much light on the situation discussed by Paul in 1 Corinthians 6.1-8. It has been suggested that it was men of relatively high social standing who were entering into vexatious litigation, and that this may well have been undertaken in order to protect reputation and status. Paul is opposed to Christians resorting to such means and he shames the Christians by arguing that even the 'despised' members of the church, those who themselves would receive no justice in the Roman legal system, are 'wise' enough to handle the civil disputes of their social superiors.

---

[47] Cf. M. Delcor, 'The courts of the Church of Corinth and the courts of Qumran', in ed. J. Murphy-O'Connor, *Paul and Qumran, Studies in New Testament Exegesis* (London, 1968), 69-84.

[48] Cf. E. Schürer, *The History of the Jewish People in the Age of Jesus Christ (175 BC-AD 135)* II (ET: Edinburgh, 1979), 208-9. Qumran also handled such disputes, Barrett, 135, Strack-Billerbeck, Vol 3, 362, M. Burrows, *The Dead Sea Scrolls* (London 1956), 235. J.A. Crook, *Law and Life of Rome*, 78-9.

[49] E. Bammel, 'The Trial before Pilate', in edd. E. Bammel & C.F.D. Moule, *Jesus and the Politics of His Day* (Cambridge, 1984), 417-418.

CHAPTER SIX

SECULAR PRACTICES OF CHRISTIAN LEADERSHIP: II. BEYOND REPROACH

1. *Introduction*

The situation described in 1 Corinthians 5.1[1] is one where gross sexual immorality, incest, is being practised within the community and being tolerated by others within the church.[2] It is not initially clear whether the relationship was one of concubinage or marriage (however the present tense of ἔχειν (1 Cor 5.1) does suggest a continuing relationship); whether the former husband and father are still alive; and consequently whether the woman is divorced or widowed; or even whether both the man and the woman are members of the church or just the man.[3]

It should be noticed that Paul appears just as concerned with the community's arrogance (πεφυσιωμένοι, καύχημα, 1 Cor 5.2, 6), and lack of action in response to this immorality, as with the offenders themselves, or indeed with the act of immorality.[4]

Commentators have concentrated primarily on the way judgment is to be handled within the community (παραδοῦναι τὸν τοιοῦτον τῷ Σατανᾷ εἰς ὄλεθρον τῆς σαρκός, ἵνα τὸ πνεῦμα σωθῇ ἐν τῇ ἡμέρᾳ τοῦ κυρίου, 1 Cor 5.5). The problem of boasting and arrogance in the community (1 Cor 5.2, 6) has

---

1   Ὅλως ἀκούεται ἐν ὑμῖν πορνεία, καὶ τοιαύτη πορνεία ἥτις οὐδὲ ἐν τοῖς ἔθνεσιν, ὥστε γυναῖκά τινα τοῦ πατρὸς ἔχειν.

2   The difficulties in interpreting the events in 1 Corinthians 5 are not related to significant textual variants. J. Héring, 36 on 1 Cor 5.6 notes, "*Ou* is omitted by Lucifer of Calaris and Ambrosiaster. If these authors have preserved the best reading, then the Apostle would have been expressing himself with bitter irony: 'This mania of boasting about yourselves suits you!'" Cf. also J. Weiß, 133. No significant difference in overall interpretation is offered by this, however.

3   J.B. Lightfoot, *Notes on epistles of St. Paul from unpublished Commentaries* (London, 1904), 202-3, suggests it was a lasting, not temporary situation (ἔχειν); that it may have been either concubinage or marriage; that the former husband and father are still alive. (This is argued from 2 Corinthians 7.12, although this is an unnecessary conclusion to draw. The case in 2 Corinthians 7 may be quite unrelated. The father may well have died. C.K. Barrett, 121, draws the inference that the father is either dead or divorced from the fact that Paul does not describe the relationship as adulterous); that there has been a divorce or separation, on the grounds that the relationship is termed πορνεία and not μοιχεία; since there is no criticism of the woman, it is assumed that she was not in the community, and therefore possibly not a Christian. Cf. also H. Conzelmann, 96, n. 25, the language γυνὴ πατρός is taken directly from the LXX of Lev 18.7-8, where this specific sin is forbidden. A distinction is drawn in Leviticus between a mother and step-mother. In 1 Corinthians 5 it would seem to be the step-mother who is referred to. Conzelmann, 96, agrees with Lightfoot that it is unlikely that an adulterous relationship is involved.

4   Weiß, 123, argues that chapter 5 is a continuation in tone from chapter 4. Paul is concerned to curb the arrogance of the community. He further points out, 125, that 1 Cor 5.2 harks back to 1 Cor 4.8.

received scant attention and none has explored possible reasons why the incestuous man was not proceeded against in Roman law.

The aim of the present chapter, therefore, is to establish first, whether there is a connection between the boasting and immorality; secondly, to assemble both the forensic and literary evidence for prohibitions of incest; thirdly, to suggest pecuniary or social motives for this immorality; and finally, to propose that the community's reluctance to bring legal proceedings against the incestuous man is because he is of such social status that he is beyond the reach of litigation for some in the community.

2. Boasting

One of the major problems of interpretation lies in determining the relationship between the arrogance within the community and the act of immorality. Is this instance of incest the object of their boasting, or is Paul's criticism that there can be no grounds for any boasting whilst there is such serious immorality in the community?[5]

A number of commentators argue that the boasting in chapter 5 is linked closely with the freedom expressed in the Corinthian slogan in 1 Corinthians 6.12, Πάντα μοι ἔξεστιν. This interpretation suggests that the Corinthians are boasting about the immorality. The community is well aware of the situation, and for some reason, possibly theological, it not only tolerates the act, but also is actually proud of it. It is not clear, however, that Paul is addressing general moral laxity at this stage in the epistle. That matter is specifically addressed later.[6]

Daube, in a number of publications, has put forward a significantly different interpretation.[7] He argues that, for the Rabbis, conversion was not a

---

[5] Fee, 196, outlines this major problem of interpretation.

[6] *Contra* Barrett, 122, Bruce, 54, and A.C. Thistleton, 'Realized Eschatology at Corinth', *NTS* 24 (1978), 515-6. Paul does not argue against their view of spiritual freedom with respect to this issue. Barrett also offers the suggestion that maybe there is here an enthusiastic antinomianism. Although Conzelmann, 96, notes that a "specific link between this case and the Corinthian slogan of freedom, that is to say a speculative ground for the incestuous man's behavior, is not suggested", he does, however, say that the link with libertinism does exist here. Robertson/Plummer, 96, 101, refutes this. Cf. also Fee, 195, who notes that the issue in 1 Cor 6.12-20 is markedly different from 1 Cor 5.1-13; and Orr, 188, says, "The scandal was not simply a case of sexual immorality, however: the attitude of the church was involved, and Paul chided the church for indulgent pride. The implication is that they were proud in the assumption that their Christian freedom was enhanced by their sympathetic understanding of this unusual sexual relationship". O.L. Yarbrough, *Not like the Gentiles: Marriage Rules in the Letters of Paul* (Atlanta, 1985), 96-7, sees no evidence here for a libertine party, nor that sexual immorality was a general problem in the community.

[7] D. Daube, 'Pauline Contributions to a Pluralistic Culture: Re-creation and beyond', in edd. D.G. Miller & D.Y. Hadidian, *Jesus and Man's Hope* II (Pittsburgh, 1971), 223-245; *The New Testament and Rabbinic Judaism* (London, 1956), 113; 'Biblical Landmarks in the Struggle for Women's Rights', *Juridical Review* 90, n.s. 23 (1978), 184-6; 'Historical Aspects of Informal Marriage', *Revue Internationale de Droits de L'Antiquité* 25 (1978), 95-97; *Ancient Jewish Law: Three Inaugural Lectures* (Leiden, 1981), 14-16; 'Onesimos', in edd. G.W.E. Nickelsburg & G.W. MacRae, *Christians among Jews and Gentiles, Essays in Honor of Krister Stendahl* (Philadelphia, 1986), 40-2; cited in, D. Daube, *Appeasement or Resistance and other essays on New Testament*

metaphorical rebirth. The new convert has none of the previous ties with his family. This frees him to marry any of his 'previously' closest relations, and therefore the prohibitions of incest no longer apply. The obvious danger that Judaism would be seen by others as morally lax where it allowed relationships considered by pagan law to be immoral, led the rabbis to make the concession that relationships of this kind for the convert would still be treated as incestuous where they were considered so by pagan law.

With regard to 1 Corinthians 5, Daube considers that the motivation for this relationship was none other than elation at new birth (indeed the whole community is 'puffed up' with that elation). He considers that Paul has accepted the Rabbinic view in general, and, like the Rabbis, considers that where pagan law forbids incest, the convert should abide by that secular law. Daube rightly points out that it is inconceivable that the Corinthians would openly have condoned gross incest.[8] Daube writes,

> It is not, then, quite accurate to describe the attitude of those rebuked in chapter 5 as antinomianism. They may, of course, have been antinomians; but in this affair they contended only that their preconversion ties had gone as a result of re-creation. Where they went wrong was in insisting on this principle absolutely, without heeding the harm likely to ensue if it was carried out beyond a certain point.[9]

Daube's assumption lacks credibility because, in this context, Paul does not address the situation along the lines of new creation. He neither confronts them on their wrong application of Rabbinic theology, nor even employs conversion language in the context.[10] The suggested action of excommunication is especially harsh if, as Daube argues, Paul actually agrees *in toto* with this view of re-birth, and simply disagrees with the Corinthians on

---

Judaism (London, 1987), 59-64. For a similar argument see also Strack-Billerbeck, *ad loc.*; J.B. Lightfoot, *Notes on epistles of St. Paul,* 203; H.A.W. Meyer, *Critical and Exegetical Handbook to the Epistles to the Corinthians* I (ET: Edinburgh, 1892), 140; and C.J. Ellicott, 83. Cf. also J.D.M. Derrett, 'Midrash, The Composition of Gospels, and Discipline', in *Studies in the New Testament* IV (Leiden, 1986), 174-5, "Paul has evidently interpreted the textual sources in such a way as to make this form of incest a crime. Even though proselytes were new creatures they were not utterly unrelated persons. Even the rabbis agreed that a converted male cannot marry his mother; a manumitted slave (who is like a proselyte) cannot with impunity commit sodomy or bestiality. It is possible to argue that a woman who has been enjoyed by a man's father must not be enjoyed by that man, since the Pentateuch explicitly refers to the physical act. One could take a different view, as for centuries rabbinical Jews did, but it was highly inexpedient to do so. Paul, as the spiritual leader of the new sect, a sect which was guided by the spirit and power of Jesus and not by the written word of the Torah or its rabbinical interpretation, has made up his mind, and the fact that such incest was criminal amongst the pagans of Corinth was highly significant in his eyes for he says so".

8   D. Daube, 'Pauline Contributions to a Pluralistic Culture', 224. It was being done under their supposed privilege as new creatures.

9   D. Daube, 'Pauline Contributions to a Pluralistic Culture', 227.

10   New Creation language is explicitly used by Paul later in the Corinthian correspondence (2 Cor 5.17), but he shows no awareness in the 1 Corinthians 5 context that it is this theological premise which is being used by the Corinthians. *Contra* Daube, see Barrett, 121, "But it is not certain, and Paul certainly does not say, that the point at issue was whether conversion, becoming a Christian 'proselyte', set a man free to have sexual relations with a woman who stood in what would otherwise be a forbidden relationship with him; the sin may have arisen directly out of Corinthian libertinism (cf. iv. 6)".

whether the pagan law overrides on the matter of incest. The interpretation is dependent on the assumption that the boasting in 1 Corinthians 5 has its object in the matter of immorality.[11]

A third interpretation is that the boasting is *despite* the immorality. Paul's contention is said to be that it is highly inappropriate for anyone to boast with spiritual pride whilst, at the same time, this incest is being practised within the community.[12] It is thus seen to be somewhat ironic that a church so confident and arrogant could be guilty of tolerating incest in its midst.[13]

Having stated in 1 Corinthians 5.1 the details of the report which has reached him, Paul reacts to the community's response, καὶ ὑμεῖς πεφυσιωμένοι ἐστέ. The use of the periphrastic perfect here gives the sense of a continuing condition.[14]

In Paul's view, the action which should have been taken is beyond question. The offending man should have been put out of fellowship, and the offence in no way tolerated (1 Cor 5.2). For some reason, however, this immorality does not appear to have been confronted by others within the community; rather it has been overlooked. Instead of displaying grief at so serious an offence, the community had exhibited proud boasting.

The Corinthians' boasting has already been referred to in the letter by Paul. This boasting has been over σοφία, leading figures in the community and Paul's return to Corinth.[15] Paul succinctly deals with this matter in

---

[11] Daube draws the contrast between the situation in 1 Cor 6.8 ff. where the believers, he says, did not consider their actions to be laudable, 'Pauline Contributions to a Pluralistic Culture', 224.

[12] Cf. J. Weiß, 133; R.C.H. Lenski, 206, 219; E. -B. Allo, 116; F. Godet, 242, "Even this fact has not sufficed to disturb the proud self-satisfaction which he has already rebuked in the Corinthians in the previous chapter, or to make them come down from the celestial heights on which they are now walking to the real state of things.—The word πεφυσιωμένοι, *puffed up*, goes back on the words, iv. 6 (φυσιοῦσθε), and especially ver. 19 (τῶν πεφυσιωμένων). What have they done, those grand talkers, in view of this monstrous scandal?"; Robertson and Plummer, 95; J.B. Lightfoot, *Notes on epistles of St. Paul*, 203-4, suggests that their boasting of intellectual insight is all the more unfounded because it is practised whilst at the same time there is "this plague-spot ... eating like a canker at the vitals of the church"; O. Yarbrough, *Not Like the Gentiles*, 90; J.S. Bosch, "'Gloriarse" segun San Pablo, Sentido y teología de καυχάομαι', *Analecta Biblica* 40 (Rome, 1970), 257, "Esa 'gloria' no es buena por cuanto que se ha convertido en una hinchazón (v. 2) que les ciega y no les de a ver que, por el «fermento» del incestuoso, están dejando de ser una masa santa". With respect to 1 Cor 5.6, C.K. Barrett, 127, suggests that the boasting is somehow separate from the immorality, and linked more closely with 1 Cor 4.6-7. It is all the more important for a church not to boast when it also is exposed to such corruption. C.K. Barrett, 122, allows for the possibility that the Corinthians may not have been "*puffed up* simply in regard to the act of fornication, proud that it should have happened; he may refer to their general state of inflation, a bubble that this pin at least should have pricked". Fee, 201-2, 215, prefers the possibility that in some sense the arrogance of the Corinthians is linked directly with the sexual aberration.

[13] Cf. the boasting referred to by Paul in 1 Cor 4.6, 18, 19.

[14] J.H. Moulton, *A Grammar of New Testament Greek* III (Edinburgh, 1963), 89, refers to the instance of a perfect periphrastic in 1 Cor 5.2. Cf. also Blass/Debrunner/Funk, § 352, for the sense of a continuing condition: "Periphrasis occasionally provides a rhetorically more forceful expression"; cf. also A.T. Robertson, *Grammar of the Greek New Testament in the Light of Historical Research* (ed 4: Nashville, 1923), 826, "This analytic tendency affected the durative and perfect kinds of action. It did not suit the purely punctiliar idea".

[15] See the relevant discussion in Chapters Seven and Eight concerning 1 Cor 1.31; 4.6, 18-19.

1 Corinthians 5. This follows on from Paul's discussion throughout the first four chapters of the epistle.

The third interpretation that the boasting is despite the man's immorality, rather than as a direct reaction to it, is to be preferred because it is more consistent with Paul's preceding argument in 1 Corinthians 4.6, 18, 19 and the context of 1 Corinthians 5.2, 6. The first interpretation, however, involves a retrojection of the "everything is lawful to me" slogan of 1 Corinthians 6.12 into chapter 5.[16]

3. *Prohibitions against Incest*

It is widely accepted that the woman referred to in the chapter is the man's stepmother. In Roman society such a relationship between a man and his stepmother would have been considered incestuous.[17] In both Jewish and Roman law the prohibitions against incest were unequivocal.[18]

a. *The Roman Legal Situation*

Roman law forbids marriage between a man and his wife's mother or his son's wife or his wife's daughter or his father's wife.[19] The punishment for such an offence, referred to as *stuprum,* would have been very severe—*relegatio ad insulam.*[20] This offence was treated under the Augustan *lex Julia de adulteriis.*[21]

---

[16] Commentators have sometimes been unduly influenced in exegesis of 1 Corinthians by Strabo's comment, *Geography* 8.6.20.C, that Old Corinth was "so rich that it owned more than a thousand temple-slaves, prostitutes, whom both men and women had dedicated to the goddess". See for example, F.F. Bruce, 18-19. The Corinth of Paul's time had the very different foundation of the Roman colony, and was subject to the Roman laws which prohibited incest. Barrett rightly notes, 2-3: "The immoral reputation of old Corinth ... may not be simply carried across a century". Cf. H. Conzelmann, 'Korinth und die Mädchen der Aphrodite, Zur Religionsgeschichte der Stadt Korinth', *Nachrichten der Akademie der Wissenschaften in Göttingen* 8 (1967-8), 247-61, where he distinguishes between the Greek and Roman Corinth.

[17] Jane F. Gardner, *Women in Roman Law and Society* (London, 1986), 126, "*Incestum* included both sexual relations between primary kin and the contracting of marriage within the prohibited degrees of relationship, whether natural or by adoption".

[18] The appropriate focus is Roman law in the time of the Principate, rather than looking at Greek law, since the Roman colony at Corinth would have been under the jurisdiction of Roman legal procedures and magistrates, (see the discussion in Chapter Five).

[19] Gaius, *Institutes* 1.63, *Item eam quae nobis quondam socrus aut nurus aut privigna aut noverca fuit. Ideo autem diximus 'quondam', quia, si adhuc constant eae nuptiae, per quas talis adfinitas quaesita est, alia ratione mihi nupta esse non potest; quia neque eadem duobus nupta esse potest, neque idem duas uxores habere.* Jane F. Gardner, *Women in Roman Law and Society*, 126, n. 34, refers also to further legal texts, from different periods, relating to incest.

[20] Cf. Jane F. Gardner, *Women in Roman Law and Society*, 126-7.

[21] Cf. P.E. Corbett, *The Roman Law of Marriage* (Oxford, 1969), 133, "The *lex Julia de Adulteriis*, passed between 18 and 16 BC, was the spearhead of Augustus' attack upon the moral corruption into which Roman society had sunk in the last century of the Republic".

Marriage within the Principate had been considerably changed from Republican times by three Augustan laws (the *Lex Julia de maritandis ordinibus,* the *Lex Julia de adulteriis* and the *Lex Papia Poppaea*).[22]

From the time of Augustus onwards adultery and incest were regarded in the most serious terms. Paulus, in *Opinions* 2.26, writes,

> In the second chapter of the *lex Julia* concerning adultery, either an adoptive or a natural father is permitted to kill an adulterer caught in the act with his daughter in his own house or in that of his son-in-law, no matter what his rank may be. ... If a son under paternal control, who is the father, should surprise his daughter in the act of adultery, while it is inferred from the terms of the law that he cannot kill her, still, he ought to be permitted to do so. ... it has been held that women convicted of adultery shall be punished with the loss of half of their dowry and the third of their estates, and by relegation to an island. The adulterer, however, shall be deprived of half his property, and shall also be punished by relegation to an island; provided the parties are exiled to different islands. ... *It has been decided that the penalty for incest, which in case of a man is deportation to an island, shall not be inflicted upon the woman;* that is to say when she has not been convicted under the *lex Julia* concerning adultery.[23]

b. *Literary Evidence*

Literary evidence also shows that incest was viewed with a sense of outrage, both in Jewish and non-Jewish writings.

The instance most widely referred to is Cicero's disgust at the adulterous relationship between a man and his mother-in-law in the *Pro Cluentio* defence.[24] It is clear that Cicero's deliberate intention would have been to highlight the atrociousness of the immorality in order to gain the most advantage in the court case. Nonetheless it is significant that the Roman sense of propriety was such that Cicero felt able to use such material. Cicero describes how Sassia, the mother of Cluentius had an affair with her son-in-law (that is the brother-in-law of Cluentius). Cicero refers to the mother's outrageous passion for her son-in-law, Melinus, as a crime (*O mulieris scelus incredibile*

---

[22] The Corinthian colony would have been subject to such laws, the aims of which have variously been described as to encourage a greater sense of morality (by stipulating serious penalties for adultery) and to increase the birth-rate (by offering financial and career inducements to the larger families). Cf. A. Wallace-Hadrill, 'Family and Inheritance in the Augustan Marriage-Laws', *Proceedings of the Cambridge Philological Society* 207 (New Series, 27) (1981), 58; cf. also H. Last, 'The Social Policy of Augustus', in edd. S.A. Cook, F.E. Adcock, M.P. Charlesworth, *The Cambridge Ancient History* X (Cambridge, 1966), 448; cf. also, R.I. Frank, 'Augustus' Legislation on Marriage and Children', *California Studies in Classical Antiquity* 8 (1975), 41.

[23] Cf. J.P.V.D. Balsdon, *Roman Women: Their History and Habits* (London, 1977), 189, 215-6, 218, "When, by the *Lex Julia de Adulteriis* of BC 18, adultery was made a public crime, a permanent court was established to hear cases against married women, and whether they were married or not, their paramours. And husbands themselves were made to walk more warily. By the new law a married man was liable to prosecution if he seduced another man's wife and she was prosecuted for adultery by her husband; if he connived at his own wife's misbehaviour; or if he practised unnatural vice (*stuprum*), an offence of which he might be guilty if he had a mistress who was not a registered prostitute; and when women with respectable origins, even married women, sought to make things easier by registering as prostitutes, the Senate closed this loophole to them". Tacitus, *Annals* 2.85.1. See also J.P.V.D. Balsdon, *idem,* 219.

[24] Cicero, *Pro Cluentio* 5.12-6.16.

et praeter hanc unam in omni vita inauditum! O libidinem effrenatam et indomitam! O audaciam singularem!)[25] Initially, this passion was curbed, but in time Sassia was so inflamed that she disregarded the expectations of decency. It next seems that the situation may be solved by the impending divorce of Melinus and Cluentia. However, Cicero, exhibits shocked surprise in recounting that the mother-in-law then marries the son-in-law.[26]

Another instance in Roman literature where incest is treated with contempt is in Apuleius' *Metamorphoses*. Although the account is fictitious, the reactions may be considered typical. In *Metamorphoses* 10.2-12 there is the description of how a woman is attracted towards her stepson. This stepson is persuaded to promise to gratify her desires once her own husband is away. Taking advice, however, the stepson wisely escapes rather than be drawn into committing so outrageous a crime. The stepmother enraged by this trickery employs her slave to kill the stepson. The plan is unsuccessful; indeed, it is the woman's true son who is accidentally poisoned. The stepson is wrongfully accused of the murder, and false corroborating evidence is brought by the slave. Eventually that evidence is shown to be untrue and justice seen to be done when both the woman and her slave are sentenced with *relegatio ad insulam,* the standard punishment for incest.[27]

This story is interesting not only for the disgust with which incest is viewed, but also for the way in which the slave adopts a position defending the honour of his mistress, rather than upholding justice. It may be that in 1 Corinthians 5 there is a situation with some parallel where the honour of a leading figure is defended, rather than justice pursued.

Both Tacitus and Dio Cassius cite an instance of incest where a man was charged with such relations with his daughter and both perished.[28] Dio Cassius refers to this as "criminal relations" (αἰτίαν τε ἔσχεν ὡς συνών οἱ ...).

Martial also uses strong language to refer to a case of incest,

> Stepson to your stepmother, Gallus, rumour had it you never were while she was your father's wife. But this could not be proved while your progenitor lived. Now your father lives nowhere, Gallus, your stepmother lives with you. Though great Tully were recalled from the nether shades, and Regulus himself were to defend you, you cannot be acquitted; for she who has not ceased to be such after your father's death, never, Gallus, was a stepmother.[29]

---

[25] Cicero, *Pro Cluentio* 5.15.

[26] It may be noted how severe the language is, *Pro Cluentio* 5.12-6.14, *Cum essent eae nuptiae plenae dignitatis, plenae concordiae, repente est exorta mulieris importunae nefaria libido non solum dedecore, verum etiam scelere coninuncta. ... ea igitur mater Habiti, Melini illius adulescentis, generi sui, contra quam fas erat, amore capta ... deinde ita flagrare coepit amentia, sic inflammata ferri libidine, ut eam non pudor, non pudicitia, non pietas, non macula familiae, non hominum fama, non filii dolor, non filiae maeror a cupiditate revocaret. ... Nubit genero socrus, nullis auspicibus, nullis auctoribus, funestis ominibus omnium.*

[27] Apuleius, *Metamorphoses* 10.2-12. The combination of crimes is described as *scelestum ac nefarium facinus,* 10.2.

[28] Tacitus, *Annals* 6.19; Dio Cassius, *Roman History* 58.22.

[29] Martial, *Epigrammata* 4.16.

The Torah also explicitly forbade intercourse either with one's mother or with the wife of one's father.[30] This was further deliberated in the later Jewish writings. The Sentences of Pseudo-Phocylides determine, "Touch not your stepmother, your father's second wife; but honour her as a mother, because she follows the footsteps of your mother" (μητρυιῆς μὴ ψαῦε τὰ δεύτερα λέκτρα γονήος, μητέρα δ' ὡς τίμα τὴν μητέρος ἴχνια βᾶσαν); and "Do not have intercourse with the concubines of your father" (μηδέ τι παλλακίσιν πατρὸς λεχέεσσι μιγείης).[31] Rabbi Ishmael equally deliberates against intercourse with a father's wife and with a mother.[32]

Josephus refers to such incest as the "grossest of sins" (κακόν μέγιστον) and "an outrageous crime" (ὡς ἔκφυλον ἔχον τὴν ἀδικίαν μεμίσκεν).[33] Philo speaks in the strongest terms of the Persian magnates who even honour those children born through incest. He remarks, "What form of unholiness could be more impious than this?" (οὐ τί ἂν γένοιτο δυσσεβέστερον ἀνοσιούργημα?)[34]

4. Possible Motives for Incest

One of the significant aspects of Roman marriage was the dowry which came with the bride as a gift from her father. Originally this was intended to cover the living expenses of the household.[35] The dowry was an important factor in both the joining and divorcing of marriage. Plutarch pointed out that there were those whose motivation for marriage was dominated more by the size of the dowry, or the looks of the girl, than the character of the prospective wife.[36]

Where no previous agreement had been reached, the law maintained that the dowry was held to be returnable to the bride's father on dissolution of the marriage, but the woman might well make a claim (actio rei uxoriae) to retain all or part of it for use should she marry again.[37] Balsdon points out, "For

---

[30] Cf. Lev 18.7-8 and 20.11; Fee, 200, n. 24, refers also to Amos 2.7 b, "father and son sleeping with the same girl".

[31] The Sentences of Pseudo–Phocylides, ed. P.W. Van der Horst (Leiden, 1978), l. 179-81. See also m. Sanh, 7.4; b. Sanh. 54 a; T. Reub. passim.

[32] Cf. G.G. Porton, The Tradition of Rabbi Ishmael, Studies in Judaism of late Antiquity III (Leiden, 1979), 96–7.

[33] Josephus, Antiquities 3.274.

[34] Philo, De Specialibus Legibus 3.13-14; see also 3.20-21, for further discussion on sexual relations with a step-mother or natural mother.

[35] Cf. J.P.V.D. Balsdon, Roman Women, 188. For further discussion see also R.P. Saller, 'Roman Dowry and the Devolution of Property in the Principate', Classical Quarterly 34 (1984), 195-205; and J.F. Gardner, 'The Recovery of Dowry in Roman Law', Classical Quarterly 35 (1985), 449-53.

[36] Plutarch, Moralia 141.C-D, "Marriages ought not to be made by trusting the eyes only, or the fingers either, as is the case with some who take a wife after counting up how much she brings with her, but without deciding what kind of a helpmate she will be"; 142.F, "In about the same way, the marriage of a couple in love with each other is an intimate union; that of those who marry for dowry or children is of persons joined together; and that of those who merely sleep in the same bed is of separate persons who may be regarded as cohabiting, but not really living together".

[37] Cf. J.P.V.D. Balsdon, Roman Women, 188; P.E. Corbett, The Roman Law of Marriage, 182-3, "The actio rei uxoriae was originally granted, according to the view now prevailing, as a penal

divorce has always had its crude financial aspect; and when a husband had no better ground of divorcing his wife than the fact that he found her company tedious, he was frequently restrained, no doubt, by the chill realization that he could not divorce her without repaying her dowry".[38] This was subject to a number of qualifications—circumstances under which the husband was allowed to retain varying fractions of the dowry.[39]

By the time of the Christian emperors it was established that a widow, on remarrying, had to give her dowry to her deceased husband's children. Until then it had been the case that a deceased man's children might not benefit from his inheritance should their mother remarry.[40] The inheritance was automatically passed on to the children on the death of their widowed mother where she did not remarry.[41] The possibility arises from this that the incestuous relationship in 1 Corinthians 5 may have been motivated by a desire on the part of the man to resist his father's inheritance passing on to another family through the remarriage of his father's wife.

Furthermore, from the time of Augustus, pressure was placed on the childless widow who was still considered of child-bearing age to remarry.[42] Balsdon writes,

> Augustus cared more for propagation than he did for sentiment. For him the romantic picture of the loyal widow sadly and faithfully devoted to the memory of her husband had no appeal. Children were what the State needed. So, by his earliest moral law a childless woman between the ages of twenty and fifty was penalized if she remained unmarried for longer than a year after the death of her husband or for longer than six months after divorce.[43]

Clearly such financial incentives could be scorned by the woman who was particularly well established.[44]

---

proceeding by which the woman divorced without fault on her part could recover, from an unjust husband, such portion of the property brought into the marriage by her as the judge might consider equitably due in the circumstances. In the classical law, this action is equally available for the woman who has herself occasioned a divorce or whose marriage has been dissolved by the death of her husband. Its penal character has long been forgotten, dowry having come to be regarded as restorable, at least in part, in all cases of dissolution where the woman survives". See also *idem*, 186, "The rule found another *raison d' être* in the expediency of keeping the marriageable woman endowed. She could prevent recovery of her dowry until satisfactorily assured that it would be available for a second marriage". For a discussion of the practices with dowry in Greek law, see B.W. Winter, 'Providentia for the Widows of 1 Timothy 5:3-16', *Tyndale Bulletin* 39 (1988), 83-5.

[38] J.P.V.D. Balsdon, *Roman Women*, 219.

[39] P.E. Corbett, *The Roman Law of Marriage*, 192, "The husband called upon to restore dowry may withhold a portion or even the whole of it on proof of certain special circumstances. He is entitled to *retentiones propter liberos, propter mores, propter impensas, propter res donatas,* and *propter res amotas*".

[40] Cf. S. Dixon, *The Roman Mother* (London, 1988), 49-50.

[41] S. Dixon, *The Roman Mother*, 50, points out that Greek law gave more authority with the dowry to the eldest son whose responsibility it was to look after his mother. Roman practice, in general, was to leave the dowry in the possession of the wife.

[42] Cf. B.W. Winter, 'Providentia for the Widows', 85; J.P.V.D. Balsdon, *Roman Women*, 208; H. Last, 'The Social Policy of Augustus', 454-5.

[43] J.P.V.D. Balsdon, *Roman Women*, 221.

[44] Cf. J.P.V.D. Balsdon, *Roman Women*, 208.

The Augustan laws introduced a complex set of inducements to marriage and child-bearing which were linked with inheritance.[45] Frank summarises them thus:

> The basic premise of this legislation was that marriage was a duty incumbent on all Roman men between 25 and 60 years of age, and on all Roman women between 20 and 50. Widowed and divorced persons within these age limits were expected to remarry. Exemptions were granted to free-born persons who had procreated at least three children, and to freed persons who had procreated four; in general these numbers represented the 'quota' expected of each citizen.[46]

In the words of Dio Cassius,

> [Augustus] laid heavier assessments upon the unmarried men and upon the women without husbands, and on the other hand offered prizes for marriage and the begetting of children. And since among the nobility there were far more males than females, he allowed all who wished, except the senators, to marry freedwomen, and ordered that their offspring should be held legitimate.[47]

It was the case that the surviving partner of a marriage was only entitled to one tenth of the inheritance if childless.[48] The effect of these laws was designed to encourage remarriage after divorce or death of a partner. Last points out that there was a penalty for those who remarried a partner who was considered beyond child-bearing age.[49] Tacitus writes of the Augustan inheritance laws, "Thenceforward the fetters were tightened: sentries were set over us and, under the Papia-Poppaea law, lured on by rewards: so that, if a man shirked the privileges of paternity, the state, as universal parent, might step into the vacant inheritance".[50]

Returning to the instance in 1 Corinthians 5, the possibility arises that the incestuous step-mother may have been childless. In these circumstances she may have been tempted to derive children through a relationship with her step-son, and so become eligible to her due inheritance.

---

[45] Cf. Plutarch, *Moralia* 142.F, where the practice of entering upon marriage purely with the motivation of producing legitimate children (with the implication of its consequent benefits) is mentioned.

[46] R.I. Frank, 'Augustus' Legislation on Marriage and Children', 45.

[47] Dio Cassius, *Roman History* 54.16

[48] Cf. L.F. Raditsa, 'Augustus' Legislation Concerning Marriage, Procreation, Love Affairs and Adultery', in ed. H. Temporini, *ANRW* II. 13 (Berlin, 1980), 323. See also H. Last, 'The Social Policy of Augustus', 451, "Spinsters and wives without children lost all capacity to take under wills when they reached the age of fifty, though in earlier life they were only deprived if they had property amounting to 50,000 sesterces; but, unlike men, they were also subject to a direct financial tax. By a rule which may well be Augustan, though its authorship is not recorded, women with property exceeding 20,000 sesterces paid to the State a yearly levy of one per cent. on their capital until such time as they might find a husband". See Dio Cassius, *Roman History* 55.5.

[49] H. Last, 'The Social Policy of Augustus', 450, 25-60 years for men; 20-50 years for women: "Matches between persons of whom one was still within these limits and the other had left them behind were discouraged by confiscation of the dowry on the husband's death, and anyone who had passed these periods of life was penalized for a failure to shoulder the burdens of parenthood by partial disability to take under the terms of wills".

[50] Tacitus, *Annals* 3.28.

A further significant inducement to procreation was the withholding of prestigious posts from childless couples. Frank writes,

> preference was given candidates for political and bureaucratic office who had three legitimate children. Thus one specific provision known to us is that such men had first choice when governorships of provinces were distributed to ex-magistrates. Of course this affected only members of the upper classes, and it has been doubted that this policy was of much significance. Nevertheless the evidence indicates that even young men just starting a career were anxious to have the privileges fatherhood brought, for those without the children went to great pains to get it by imperial grant. Indeed, one can say that for 300 years this was an important factor in the life of every young man anxious to make a career in the bureaucracy.[51]

Linked with this was the practice of rewarding *delatores* or informers, who would inform the authorities of marriage violations.[52]

It is clear that there would have been much opposition to these laws. Dio Cassius describes an incident where Augustus, when faced with senatorial bad feeling over these issues, divided a public meeting of men into those who had offspring and those without. Augustus is then said to have praised assiduously the former, and humiliated the latter.[53]

Suetonius also points out the senatorial disfavour with the laws, and argues that Augustus was under pressure to lessen the severity of his initial regulations;

> He revised the existing laws and enacted some new ones for example, on extravagance, on adultery and chastity, on bribery, and on the encouragement of marriage among the various classes of citizens. Having made somewhat more stringent changes in the last of these than in the others, he was unable to carry it out because of an open revolt against its provisions, until he had abolished or mitigated a part of the penalties besides increasing the rewards and allowing a three years' exemption from the obligation to marry after the death of a husband or wife. When the knights even then persistently called for its repeal at a public show, he sent for the children of Germanicus and exhibited them, some in his own lap and some in their father's, intimating by his gestures and expression that they should not refuse to follow that young man's example. And on finding that the spirit of the law was being evaded by betrothal with immature girls and by frequent changes of wives, he shortened the duration of betrothals and set a limit on divorce.[54]

It is clear that the Augustan marriage laws were particularly restrictive. Incest was forbidden and punishment for disobedience severe; adultery, defined by the laws, was viewed in the most serious of terms; the divorced and widowed, who were of suitable age, were given strong incentive to remarry; and

---

[51] R.I. Frank, 'Augustus' Legislation on Marriage and Children', 45-6.

[52] Cf. R.I. Frank, 'Augustus' Legislation on Marriage and Children', 46. See also, P. Csillag, *The Augustan Laws on Family Relations* (Budapest, 1976), 22, "Another measure of Augustan legislation triggering off demoralizing effects was the rewards paid to delatores. These were enticed by the provisions of the Lex Julia et Papia Poppaea to denunciations against persons who, owing to caelibatus or orbitas, were incapacitated from inheriting".

[53] Cf. Dio Cassius, *Roman History* 56.1-10.

[54] Suetonius, *Augustus* 34.

childlessness was frowned upon. In addition to this it may be seen how the dowry in Roman marriage had a significant influence.

It is important to reconstruct the situation which is incompletely described in 1 Corinthians 5 in the light of these marriage regulations. Could it be that the motives for this relationship were financial (either because of the dowry or the possibilities of inheritance), or that the social status of the woman made her continuation in the household a social asset? Or was the relationship based on attraction—something no more complex than the lust of the woman for her step-son? Such an action is by no means without precedent in the contemporary literature.[55]

Either the woman's father and her earlier husband may be presumed to be dead, or the woman is divorced. Otherwise both father and husband of the woman would have been under pressure to bring legal proceedings against their wife and daughter, or risk being implicated in the crime themselves. This may be assumed to be the case since the husband, once made aware of his wife's adulterous relationship, was under pressure at once to divorce her, and within two months to bring legal proceedings against her. Failing this, he could be accused of condoning the crime, and thus, by implication, be guilty of adultery himself.[56] If still married, it would seem reasonable that the husband would not have been ignorant of the relationship since Paul argues that the incident is plainly known—1 Corinthians 5.1, Ὅλως ἀκούεται.

On the basis that the incestuous man is of such high social standing that there was no one who was able to bring legal proceedings, in the absence of either father or previous husband, against them, the more likely possibility is that the incestuous woman is widowed.

If, then, the woman were either widowed or divorced, the relationship would not necessarily be adulterous. It may still be that of a man and his concubine. (If of suitable age, the woman would then be avoiding her responsibility to remarry, and still guilty of incest). In these circumstances the motivation for this relationship may have been financial. On the man's side, he may have wanted to avoid a situation where his step-mother remarried, and thus he would lose his father's inheritance. An alternative situation, but less

---

[55] As has been seen in Apuleius, *Metamorphoses* 10.2-12, and Cicero, *Pro Cluentio* 5.12-6.16.

[56] Cf. J.P.V.D. Balsdon, *Roman Women*, 218. *Digest*, 48, 5, 30. Cf. L.F. Raditsa, 'Augustus' Legislation Concerning Marriage, Procreation, Love Affairs and Adultery', 310-1, "Augustus made love affairs and adultery public crimes, liable to *accusatio publica*. ... A husband who knowingly tolerated his wife's adventures or for that matter derived profit from them also was liable to prosecution for pimping (*lenocinium*) (D. 48, 2, 2)". Cf. also *idem*, 313. H. Last, 'The Social Policy of Augustus', 446, "Divorce was an essential preliminary to any charge of adultery. In the rare cases where the husband had caught his wife *in flagranti* and had killed her paramour it must be made at once and the affair put into the hands of a magistrate within three days; but in more normal circumstances, when the evidence had to be weighed with care, the right to prosecute was reserved to the husband (and his father-in-law) for sixty *dies utiles,* at the end of which any accuser more than twenty-five years old might act". P.E. Corbett, *The Roman Law of Marriage*, "All persons who lent their aid for the commission of *stuprum* or adultery, or who took money or other valuables as an inducement not to prosecute, rendered themselves liable to the same punishment as the principals. But principals and accessories were punishable only if they had acted with guilty knowledge".

likely, may have been that the woman may have not produced sufficient children to benefit under the Augustan laws. This relationship may, in her eyes, have provided the possibility of producing more children. This is less likely in that any offspring through the incestuous relationship would have been considered illegitimate.

It is then possible to argue, although it is clear that the text allows no certainty, that the motivation for this incestuous relationship was financial. If this is the case it adds weight to the suggestion that the relationship is between a man and woman of some social standing.

5. Clients' Silence on Patron's Morality

Since the Corinthians are neither boasting *because of* the πορνεία, nor does their 'libertarianism' enable them to be arrogant *despite* the incest, some further explanation must be found. The answer may well be related to the social status of the incestuous man.

If, as argued above, the incestuous man is of high social standing, he would in this instance be to some extent beyond reproach or criticism. His position within the community would have been such that it would have been inexpedient to confront him with the seriousness of his actions.[57] Instead it would have been the case that members within the community had chosen to remain uncritical of the incestuous brother. This would be the case if in some way the offender were of considerable importance to the church. To lose the favour of a key benefactor, for example, would have been unthinkable in Graeco-Roman society, and would invite hostility.[58] It would have been more expedient for such a leading figure to be protected from criticism which might lead to his excommunication. There may be, in other words, a situation where clients

---

[57] Cf. J. Chrysostom, 'Homilies on the Epistles of Paul to the Corinthians', in ed. P. Schaff, *A Select Library of the Nicene and Post-Nicene Fathers of the Christian Church* XXI (Grand Rapids, 1969), 83-85; H. Grotius, *Annotationes in Novum Testamentum* II (Paris, 1746), 367, 369; K.F.G. Heinrici, *Das erste Sendschreiben des Apostels Paulus an die Korinther* (Berlin, 1880), 165; H. Hammond, *A Paraphrase and Annotations upon all the Books of the New Testament briefly explaining all the difficult places thereof* (ed 7: London, 1702), 474; D. Whitby, *A Paraphrase and Commentary on the New Testament* II (ed 7: London, 1760), 126-7; C.F. Kling, *The First Epistle of Paul to the Corinthians* (ET: ed 4: 1869), 114, although he himself disagrees with the position adopted. H.A.W. Meyer, *Critical and Exegetical Handbook to the Epistles to the Corinthians* I, 141, argues, that it is "not pride in the incestuous person himself, who is conceived to have been a highly-esteemed teacher". Cf. also *idem,* 147, "what is meant by it is not the incestuous person ... as a man of high repute for wisdom in Corinth, but the condition of the Corinthians as a Christian church, inasmuch as they boasted themselves of this so confidently, while morally it was foul enough and full of shameful abuses!" See also R.C.H. Lenski, 207-8, "Were the members at Corinth so taken up with their factional wrangling that their eyes were closed even to this kind of moral turpitude? Or did this man occupy such a prominent place in the congregation that the members did not venture to challenge his crime? We may assume that the former was the case".

[58] In the same way it may be seen in Romans 5.7 that a man who had displayed his generosity as a benefactor was more highly valued than one who was merely morally correct. Cf. the author's article, 'The Good and the Just in Romans 5:7', *Tyndale Bulletin* 41 (1990), 128-142, and Appendix B.

have chosen to ignore the sinful actions of their benefactor rather than lose the favour of so prominent a person.

The dynamic of patronage was such that it was incumbent on the clients of a patron to show due gratitude.[59] Enmity was expected to be incurred by any lack of suitable gratitude to the patron—a relationship which would have been seriously deleterious to the man of lower social status. Even for a social equal, it will often have been too costly to initiate enmity with someone. On these grounds there may be a reason for the apparent reluctance to bring litigation against the incestuous man in 1 Corinthians 5.

Besides the matters of expediency and *gratia,* socially inferior people also faced legal obstacles against bringing those from the social élite to court. There was legal protection against those of the lower classes bringing *infamia* on a social superior. This was done by forbidding any person to enter into litigation with their superior.[60]

The law insisted that certain people were protected from having a summons brought against them. These included the plaintiff's parents and patron, or the city's magistrates and priests.[61] The reason for this was in order to protect *existimatio,* since it would have been possible for a man of low status to damage seriously the career of, for example, an accomplished politician by taking him to court.[62] If, then, the incestuous man in 1 Corinthians 5 were a significant patron within the church, it may have been impossible for his clients within the church, even where willing, to bring legal proceedings against him.[63]

Paul has already pointed out that some within the congregation had become 'puffed-up' over various leading figures in the community (1 Cor 4.6). He has made plain that this in itself is wrong. The irony in 1 Corinthians 5 lies in that they can remain 'puffed-up' over a man who is σοφός, δυνατός and εὐγενής,

---

[59] See the relevant discussion in Chapter Three, 31-36.

[60] Cf. P.D. Garnsey, *Social Status and Legal Privilege in the Roman Empire* (Oxford, 1970), 184. See also the relevant discussion in Chapter Five.

[61] Cf. P.D. Garnsey, *Social Status and Legal Privilege,* 181. *Digest* 4.3.11.1, "An action will not be given to certain persons, for example, to sons or freedmen proceeding against parents or patrons, since it carries *infamia.* Nor, however, should it be given to a man of low status against someone pre-eminent in status—for example, to a commoner against a consular of assured prestige, or to a man of wanton and wasteful life, or someone worthless in some other way, against a man of faultless life. Labeo says this". Cf. also *Digest* 37.15.2; 44.4.4.16. P.D. Garnsey, *op. cit.,* 187, suggests that merely on the grounds that a prosecutor was of a lower social status than his opponent, his case might be refused. *Idem,* 202, fn 2, points out the restrictions on bringing *iniuria* on a patron, which would have included taking him to court, "Institutiones, Justinian, 4.4.9: 'An injury is judged to be grave ... because of the person to whom it is done; if, for example, a magistrate has suffered an injury, or a senator at the hands of a man of low status, or a parent or patron at the hands of children or freedmen: injury is judged differently depending upon whether it is done to a senator, parent, and patron, or to a stranger and man of low status".

[62] Cf. P.D. Garnsey, *Social Status and Legal Privilege,* 184, 186.

[63] In Seneca's *Controversiae* 10.1, a rich man is depicted taunting his inferior. The taunter can be confident that he is unlikely to be taken to court even though he has murdered the poor man's father. The poor man is aware that this is a futile situation. Either he will be forbidden to enter upon litigation, or, if allowed, he would almost certainly prove unsuccessful.

and yet also guilty of πορνεία. It seems to be the case therefore that the sexual immorality itself is not being exalted, but the offender himself is the object of boasting, and this despite the fact that he is involved in sexual immorality. Their arrogance over other issues allows them to overlook the far more serious instance of immorality, instead of them approaching the situation with the more appropriate solemn mourning (1 Cor 5.2).

Paul makes no suggestion in 1 Corinthians 5 that any theological libertarianism is the cause of their response to this matter of incest (although he does refer to such freedom at a later stage in the letter, 1 Cor 6.12-13; 10.23). Rather, the immediate antecedent in this discussion is the way in which people have become puffed-up regarding one another (εἷς ὑπὲρ τοῦ ἑνὸς φυσιοῦσθε κατὰ τοῦ ἑτέρου, 1 Cor 4.6), and are arrogant about Paul not returning (ὡς μὴ ἐρχομένου δέ μου πρὸς ὑμᾶς ἐφυσιώθησάν τινες· 1 Cor 4.18).[64] It may be the case that the reference by Paul to the fact that, although absent in body, he is present in spirit is linked with the arrogance alluded to in 1 Corinthians 4.18, where some boast because Paul has not returned to them.[65] This provides a link in argument with the previous discussion, and further suggests that it was arrogance over people that was the root cause in 1 Corinthians 5.

It is, therefore, the case that the church is not condoning incest, but rather that it may be ignoring it.[66]

Why was the man not put out of fellowship? Why was he not indeed taken to court for so serious a crime? It may have been simply that there was no one who was prepared, or able, to take him to court. It may simply have been that it was not expedient to risk damaging the high status of someone in the community of such standing, maybe a benefactor.[67]

Paul is concerned here that those within the community are more concerned with the status of a person (the grounds for their boasting), than they are about his immorality.[68] The suggestion that none in the church should mix with this

---

[64] Conzelmann, 95, argues that there is no immediate antecedent to the discussion in 1 Corinthians 5. H.A.W. Meyer, *Critical and Exegetical Handbook to the Epistles to the Corinthians* I, 138, suggests there is a stark change in content between chapters 4 and 5. Barrett, 120, however, does see arrogance and high-flown wisdom as the dominating influence in the epistle, and that 1 Corinthians 5 is simply another expression of this. He does suggest the possibility that the arrogance is here demonstrated by an enthusiastic antinomianism. Fee, 194-5, also notes the link with 1 Corinthians 4.18-19. J.B. Lightfoot, *Notes on epistles of St. Paul*, 202, notes that links with the previous chapter include "the condemnation of their vanity, involving the contrast between the spiritual pride of the Corinthians and the state of their Church, comp. iv. 18, 19 with v. 2".

[65] Cf. Fee, 205, "His actual presence by the Spirit probably harks back to the 'arrogance' of those who say that he is not returning (4.18)".

[66] *Contra* Fee, 203, who suggests that it is the Corinthians' lack of a sense of sin which is the root problem.

[67] H.A.W. Meyer, *Critical and Exegetical Handbook to the Epistles to the Corinthians* I, 140, states the possibility that the magistrates in Corinth may well have commonly turned a blind eye to such immorality.

[68] Conzelmann, 95, agrees with K. Barth, *The Resurrection of the Dead* (ET: London, 1933), 30, that the Pauline accusation is not against pagan immorality, nor yet principally against any individuals. It is more that the community has not acted rightly in their treatment of the offender. Fee, 195-6, correctly points out, "In fact what is most remarkable about 5.1-13 and 6.1-11 is how little time

man, not even eat with him, would have been a most serious slight to the man's standing in society. Status was so important that a slight of this kind could ruin a prominent man's career entirely. Paul does not commend that he be put before the legal courts for the appropriate punishment. His concern is simply to maintain the purity of the community.[69]

6. *Conclusions*

A number of conclusions may tentatively be drawn from these findings. It has been argued from the context of 1 Corinthians 5 that the boasting within the community corresponds to pride in the incestuous man, and not boasting in the liberty of incest or the incestuous relationship. It has furthermore been demonstrated that both Roman and Old Testament law strictly forbade incest, and that such sexual immorality was deeply frowned upon in Graeco-Roman society. Some possible motives, on the part of the incestuous man and woman, for the sexually immoral relationship have been suggested, which indicate that both may have been from the social élite in society. Finally, some possible motives on the part of the Corinthian community for apparently remaining quiet regarding the incest were suggested; namely, that they were bound by conventions as clients to a patron, and either through loyalty to him or dependence on him did not charge the man.

Paul, on the contrary, does not tolerate the incest, and disregards the man's status. His reaction is to expel the immoral brother, treating him as an outsider, and in this way heap shame upon him. This shows Paul to be no respecter of special privilege for people of status within the church.

It should be noted that there is little evidence to provide grounds for any certain reconstruction of the situation in 1 Corinthians 5. It has been shown, however, that both the social and legal background to first century society in Corinth does shed further light on the Pauline material. By assessing this background it has been possible to suggest a reconstruction which remains consistent with both the socio-historical information and the text of 1 Corinthians 5. Taken by itself, this reconstruction remains only a possibility. Taken, however, alongside the thrust of Paul's argument throughout 1 Corinthians 1-6 this reconstruction becomes a probability.

---

he devotes to the 'sins' (and 'sinners'). He does threaten the latter with the grave consequences of their wrongdoing, but he is far more exercised in both cases with the church and its attitudes". Status in secular Corinth has already been shown by Paul to have been an issue which the Corinthian Christians have been boasting about (1 Cor 1.18-31); see Chapter 7.

[69] 1 Cor 5.12. Cf. H.A.W. Meyer, *Critical and Exegetical Handbook to the Epistles to the Corinthians* I, 140, "The objection, again, that Paul does not insist upon a divorce, is of no weight; for he does insist upon excommunication, and, after that had taken place, the criminal marriage—if the offender were not thereby sufficiently humbled to dissolve the connection of his own accord— would no longer concern the Christians".

CHAPTER SEVEN

SECULAR PERCEPTIONS OF CHRISTIAN LEADERSHIP

1. *Introduction*

It has been argued in the preceding chapters that Paul specifically addresses the adoption of secular practices of leadership within the church of Corinth in 1 Corinthians 5 and 6. Both in terms of the deference paid to significant patron figures, and in the practice of taking fellow Christians to the lawcourts, leading Christians have adopted the secular practices of the surrounding Corinthian society and have been using secular conventions to their advantage within the Corinthian church.

As well as these specific instances of secular practices in 1 Corinthians 5 and 6, it will be argued in the present chapter that leading Christians within the church have also adopted other secular perceptions of leadership.

Some of these secular perceptions can clearly be seen in 1 Corinthians 1-6: first, the Corinthians have adopted a form of personality-cult in regard to some of the 'apostolic' figures; secondly, the Corinthians were puffed-up and boastful in a secular fashion; thirdly, their actions were characterised by ἔρις and ζῆλος; fourthly, there was a preoccupation in the Corinthian community with secular σοφία; and finally, the Corinthian leaders may well have been influenced by the libertarian lifestyle of secular leaders.

In the present chapter, it will be demonstrated from 1 Corinthians 1-6 that these characteristics of leadership were adopted by the Corinthian Christians, and also that they have direct parallels with secular leadership in Graeco-Roman society.

2. *Exclusive Allegiance to Christian Leaders*

The so-called 'parties' in Corinth have been at the centre of a number of developed nineteenth and twentieth century theories regarding Corinthian, and sometimes more widely New Testament, church theologies.[1] Common to many of these theses is the assumption that the distinction between the groups is theological. It has been held that from the evidence of 1 Corinthians it is possible to define how many groups there were and also determine, in whole or in part, the distinctive theologies of the opposed parties.

---

[1] N.A. Dahl, 'Paul and the Church at Corinth according to 1 Corinthians 1:10-4:21', in edd. W.R. Farmer, C.F.D. Moule, R.R. Niebuhr, *Christian History and Interpretation: Studies Presented to John Knox* (Cambridge, 1967), 314, gives a brief summary of some of these theories.

By re-examining the evidence afforded by 1 Corinthians, it may be questioned whether it is indeed possible to define in any developed way how the groups may have differed theologically, or even whether the parties were founded on theological preferences at all.[2]

a. *Evidence for the 'Belonging'*

It is clear that within the community, the Corinthians are siding their loyalties with specific leading individuals, Paul, Apollos, Cephas and possibly also the figure of Christ.[3] Paul explains how this is demonstrated in 1 Corinthians 1.12: ἕκαστος ὑμῶν λέγει, ἐγὼ μέν εἰμι Παύλου, ἐγὼ δὲ Ἀπολλῶ, ἐγὼ δὲ Κηφᾶ, ἐγὼ δὲ Χριστοῦ.

The word ἕκαστος determines that this practice is not limited to a select few within the community, and this is corroborated by Paul's insistence that, within the community, *everyone* should agree together (1 Cor 1.10, ἵνα τὸ αὐτὸ λέγητε πάντες).[4] It is clearly widespread amongst the Corinthian Christians who adopted one or other of these 'apostolic' individuals as their figure-head.

This practice is referred to again in 1 Corinthians 3.4 simply with reference to Apollos and Paul and again in 1 Corinthians 3.22 with reference to Paul, Apollos and Cephas.[5]

It may be seen that the evidence for the parties is at the same time a prominent element of Paul's opening section,[6] and also an aspect which is only mentioned further in the letter *en passant*.[7] Paul writes to the church as though he considered it to be a single body. He does not address four organised,

---

[2] L.L. Welborn, 'On the Discord in Corinth: 1 Corinthians 1-4 and Ancient Politics', *JBL* 106 (1987), 86, suggests that Schmithals, Lütgert, Schlatter and Wilckens have all seen the controversy in religious terms, and thus have avoided having to look at any possible political background by which to understand the situation in Corinth.

[3] The number of parties is much debated, with some arguing that there were only two groups, and more questioning whether Paul's statement regarding those of Christ is to be considered on the same level as his statements regarding himself, Cephas and Apollos. It cannot be decisively argued why Paul refers to those of Christ here. It has been suggested that this slogan was introduced by Paul simply to show how absurd their allegiances to personalities are, or indeed that this was a description of Paul's own stance in the face of such slogans. Identifying the nature of a 'Christ-party', if there was one in the church at Corinth, has proved most contentious. The argument which will be put forward here applies whether or not Paul's reference to a 'Christ-party' is rhetorical.

[4] The impact of the pronoun ἕκαστος is strengthened also by the addition of the further pronoun ὑμῶν, cf. Liddell and Scott s.v., thus, "each one of you ...". J.B. Lightfoot, *Notes on the Epistles of Saint Paul from Unpublished Commentaries* (London, 1904), 153, paraphrases, "there is not one of you, but has his party leader. The whole body is infected with this spirit of strife". Both H. Conzelmann, 32 and W. Schrage, *ad loc.*, suggest, however, that ἕκαστος should not be pressed.

[5] Cf. J. Polhill, 'The Wisdom of God and Factionalism: 1 Corinthians 1-4', *Review and Expositor* 80 (1983), 333.

[6] Paul introduces the discussion with an emphatic entreaty, Παρακαλῶ δὲ ὑμᾶς, ἀδελφοί, διὰ τοῦ ὀνόματος τοῦ κυρίου ἡμῶν Ἰησοῦ Χριστοῦ, 1 Cor 1.10; cf. C.K. Barrett, *ad loc.*

[7] Conzelmann has suggested that after the first major section of the epistle, 1 Cor 1.10-4.21, the personality-centred groups are not specifically alluded to, excepting perhaps in the section including Paul's *apologia pro sua vita* in 1 Cor 9. Conzelmann, 32-3, rightly argues with respect to 1 Cor 1.10 that, although we read of the possibility of divisions, they are not to be regarded as divisions which suggest distinctions in theology.

specific and individual parties.[8] It will be seen, however, that the major emphasis of these opening sections is Paul's antithetical approach to the secular practices which are adopted by those in the Corinthian community.

b. *Nature of the 'Belonging'*

The Corinthian Christians within the church were aligning themselves behind their favourite leaders with the result that there was disagreement and distinction. The significant words in 1 Corinthians 1.10-11 are Paul's appeal ἵνα τὸ αὐτὸ λέγητε πάντες, καὶ μὴ ἦ ἐν ὑμῖν σχίσματα, ἦτε δὲ κατηρτισμένοι ἐν τῷ αὐτῷ νοΐ καὶ ἐν τῇ αὐτῇ γνώμῃ. ἐδηλώθη γάρ μοι περὶ ὑμῶν, ἀδελφοί μου, ὑπὸ τῶν Χλόης ὅτι ἔριδες ἐν ὑμῖν εἰσιν.

Munck's paper, *The Church without Factions,* has long argued for the diminished significance of parties within the Corinthian community.[9] The αἱρέσεις of 1 Corinthians 11.19 are understood by him to be eschatological phenomena and the σχίσματα of 1 Corinthians 1.10, 11.18 and 12.25 are not regarded as lasting separations.[10] On these grounds the situation in Corinth is understood to be no more than 'bickerings' as different members of the church profess allegiance to different leading figures.[11]

It must be seen that the theological differences in the community, raised later in the epistle, do not describe particular personality-centred groups and the factions are not specifically referred to elsewhere in 1 Corinthians.[12] Furthermore, in his writing, Paul takes no opportunity to accuse any of the specific parties of faulty theology.[13] At no point in 1 Corinthians does Paul link together wrong theology with any of the specific groups referred to in 1 Corinthians 1.[14] His concern is not with the respective theologies of different

---

[8] 1 Cor 1.4-9 appears to be addressed to a church which has in no sense split into distinct groups. On the contrary, Paul's remembrance of the Corinthians is as one church, and his consideration of God's grace to them is as to one church.

[9] In J. Munck, *Paul and the Salvation of Mankind* (London, 1959).

[10] J. Munck, *Paul and the Salvation of Mankind,* 138-9, "It is therefore a question, not of factions, but simply of divisions among church members for non-theological reasons". Cf. also, N.A. Dahl, 'Paul and the Church at Corinth according to 1 Corinthians 1:10-4:21', 315, "it is fairly generally agreed that in 1 Corinthians 1-4 Paul is addressing the church at Corinth as a whole, and that it is not possible to take any one section to refer to any one of the 'parties', if there were any parties at all". Fee, 53, n. 27, also argues that the sense of σχίσματα here is of dissensions, rather than schisms.

[11] J. Munck, *Paul and the Salvation of Mankind,* 139.

[12] Many commentators, however, feel that the Christ-party may appear in 2 Cor 10.7.

[13] H. Conzelmann, 34, writes, "It should be noted that the object of Paul's attack is not Peter and his party, but all parties". Cf. also J. Weiß, XXX-I, "Denn P. nimmt sich nicht eine Partei nach der andern vor, um nach gründlicher Exposition ihrer Ansichten diese zu widerlegen; darum ist es fast unmöglich, die gerügten Mißstände und seine Widerlegungen sauber auf einzelne Gruppen zu verteilen ... Darum wird es sehr schwer sein, die einzelnen Stücke seiner Polemik richtig zu beziehen und aus ihr Schlüsse auf die Parteien zu ziehen".

[14] N. Hyldahl, 'Den korintiske Situation—en skitse', *Dansk Teologisk Tidsskrift* 40 (1977), 24, correctly points out, "Man herfra og til at hævde, at menigheden var 'uden partier', er der et langt spring. At det ikke drejede sig om teologiske eller idealogiske modsætninger, berettiger ikke til at bagatellisere dem eller helt negligere dem. Tværtimod må det i så fald gælde om så meget mere ihærdigt at få præciseret, hvori persondyrkelsen og de deraf udsprungne modsætninger bestod".

groups, but solely that the Corinthians were aligning themselves with these specific personalities in a personality-cult.[15]

Paul's statement in 1 Corinthians 3.5 further suggests that theological distinctions are not his concern. "What is Apollos? What is Paul?" demonstrates that it is people and personalities which are at the centre of the division, and not philosophies. This is reinforced in 1 Corinthians 3.21 and 4.6 where Paul makes plain that it is the "boasting in men" which has dominated the Corinthian divisions, and not the defending of theologies. In 1 Corinthians 3.21, he urges the Corinthians to stop boasting in men and immediately links it with further discussion of the party slogans. In contrast to the statements of 1 Corinthians 1.12 saying "I am of ...", Paul affirms that it is in fact just those leaders who *belong* to the Corinthian Christians; πάντα γὰρ ὑμῶν ἐστιν, εἴτε Παῦλος εἴτε Ἀπολλῶς εἴτε Κηφᾶς εἴτε κόσμος εἴτε ζωὴ εἴτε θάνατος εἴτε ἐνεστῶτα εἴτε μέλλοντα, πάντα ὑμῶν, ὑμεῖς δὲ Χριστοῦ, Χριστὸς δὲ θεοῦ.

Paul points out his thankfulness that few can look to him as their figurehead through his baptizing of them, 1 Cor 1.14-16. It is actions such as these which were being interpreted in the Christian community as indicative of patronal relationships. Paul's mission as preacher, and not baptizer, meant that few could suggest that they were "of Paul" through baptism. Paul stresses rather that it is both the death of Christ, and baptism into the name of Christ, which are significant (1 Cor 1.13-17).

Welborn is, therefore, correct when he writes,

> It is no longer necessary to argue against the position that the conflict which evoked 1 Corinthians 1-4 was essentially theological in character. The attempt to identify the parties with the views and practices condemned elsewhere in the epistle, as if the parties represented different positions in a dogmatic controversy, has collapsed under its own weight.[16]

c. 'Belonging' in Secular Society

Such personality-centred politics within the church were characteristic of the surrounding Graeco-Roman society.[17] It may be assumed that those in the Corinthian Christian community who were also significant in the society of the

---

[15] J. Munck, *Paul and the Salvation of Mankind,* 150, "In connection with Paul's treatment of the supposed factions it is a matter of marked indifference to him what the different faction leaders represented, or what was preached by the leaders who were invoked. It is not those leaders, but only the Corinthians' attitude towards them, that Paul is attacking". Amongst others, W.O. Fitch in 'Paul, Apollos, Cephas, Christ, Studies in Texts: 1 Corinthians 1:12', *Theology* 74 (1971), 18-24, is wrong to suggest that the differences are theological. Conzelmann, 32 states, "The word σχίσματα, 'divisions,' implies in itself merely a neutral statement of the existence of divisions. It does not mean the existence of different systems of doctrine". N. Hyldahl, 'The Corinthian "Parties" and the Corinthian Crisis', *Studia Theologica* 45 (1991), 20, points out the agreement between N.A. Dahl and J. Munck on the fact that whatever the differences between Paul and the Corinthians, they were not matters of doctrine.

[16] L.L. Welborn, 'On the Discord in Corinth: 1 Corinthians 1-4 and Ancient Politics', 88.

[17] Cf. D.F. Epstein, *Personal Enmity in Roman Politics—218-43 BC* (London, 1987), 31, "Personal relationships, not ideology, provided the most common bonds among Roman leaders competing for power".

colony were simply continuing to practice in the church what was considered acceptable in secular society.

i. *Patronage*

It appears that the standard expectations of patronage and benefaction were dictating the dynamic of relationships within the church. A secular understanding of the underlying distinctions in rank and status between those in the church and the 'apostolic' figures of Paul, Cephas and Apollos demanded that it would be personally advantageous to be associated with one or other of these figures.

An individual in the church could benefit in reputation and status through even the unequal friendship with an apostolic figure. It is for this reason that in the church people were saying for example, "I am of Paul" and "I am of Apollos".

Plutarch describes the well-known advantage of establishing one's own reputation by initially attaching oneself to a greater man's reputation. In discussing how a young man might eventually make his mark in high office, he says,

> But the safe and leisurely way has been chosen by many famous men … For just as ivy rises by twining itself about a strong tree, so each of these men, by attaching himself while still young to an older man and while still obscure to a man of reputation, being gradually raised up under the shelter of his power and growing great with him, fixed himself firmly and rooted himself in the affairs of State.[18]

This may be similar to the way in which certain members of the Corinthian church linked themselves with those of established reputation—Apollos, Cephas and Paul (1 Cor 1.12.)

A group so strongly influenced by the expectations of their surrounding society would feel bound by the conventions and obligations which were the norm.[19] A debt of gratitude could be repaid by giving honour and prestige to a leading figure, and such honour would often be reinforced by a display of popularity and public recognition.

Paul, for his own part, deliberately tries to deter any such attachment to himself by reminding the Corinthians that it was Christ, not Paul, who was crucified and it was into Christ's name, not his own, that they had been baptised (1 Cor 1.13).

ii. *Sophists*

It is also possible to see in these verses a problem that is wider than simply the groupings in the church. Individuals in the community are being strongly influenced by the sophistic tradition which had taken root in secular Corinth.

---

[18] Plutarch, *Moralia* 805.E-F.
[19] See the discussion in Chapter Three above, 31-36.

Winter has argued strongly for a sophistic background to the actions of the Corinthians regarding the 'apostolic' leading figures.[20] He suggests that one of the characteristics of the sophists is the imitation by loyal students of their respective teachers.[21]

Winter argues with respect to 1 Corinthians 1.10-17 that:

> the reason for the Corinthians' intense response to Paul and others has been explained by the precedent created for followers of the sophists with their commitment and zealousness to a particular teacher. Just as one enrolled in the school of a sophist or became their zealous follower and admirer at public declamations, so too the newly baptized would receive instruction from their Christian teacher. Where household baptisms occurred, the coming of a teacher into that social unit certainly had its cultural precedent in the sophistic movement. It seems reasonable to explain the nexus between leaders, parties and baptism in this way.[22]

It may be surmised, therefore, that these groupings may have consisted in primary affiliations to favourite teachers and rhetors.[23]

iii. *Politics*

Welborn has plausibly argued for a further element to lie at the root of the parties in the Corinthian church. Much of the language used by Paul with regard to the situation suggests a political background.[24] The person-centred politics suggested by the party slogans is entirely to be expected where parties were normally named after individuals, not beliefs.[25] Epstein writes, "Roman politics was dominated by factions, loose organisations of politicians, united primarily by personal bonds rather than by ideology".[26] Welborn draws evidence which shows that such political wranglings were particularly factious and heated.[27]

In secular society, therefore, the conventions of patronage, politics and the sophistic loyalty between pupil and teacher all have strong parallels with the situation in the Corinthian church. It is not that any one of these influences is supreme.[28] Regarding the apostolic figures of Paul, Cephas and Apollos, the Corinthian Christians have broadly adopted a number of characteristics which

---

[20] For full details see the developed argument in B.W. Winter, *Philo and Paul among the Sophists, A Hellenistic Jewish and a Christian Response,* unpublished PhD Thesis (Macquarie University, 1988), 177-85.

[21] B.W. Winter, *Philo and Paul among the Sophists,* 203-4.

[22] B.W. Winter, *Philo and Paul among the Sophists,* 192-3.

[23] Cf., for example, Paul's fear that, through some early affiliation, some may have been able to say, 'I was baptised by Paul', (1 Cor 1.14-15).

[24] Cf. σχίσματα, ἔριδες, ζῆλος and μερίς. The textual variant in 1 Cor 3.3 where $\mathfrak{P}^{46}$ and other texts add Καὶ διχοστασίαι offers another political term, but this appears to be a gloss. (W. Schrage, G.D Fee and Orr/Walther suggest the possible influence of Gal 5.20).

[25] L.L. Welborn, 'On the Discord in Corinth: 1 Corinthians 1-4 and Ancient Politics', 91, writes of, "a picture of ancient politics as a dynamic world of personal alliances, a cosmos of blood relations, clients, and friends, constellated around a few men of noble houses who contended for power against the background of the class struggle".

[26] D.F. Epstein, *Personal Enmity in Roman Politics,* 80.

[27] L.L. Welborn, 'On the Discord in Corinth: 1 Corinthians 1-4 and Ancient Politics', 92-3.

[28] *Contra* L.L. Welborn, 'On the Discord in Corinth: 1 Corinthians 1-4 and Ancient Politics'.

were prevalent in the surrounding secular society of Roman Corinth. The consequent effect is that there is a dynamic of relationship which Paul asserts is inappropriate in the Christian church.

It may be seen, in conclusion, that Baur's highly developed thesis of a Hegelian Pauline-Petrine division within the church cannot be defended in the light of this understanding of secular influences within the church at Corinth.[29] The distinctions between the parties are not the theological distinctions between Hellenistic and Jewish Christianity, but rather the personality distinctions based on reputation in secular terms.[30] The dynamics which were so strong an aspect of secular Corinthian society in the first century then become the most obvious background for understanding the situation which Paul is addressing regarding the Corinthian parties.[31]

3. Boasting in the Corinthian Community

a. Evidence for 'Boasting' in 1 Corinthians

The second aspect of secular leadership which had been adopted by the Corinthian church was its tendency towards boasting and taking pride in men.

Bultmann indicates that the verb καυχᾶσθαι is used in the New Testament almost exclusively by Paul.[32] Fee notes that the καυχᾶσθαι word-group is principally used by Paul in the context of the Corinthian correspondence, and then almost always in a pejorative sense.[33] Furthermore Marshall comments

---

[29] N. Hyldahl, 'Den korintiske situation—en skitse', 23-4, succinctly states, "At den teologiske modsætning mellem Paulus-partiet på den ene side og Kefas-partiet på den anden skulle vedrøre ekklesiologien, og at der overhovedet bestod teologiske—eller ideologiske—modsætninger mellem menighedsgrupperne, så at det ville være berettiget at tale om egentlige partier, er efter mit skøn grebet ud af luften og kaster ikke lys over teksten i 1 Kor., men siger til gengæld så meget desto mere om F.C. Baurs og Tübingerskolens stadig væk kun lidt svækkede indflydelse i tysk nytestamentlig eksegese".

[30] Contra Baur's influential thesis, Paulus, der Apostel Jesu Christi I (ed 2: Leipzig, 1866). Cf. J.A. Davis' assessment in Wisdom and Spirit: An Investigation of 1 Corinthians 1.18-3.20 Against the Background of Jewish Sapiential Traditions in the Greco-Roman Period (Lanham, 1984), 141, "Baur's attempt to make 1 Corinthians conform to his own dialectical understanding of the whole of early church history drew searching criticism from those who were convinced that his interpretation of 1 Cor 1.12 was incorrect. They argued that Baur had blurred the distinction between the internal problems of 1 Corinthians and the conflicts caused initially in Galatia, and perhaps later on in Corinth as well by the entrance of 'judaizers' into the fellowship ... The weakness of Baur's dialectical theory applied without qualification or nuance to the interpretation of 1 Corinthians is glaringly and justly exposed by such criticism".

[31] In addition to the secular political nuances which may be seen in the Corinthians' statement, 'I am of Paul', it should be noted that there was also a pagan background in Corinth to such a slogan. An interesting parallel may be noticed with the Corinthian bronze bowl of Aphrodite with the inscription τᾶς Ἀφροδίτας ἐμί. This sixth or fifth century B.C. bowl is cited in B.W. Winter, 'Theological and Ethical Responses to Religious Pluralism—1 Corinthians 8-10', Tyndale Bulletin 41 (1990), 224, n. 54; see also, A.E. Newall, American Journal of Archaeology 35 (1931), 1-2, L.H. Jeffery, Local Scripts of Archaic Greece (Oxford, 1990), 132, no. 35, plate 21; A.N. Stillwell, Corinth, 15.1, 115, no. 1, and SEG XI 200.

[32] R. Bultmann, 'καυχάομαι, καύχημα, καύχησις', TDNT III (Grand Rapids, 1989), 648. Cf. also Fee, 84.

[33] Fee, 84, n. 28.

that φυσιοῦν—"puff up, to be conceited, proud or arrogant"—is also used almost exclusively by Paul in relation to the Corinthians' conduct.[34] Boasting, consequently, appears to be a peculiarly prominent characteristic of the Corinthians within the Pauline corpus.[35]

i. *Boasting in Symbols of Status*

Boasting is specifically referred to for the first time in the letter in 1 Corinthians 1.29 and 31. Paul explains that God's plan of salvation was so designed as to preclude any grounds for boasting before the Lord. The paraphrase from Jeremiah 9.23-24 is anticipated in 1 Corinthians 1.26 where Paul uses the parallel terms of the σοφός, δυνατός and εὐγενής. The passage from Jeremiah instead uses the nouns σοφός, ἰσχυρός and πλούσιος.[36]

Paul, at this point, perceives the boasting to be over symbols of status, such as wisdom, influence and nobility. The connections with Jeremiah more clearly illustrate Paul's perception of the basis of the boasting which is apparent in the community. The Corinthians are elevating aspects of social status, for example, wealth, influence and wisdom. It is not, however, until 1 Corinthians 3.21, 4.7 and 5.2, 6 that Paul openly accuses the Corinthians themselves of boasting.[37]

Marshall shows that Paul's principle opposition comes from those of high status within the community. He writes, "the traditional antithesis of notions of honour and shame and associated ideas present here and throughout 1.10-4.21 refer primarily to social status, and indicate the attitudes and behaviour of certain upper class Christians toward Paul and toward Corinthians of lowly status".[38] He considers that ὕβρις is a significant characteristic displayed by the Corinthians and alluded to by Paul in 1 Corinthians 4. ὕβρις is generally translated 'pride' or 'arrogance', but Marshall suggests that the concept is far wider: "*Hybris* is … having energy or power and misusing it self-indulgently".[39] Characteristic of hybristic behaviour is excessive superiority and self-confidence.[40]

---

[34] P. Marshall, *Enmity in Corinth: Social Conventions in Paul's Relations with the Corinthians* (Tübingen, 1987), 204.

[35] T.B. Savage, *Power through Weakness: An Historical and Exegetical Examination of Paul's Understanding of the ministry in 2 Corinthians,* unpublished PhD dissertation (Cambridge University, 1986), 42-3, lists some secular literary sources which argue that the Corinthians were 'boastful'. Cf. also D. Engels, *Roman Corinth, An Alternative Model for the Classical City* (Chicago, 1990), 110.

[36] See also E.E. Ellis, 'How the New Testament uses the Old', in ed. I.H. Marshall, *New Testament Interpretation* (Exeter, 1977), 204.

[37] Arrogance, φυσιοῦν, is also referred to in 1 Cor 4.18-19.

[38] P. Marshall, *Enmity in Corinth,* 181.

[39] P. Marshall, *Enmity in Corinth,* 182.

[40] Marshall notes the description by Philo of the hybrist who "considers himself superior to all in riches, estimation, beauty, strength, wisdom, temperance, justice, eloquence, knowledge; while everyone else he regards as poor, disesteemed, unhonoured, foolish, unjust, ignorant, outcast, in fact good for nothing". Philo, *On Virtues,* 174. Cf. P. Marshall, *Enmity in Corinth,* 208.

ii. *Boasting in Men*

A second significant focus of the Corinthians' boasting is their taking pride in men.[41] Paul notes this specifically both in 1 Corinthians 3.21, ὥστε μηδεὶς καυχάσθω ἐν ἀνθρώποις; and also in 1 Corinthians 4.6, ἵνα μὴ εἷς ὑπὲρ τοῦ ἑνὸς φυσιοῦσθε κατὰ τοῦ ἑτέρου. The specific manifestation of this "taking pride in one man over against another" has already been noted, in Chapter Six above, as a strong possibility in the situation of the incestuous patron of 1 Corinthians 5. There the boasting of the Corinthians is twice referred to by Paul, 1 Corinthians 5.2 and 6. The other major instance of boasting may be seen in Paul's discussion in 1 Corinthians 1.10-12 of the personality-centred parties.

Fiore rightly describes the focus of the problem in the community as these two objects of their boasting:

> The immediate situation seems to be a misapprehension of the relative merits of the community's teachers, which leads to factions grouped around different favorite personalities (1.12; 3.4, 21). But this manifests a far-reaching failure in the community members' own self-estimation, with its exaggerated pretensions to knowledge (3.18-19) and faulty regard or denigration of others (4.6-7).[42]

Dahl links these two aspects of their boasting in saying, "Paul takes boasting of the teachers to imply boasting of their own wisdom (cf. 3:18-21; 4:7-10)".[43]

It may thus be seen from these early chapters of 1 Corinthians that boasting is a particularly strong element of the Corinthians' conduct. Their boasting is over those qualities of status—wealth, high-birth and wisdom—which are highly acclaimed in secular society, and over the leading personalities.

b. *Secular Practice of Boasting in Society*

A study of the Greek verb καυχᾶσθαι and its related forms shows that before the first century AD it was relatively infrequently used in literary sources.[44] That is not to suggest that the *concept* of boasting was infrequent in the Hellenistic world. A number of other words were more commonly used to describe it. Related nouns include, περιαυτολογία, ὕβρις, ὑπεροψία and ἀλα-ζονεία.[45] Betz notes that Plutarch never uses the term καυχᾶσθαι himself, but rather employs other synonyms, μεγαλαυχία and μεγαληγορία.[46]

---

41 N.A. Dahl also notes this in 'Paul and the Church at Corinth according to 1 Corinthians 1:10-4:21', 320.

42 B. Fiore, '"Covert Allusion" in 1 Corinthians 1-4', *The Catholic Biblical Quarterly* 47 (1985), 86-7. Cf. also D.M. Stanley, '"Become Imitators of Me": The Pauline Conception of Apostolic Tradition', *Biblica* 40 (1959), 871.

43 N.A. Dahl, 'Paul and the Church at Corinth according to 1 Corinthians 1:10-4:21', 320.

44 It is much more frequently used by the later Christian Fathers, especially Gregory Nazianzen, Gregory Nyssa, Basil, *et alii*. This conclusion is derived from the texts included in the CD ROM version of *Thesaurus Linguae Graecae, Canon of Greek Authors and Works* (Oxford, 1986), using the Ibycus Scholarly Computer.

45 C. Forbes, 'Comparison, self-praise and irony: Paul's boasting and the conventions of Hellenistic rhetoric', *NTS* 32 (1986), 13.

46 H.D. Betz, *Plutarch's Ethical Writings and Early Christian Literature* (Leiden, 1978), 375.

Dowdy rightly points out that the sense of καυχᾶσθαι was largely negative during the first century AD.[47] In support of this it may be noted in Diogenes Laertius, *Vitae Philosophorum* 10.7.13, that Epicurus is credited with these harsh words, "Nay, let them go hang; for, when labouring with an idea, he too had the sophist's off-hand boastfulness like many another servile soul" (ἀπὸ τοῦ στώματος καύχησιν τὴν σοφιστικήν).[48]

Plutarch wrote a treatise entitled "On Praising Oneself Inoffensively" (*De se ipsum citra invidiam laudando*) in which the subject of 'boasting' is dealt with in some detail. He gives an account of those necessary qualifications to self-praise which may make boasting less offensive.[49] On the negative side, boasting is said to bring about distress because it causes embarrassment to the listener; because it is properly to be given by another; and furthermore because the listener is put in a position where he must either appear rude by remaining silent, or endorse the praise he is hearing.[50] Boasting of one's own deeds was considered inappropriate; but pride in another was laudable.

Self-praise was a widely accepted practice in the Graeco-Roman world, and yet at the same time, it was also frowned upon. Plutarch writes, "In theory ... it is agreed that to speak to others of one's own importance or power is offensive, but in practice not many even of those who condemn such conduct avoid the odium of it";[51] furthermore,

> For while praise from others ... is the most pleasant of recitals, praise of ourselves is for others most distressing. For first we regard self-praisers as shameless, since they should be embarrassed even by praise from others; second as unfair, as they arrogate to themselves what it is for others to bestow; and in the third place if we listen in silence we appear disgruntled and envious, while if we shy at this we are forced to join eulogies and confirm them against our better judgement, thus submitting to a thing more in keeping with unmanly flattery than with the showing of esteem—the praise of a man to his face.[52]

He also writes, "... towards one who praises himself the generality of men feel a great hostility and resentment, but do not feel so strongly against one who praises another, but often even listen with pleasure and voice their agreement".[53]

---

[47] B.A. Dowdy, *The Meaning of KAUCHASTHAI in the New Testament*, PhD Thesis (Vanderbilt University, 1955).

[48] C. Forbes, 'Comparison, self-praise and irony: Paul's boasting and the conventions of Hellenistic rhetoric', 8, suggests "However, it was widely conceded that self-praise was an odious business, and one that no decent person would indulge in, except in certain fairly clearly defined circumstances".

[49] Barrett points out that self-praise in the Greek philosophical tradition was largely criticized, 'Boasting (καυχᾶσθαι, κτλ.) in the Pauline Epistles', in ed. A. Vanhoye, *L'Apôtre Paul— Personnalité, Style et Conception du Ministère* (Leuven, 1986), 368.

[50] H.D. Betz, *Plutarch's Ethical Writings and Early Christian Literature*, 375-6.

[51] Plutarch, *Moralia* 539.A.

[52] Plutarch, *Moralia* 539.D.

[53] Plutarch, *Moralia* 542.C.

It is pointed out that the aim of much self-praise is none other than the gratifying of personal ambition.[54] Plutarch also suggests that there were ways in which, when being praised for being eloquent, rich or powerful, one should rather refer to one's better character.[55]

Boasting was a significant aspect of the sophists' display.[56] It was not limited, however, to the sophists. An important and accepted aspect of leadership in the Graeco-Roman world was self-display. Leaders would elevate themselves; their followers, with a certain element of self-interest, would praise their leaders. In the Corinthian community such καύχησις was also a part of the leadership dynamic. Plutarch talks of kings and πλούσιοι employing self-praise,[57] and he points out that hearing influential people boasting about themselves is odious: "These are the feelings and language to which we are prompted not only by στρατιῶται and the νεόπλουτοι with their flaunting and ostentatious talk, but also by σοφισταί, φιλόσοφοι, and στρατηγοί who are full of their own importance and hold forth on the theme".[58]

Paul's perception of the Corinthians as boastful is consequently a strong criticism of a characteristic which was widely used in the city's secular context. The Corinthians had carried over into the context of the church the practice, acceptable in Corinthian secular society, of enhancing one's own reputation by becoming a supporter of an established figure. They had also introduced into the church a form of boasting which was more properly at home within the secular ἐκκλησία.

4. "Ερις and Ζῆλος in the Christian Community

a. Enmity in the Christian Community

Divisiveness within the church has remained a significant aspect in discussion of the Corinthian community. Even where Munck maintained that it was a "church without factions", it was clear to him that this did not exclude the fact that there were internal bickerings.[59]

Paul is adamant that there is both ἔρις and ζῆλος within the church, and also that this is entirely symptomatic of 'worldly' behaviour. He states in 1 Corinthians 3.3: ὅπου γὰρ ἐν ὑμῖν ζῆλος καὶ ἔρις, οὐχὶ σαρκικοί ἐστε καὶ

---

54 Plutarch, Moralia 540.A, "Now the praise is frivolous which men are felt to bestow upon themselves merely to receive it; and it is held in the greatest contempt, as it appears to aim at gratifying ambition and an unseasonable appetite for fame".

55 Plutarch, Moralia 543.A, "With the fair-minded it is not amiss to use another device, that of amending the praise: when praised as λόγιος, πλουσιός, or δυνατός, to request the other not to mention such points but rather to consider whether one is of worthy character, commits no injuries, and leads a useful life". The similarity between these terms and those of 1 Cor 1.26 and Jeremiah 9.22-3 should be noted.

56 See the argument in B.W. Winter, Philo and Paul among the Sophists, 195-203.

57 Plutarch, Moralia 547.E.

58 Plutarch, Moralia 547.E.

59 J. Munck, Paul and the Salvation of Mankind, 139.

κατὰ ἄνθρωπον περιπατεῖτε? In 1 Corinthians 11.17-22 Paul refers again to the existence of divisions within the community leading to tensions within the celebration of the Lord's Supper.[60]

Welborn convincingly demonstrates the significance of secular political influences as an explanation for the discord within the community at Corinth. This is seen in Paul's choice of language particularly in 1 Corinthians 1.12, 1.17-2.5, 2.6-3.3, 4.1-21 and 11.17-34. It is with regard to the ἔρις and ζῆλος of 1 Corinthians 3.3 that Welborn could have expanded his argument further regarding the discord in the Corinthian community.[61]

b. The Importance of Enmity in Secular Politics

Epstein, in *Personal Enmity in Roman Politics 218 - 43 BC,* explores at length the importance of enmity for successful politics within the Roman world. It has already been shown that the colony of Corinth was bound to the Roman influences in both its administration and politics, and it is interesting to note parallels between Epstein's findings and the situation within the church at Corinth during the imperial period.[62]

Enmity, in Roman politics, was both a tool of great influence and a stumbling block. It was seen as a necessary evil in the path of self-advancement, and yet also something to be overlooked if necessary at the time of an election.[63] A client would go to great lengths to defend the name of his patron even whilst his patron was away. Epstein notes that *amicitia* was of considerable importance where a man was not in a position to defend his own name.[64] In the case of Apollos, Paul and Peter, the Corinthians may have taken it upon themselves to defend their absent patrons, and in the process of doing this create between themselves *inimicitia.*

Paul rebukes the Corinthians for such differences between them, and terms this as 'worldly' in 1 Corinthians 3.3. It has already been seen that enmity and personal influence were important aspects of the situation in 1 Corinthians 6 where two significant members of the Christian community were going to the civil law-courts. Such enmity appears to have been widespread within the church.

The link between personal reputation and ἔρις may be seen in this comment by Dio Chrysostom: "the high-minded, perfect man is above material wealth; but in the matter of reputation would he perhaps quarrel (ἐρίζοι) with and envy

---

[60] See the recent article, A. Campbell, 'Does Paul Acquiesce in Divisions at the Lord's Supper?', *Novum Testamentum* 33 (1991), 61-70.

[61] He does note briefly the political nuances in the words ἔρις and ζῆλος; L.L. Welborn, 'On the Discord in Corinth: 1 Corinthians 1-4 and Ancient Politics', 87.

[62] See the discussion in Chapter Three above.

[63] D.F. Epstein, *Personal Enmity in Roman Politics,* 28, writes, 28, "The pursuit of *inimicitiae* and the destruction of one's enemies were firmly entrenched among those virtues Romans thought necessary for the acquisition of *dignitas, virtus,* status and nobility—qualities the Roman aristocracy pursued from birth".

[64] D.F. Epstein, *Personal Enmity in Roman Politics,* 47.

(φθονοῖ) those whom he sees more highly honoured by the crowd and winning greater plaudits?"[65]

Ἔρις was widespread in secular politics and the dynamics of social advancement. In the church at Corinth, Paul accuses the Christians of adopting the same character traits, and links this with acting in a secular fashion, κατὰ ἄνθρωπον περιπατεῖτε, 1 Cor 3.3.

5. Secular Σοφία

a. Contrast between Worldly Wisdom and Godly Wisdom

Wisdom has widely been recognised as one of the major aspects of Paul's opening chapters to the Corinthians in the epistle. There is dispute over what sort of wisdom the Corinthian Christians were boasting.[66] Although many different theories have been used to explain the meaning of σοφία in the context of 1 Corinthians, the weight of evidence today supports the thesis that Paul is objecting to the excessive significance placed on Hellenistic wisdom, characteristic of the sophists of the day.[67]

In 1 Corinthians 1-3 a number of different contrasts or comparisons are made by Paul. It is clear that he is contrasting the methods and standards used in the world and in some instances comparing them with those of God.

1.17	ὁ σταυρὸς τοῦ Χριστοῦ	σοφία λόγου
1.20-21	ἡ σοφία τοῦ θεοῦ	ἡ σοφία τοῦ κόσμου
1.25	τὸ μωρὸν τοῦ θεοῦ	ἡ σοφία τῶν ἀνθρώπων
1.25	τὸ ἀσθενὲς τοῦ θεοῦ	ἡ ἰσχύς τῶν ἀνθρώπων

---

[65] Dio, *Orationes* 77/8.17. Cf. also for other associated uses of ἔρις in Dio's *Orationes* 11.78; 32.15; 34.17; and 39.8.

[66] Cf. Fee, fn 79, 64-5, "Traditionally it was assumed that it reflects the Greek philosophical or sophist tradition. The most comprehensive advocacy of this position can be found in Munck (*Paul*, pp. 148-54) ... . Some who see the background as Greek argue for a hypostatic (personal) understanding of *sophia*. Thus they see the Corinthians as having equated Sophia with the so-called heavenly redeemer of Gnosticism (see esp. Wilckens, 68-76). Others have viewed the emphasis on wisdom as belonging to the Jewish wisdom tradition, either the personified wisdom of Proverbs (e.g., 8.1-9.6) and Sirach (e.g., 1.4, 9) or its Hellenized form in Philo of Alexandria (see Pearson, 27-39; Horsley, 'Wisdom' and 'Marriage'; and Davis). But the problems with these two views are twofold: (1) There does not seem to be any viable evidence that the Corinthians had a personalized view of wisdom; indeed, the evidence goes in the other direction ... ; (2) the background seems unlikely to be Jewish, since Paul explicitly says that *Jews* demand *signs* and it is the Greeks who seek for wisdom. Davis, 189 n. 26, calls this objection 'misguided'. But to do so he must dismiss Paul's explicit statement in favor of a highly speculative midrashic analysis of the text. Whether rhetorical or not, Paul's clear *statement* is that *Greeks*, not Jews, pursue wisdom. Some of course (e.g., Ellis, 45-62) reject wisdom as a Corinthian concern and see it as Paul's own point of view, which is then argued for as having a Jewish background. But the context of the whole argument seems to speak too strongly against this option. Even Paul's affirmations of wisdom in 2.6-16 seem to have been dictated by the position of the church. Elsewhere he simply does not reflect this emphasis or understanding".

[67] Cf. especially B.W. Winter, *Philo and Paul among the Sophists*, 230-1, where he refers to Paul's accusation of the Corinthians κατὰ ἄνθρωπον περιπατούμενοι, 1 Cor 3.3. C.K. Barrett, 67-8, suggests that Paul uses the notion of 'wisdom' in a variety of different senses, some good and some bad. He writes, "Wisdom is used in a bad sense when it denotes simply the skilled marshalling of human arguments, employed with a view to convincing the hearer".

1.27	τὰ μωρὰ τοῦ κόσμου	οἱ σοφοί
1.27	τὰ ἀσθενῆ τοῦ κόσμου	τὰ ἰσχυρά
1.28	τὰ ἀγενῆ τοῦ κόσμου καὶ τὰ ἐξουθενημένα	τὰ μὴ ὄντα
2.1-3	ἐν ἀσθενείᾳ καὶ ἐν φόβῳ καὶ ἐν τρόμῳ πολλῷ	ὑπεροχή λόγου ἢ σοφίας
2.5	ἡ δύναμις θεοῦ	ἡ σοφία ἀνθρώπων
2.6-7	σοφία ἐν τοῖς τελείοις	σοφία τοῦ αἰῶνος τούτου
2.12	τὸ πνεῦμα τὸ ἐκ τοῦ θεοῦ	τὸ πνεῦμα τὸ ἐκ τοῦ κόσμου
2.13	διδακτοί πνεύματος	διδακτοί ἀνθρωπίνης σοφίας λόγοι
3.1	πνευματικός	σάρκινος
3.18	σοφός (i.e. the Christian σοφός)	σοφός ἐν τῷ αἰῶνι τούτῳ
3.19	μωρία παρὰ τῷ θεῷ	ἡ σοφία τοῦ κόσμου τούτου

The contrasts which are made by Paul are between the things of God and the things of the world; it has been seen that the divisions within the church are an aspect of secular leadership; the boasting which was characteristic of secular leadership is paralleled by the Corinthian Christians; the ἔρις and ζῆλος which was a part of the Corinthian community was also an acceptable part of secular politics; the patronage dynamics were exercised in regard both to the 'apostolic' figures and the incestuous man; and influence over other Christians was enhanced by resorting to the secular law-courts. In all these matters the Corinthian Christians are found to be secular in their practices and perspectives. It is then no surprise to find that the wisdom which is so highly regarded by those in the church is also the wisdom of the world. It is unnecessary to look further than this consistent background of secular influence to find an understanding of the nature of the Corinthian σοφία.[68]

b. *The Sophistic Background to Σοφία*

In 1954, Johannes Munck made the suggestion in his controversial chapter, *The Church without Factions,* that there were similarities between the Corinthians and the Greek sophists of the day. This was the case in their "craving for applause, riches, and fame".[69]

Munck describes the Corinthian situation:

> That new, overflowing life is wisdom, and they have received it from a teacher of wisdom; and in their childish vainglory each boasts of having had the best and most eminent teacher of wisdom. And because they know only the popular philosophy and the professional orator or sophist, who understood how to captivate a Greek audience by his learning and eloquence, the outward form is conclusive for them. The apostle, who has not forgotten the apprehension with which he began to preach about Christ in Corinth, suddenly sees himself compared with a professional sophist who, with painted face and theatrical gestures, invites an audience of a thousand people to suggest to him a theme on which to improvise.[70]

---

[68] The developed theses of gnosticism and Hellenistic mystery religions are an unnecessary framework to place upon the text when the plain context of a community overly influenced by their surrounding secular society also fits the notion of σοφία.

[69] J. Munck, *Paul and the Salvation of Mankind,* 152.

[70] J. Munck, *Paul and the Salvation of Mankind,* 153. See also *idem,* 154, "the acceptance of the Gospel led the Corinthians to feel rich and wise in the possession of new life and spiritual gifts. That feeling was expressed in their calling Christianity a kind of wisdom, its leaders teachers of wisdom,

These conclusions have broadly been accepted by only a few commentators today. Fee in particular follows the argument closely, suggesting that it is the sophistic tendency which is the root of the problem.[71] Barrett suggests that Paul's reason for writing to the church in the first place was their "glorying in men" and their wrongful evaluation of their own gifts.[72]

B.W. Winter's *Philo and Paul among the Sophists* develops Munck's preliminary suggestion that the Corinthians were sophistic in their outlook.[73] Winter analyses the Sophistic movement of the first century and its impact on the city of Corinth, and from this basis notes significant parallels with the Corinthian community. In opposition to this tendency within Corinth, Winter argues that Paul is deliberately anti-Sophistic during his initial visit to the city. This stance is described by Paul himself in 1 Corinthians 2.1-5 where he avoided any identification of his ministry with the practices of the sophists.[74] Winter further argues that the Corinthians viewed their respective leaders and apostolic figures with sophistic expectations. A sophist, on his first visit to a city, would give a public lecture in order to display his skill and win acclaim. He further describes in some detail the exclusive relationship which sophistic disciples had with their preferred teachers. This wrong perspective is said to have been aggravated by the methods which Apollos adopted whilst in the community.

From 1 Corinthians 1-4, Winter describes three specific aspects which Paul criticizes—their perception of status;[75] their imitation of revered teachers;[76] and their boasting in their teachers.[77] Winter considers that the σχίσματα were caused by the Corinthians' sophistic perception of themselves as exclusive disciples of the different teachers, Paul, Apollos and Cephas.

The sophists made a point of displaying their social status—grounded in their right to being described as wise, well-born and influential. In 1 Corinthians 1.26-28, he suggests that Paul is deliberately inverting those qualifications which the sophists were inclined to boast about.[78]

There were strong parallels between the sophists and the practice of secular boasting, already referred to. Winter writes: "The over-arching theme upon which Paul took his opponents to task was that of their 'boasting' about their

---

and themselves—this was the most important for them—wise men who had drawn on that wisdom through the Christian leaders. The poor, insignificant Corinthians, with neither distinguished ancestry nor pagan wisdom to support them, had become so rich through the new proclamation that they seized on the Greek terminology that was there for them, and used it to express their new glory".

[71] Cf. Fee, 49, 80, 94. Conzelmann, Lightfoot, Meyer, Orr/Walther, Robertson/Plummer do not treat the Corinthian boasting as a central issue. Héring refers to sophists in his discussion of 1 Cor 1.20.

[72] Cf. Barrett, 59.

[73] B.W. Winter, *Philo and Paul among the Sophists*, 156-7.

[74] See discussion in B.W. Winter, *Philo and Paul among the Sophists*, 151 ff.

[75] 1 Cor 1.4-7, 30; 4.8-13.

[76] 1 Cor 1.10-16; 3.18-23; 4.10-17.

[77] 1 Cor 1.17-31; 3.18-23; 4.6 ff.

[78] B.W. Winter, *Philo and Paul among the Sophists*, 201.

achievements".[79] "Sophistic boasting was the fundamental issue which had drawn subsidiary ones together as Paul's critique of the sophistic tradition in 1 Cor 1-4 unfolded. It would naturally be the same issue on which he would pass judgement against the proponents of sophistic tradition".[80]

Forbes argues that self-praise was an invidious practice of the sophists as opposed to the "more genuine in their professions".[81] Sophists were viewed by many in a bad light, often for their excessive self-display. Plutarch suggests, "Whereas the rhetorical sophists who at their displays of eloquence accept from the audience the cries of 'how divine' and 'spoken like a god' lose even such commendation as 'fairly said' and 'spoken as becomes a man'".[82]

Thus Munck writes,

> It is the church itself that loves those wrangles in which the church members exalt themselves by supposing that their wisdom has been taken over from one of the great Christian sophists, one of those close and well known to them, Paul and Apollos, or one of those known by what Paul has told them, Peter, the apostle to the Jews, or by the Lord and Master himself, Christ.[83]

c. *Importance of Oratory for Secular Status*

In a recent study, Litfin suggests that the principal criticism which the Corinthians held against Paul is the fact that Paul did not measure up to the expectation of Graeco-Roman eloquence which the pretentious Corinthians so venerated.[84] His rhetorical shortfall in their eyes was made all the more apparent by the rather more evident skills of Apollos in oratory. The Corinthians had hoped for an orator who, in the style of the greatest public speakers, could adapt his message in order to achieve the best results in terms of fame, reputation and appreciation. Paul on the other hand was quite unprepared to adapt his message in this way.

Litfin considers 1 Corinthians 1-4 to be the *locus classicus* in the Pauline corpus where Paul's theology of proclamation can be seen. The boasting which we read of in these chapters is characteristic of the rhetors of Paul's day who were principally motivated to create a reputation for themselves. Paul's theology of proclamation is in direct opposition to this. Litfin defends a case that oratory was appreciated by the average listener, and, in the first century AD, it was by no means an exclusive pastime for the exceptionally educated alone.[85] The implications are that those in the Corinthian church would have

---

[79] B.W. Winter, *Philo and Paul among the Sophists,* 232.

[80] B.W. Winter, *Philo and Paul among the Sophists,* 232-3.

[81] C. Forbes, 'Comparison, self-praise and irony: Paul's boasting and the conventions of Hellenistic rhetoric', 9.

[82] Plutarch, *Moralia* 543.F.

[83] J. Munck, *Paul and the Salvation of Mankind,* 150.

[84] A.D. Litfin, *St. Paul's Theology of Proclamation: An Investigation of 1 Corinthians 1-4 in the Light of Greco-Roman Rhetoric,* unpublished D.Phil dissertation (Oxford University, 1983), 228.

[85] Cf. A.D. Litfin, *St. Paul's Theology of Proclamation,* 217, and B.W. Winter, *Philo and Paul among the Sophists,* 137, where they refer to Favorinus' comment on women and children appreciating oratory, Dio, *Orationes* 37.33.

been most familiar with the tricks and expectations of popular oratory.[86] These Christians were evaluating Paul in terms of his rhetorical expertise and the way he handled his message of the crucified Christ.

It is not held that the Corinthians themselves were proficient orators. However he does argue, "Though they were themselves on the outside—or perhaps even in some cases still more tantalizingly, on the fringe—of the circles of status, influence and sophistication in Corinth, they exalted those on the inside and themselves put on the airs of the aristocracy, affecting the stance of sophisticated critics as best they could".[87] It is suggested that their boasting was all the more vain because few from the church did in fact belong to the social class of the élite.[88]

Munck draws the similar conclusion,

> The Corinthians regarded the Christian message as wisdom like that of the Greeks, the Christian leaders as teachers of wisdom, themselves as wise, and all this as something to boast about. Paul asserts, on the contrary, that the Gospel is foolishness, that the Christian leaders are God's servants whom God will judge, that the Corinthians are of the flesh and therefore without wisdom, and that none of this redounds to the glory of any human being, but that he who boasts is to boast in the Lord.[89]

6. Lifestyle

A further aspect which suggests secular influences is the lifestyle of some of the Corinthian Christians. Philo, in his treatise *Quod Deterius Potiori Insidiari Solet,* records verbatim the way the ruling classes of Alexandria boasted about their lifestyle:

> The mode of life of these two classes is a witness to the truth of what I say. ... Those ... who take care of themselves are men of mark and wealth, holding leading positions, praised on all hands, recipients of honours, portly, healthy and robust, revelling in luxurious and riotous living, knowing nothing of labour, conversant with pleasures which carry the sweets of life to the all-welcoming soul by every channel of sense.[90]

This lifestyle of secular leaders was justified by them on the grounds that

> Are not eyes and ears and the band of the other senses bodyguards and courtiers, as it were, of the soul? Must we not then value allies and friends equally with ourselves? Did nature create pleasures and enjoyments and the delights that meet us all the way through life, for the dead, or for those who have never come into existence, and not for the living?[91]

---

[86] A.D. Litfin, *St. Paul's Theology of Proclamation,* 203.

[87] A.D. Litfin, *St. Paul's Theology of Proclamation,* 245. It would be wrong, however, to say that none in the church had established secular status.

[88] A.D. Litfin, *St. Paul's Theology of Proclamation,* 247.

[89] J. Munck, *Paul and the Salvation of Mankind,* 152.

[90] Philo, *Quod Deterius Potiori Insidiari Solet* 33.

[91] Philo, *Quod Deterius Potiori Insidiari Solet* 33.

Thus, leading figures felt they could indulge their senses by right.[92]

In 1 Corinthians 6.12 ff. there appears to be a similar readiness to justify the indulgence of the senses. It is not necessary to assume that the Corinthian slogan πάντα μοι ἔξεστιν suggests a libertarianism which has a theological justification. Rather it could have been derived from a philosophical justification based on Plato's *Timaeus* which was widespread in the first century. Such a lifestyle may well have been defended by Corinthian Christians because it was expected of leading citizens, indeed it distinguished them from the lower classes.[93] The second slogan, τὰ βρώματα τῇ κοιλίᾳ, καὶ ἡ κοιλία τοῖς βρώμασιν· suggests that it is not merely sexual immorality which is rife in the church. The lifestyle is more generally one of indulgence, similar to that recorded in Philo's *Quod Deterius Potiori Insidiari Solet*.[94]

7. *Conclusions*

It is the studies by Winter, Marshall and Litfin which give due recognition to the high profile which Paul gives to the secular perspectives of the Corinthians. Winter regards their boasting to be typical of the sophists of the day, and consequently the norm also for disciples of sophists. Litfin considers their boasting to have been a misplaced attempt at self-aggrandisement by displaying their own penchant for 'wisdom' and 'eloquence' whilst exposing Paul's inadequacy in oratory. Marshall draws parallels between the Corinthians' attitudes and the vulgar characteristic of ὕβρις.

In each of these studies, there is the clear characteristic of a sense of élitism which is variously displayed by a stress on reputation, honour, eloquence or wisdom—just those qualities which were of considerable importance in the surrounding cultural context of secular leadership. The social commonplaces of rhetoric and sophism, the cultural conventions associated with giving and receiving benefits, and the prowess displayed by the socially advantaged and established are all aspects which are to be seen within 1 Corinthians. The question which has not been addressed in these studies is the extent to which we can see aspects of secular local church leadership behind these behavioural patterns.

Each of these studies has concentrated its exegesis on different sections of the Corinthian correspondence, and proved valuable for its complementary perspectives. None of them, however, has included within its scope the particular aspect of leadership within the community. They have more generally

---

[92] D.T. Runia, *Philo of Alexandria and the Timaeus of Plato* (Leiden, 1986), 306-8, shows that this language of "the senses as guardians of the soul" can be traced back to Plato and was an accepted first century understanding.

[93] Philo's treatise is just such a comparison.

[94] Paul, on the contrary, displays a self control which is distinguished from the Corinthian lifestyle; cf. 1 Cor 9.27. See also the discussion in B.W. Winter, *Philo and Paul among the Sophists*, 104-5.

applied the results of their research to the broader community. The step which has been taken in this chapter is an analysis of leadership within the Corinthian church in the light of these background studies.

In each of chapters 1-6 of 1 Corinthians there is consistent evidence that the Corinthian Christians were using in the church principles of leadership which were taken directly from surrounding secular society.

Regarding the "Corinthian parties", it has been possible to see that a wrong assumption of many commentators is that the distinctions between the groups are principally theological. Here it has been demonstrated that the basis of the parties is the secular practice of aligning oneself with someone of established status and reputation in order to advance one's own status. This has been clearly seen in the dynamics of patronage, politics and sophistic practices. As a result of the common assumption, attempts to distinguish between the groups and define their beliefs has been wrongly founded.

It is not necessary to interpret the pride and boasting of the Corinthians as a Judaistic tendency introduced by Apollos.[95] The connection with either Apollos or a Judaizing party is not a defensible conjecture. Boasting was an established aspect of self-advancement in secular society, where people boasted about wealth, reputation and wisdom, and, for pragmatic reasons, also took pride in other men. Enmity was also an established key to self-advancement in politics and litigation in Roman Corinth. Finally, the display of wisdom is strongly attested in the high circles of the sophistic movement of the first century.

In all these aspects, the Corinthian Christians have carried with them into the church those aspects of the surrounding society which were normally accepted. In doing this, Paul accuses them of being thoroughly secular.

---

[95] *Contra* N. Hyldahl, in 'The Corinthian 'Parties' and the Corinthian Crisis', 24-5, and 'Den korintiske Situation—en skitse', 27-30.

CHAPTER EIGHT

PAUL'S PRINCIPLES OF CHRISTIAN LEADERSHIP

1. *Introduction*

It has been argued in Chapters Four to Seven of the present study that there were in the Corinthian congregation those who exercised authority in a way which patterned leadership in Graeco-Roman society. At this stage it is necessary to demonstrate from 1 Corinthians 1-6 the contrast of Paul's own definition of Christian leadership, and to describe his critique of the secular patterns which have been adopted.

In the present chapter the evidence that Paul is specifically bringing a charge against the Corinthians of acting in a secular fashion in the church will be drawn together in summary. It will also be shown that Paul is presenting a firm critique of that secular leadership. Finally, the ways in which Paul defines for the Corinthians a Christian understanding of leadership will be discussed— his use of leadership terminology and his references to good leadership examples.

2. *Paul's Charge of Secular Leadership Practices*

The definition of Christian leadership over against 'worldly' leadership is a key element of Paul's discussion in the early chapters of 1 Corinthians. In each of chapters 1-6 of the epistle, the impact of secular society on the Corinthians' understanding of leadership may be seen. However, Paul's most direct accusation of the Corinthians for being secular in their leadership is seen in 1 Corinthians 3.3-4.

In this passage, Paul makes four clear statements that the Corinthians are worldly in their actions and behaviour. The statement that the Corinthians are σαρκικοί is first given in 1 Corinthians 3.3. Fee is quite correct in his comment upon this verse, "With this charge Paul exposed himself to centuries of misunderstanding. But his concern is singular: not to suggest classes of Christians or grades of spirituality, but to get them to stop *thinking* like the people of the present age".[1] In these early chapters of the epistle, Paul has given instances of their 'worldly' behaviour, and he now accuses them outright of being σαρκικοί, in the sense of 'worldly'.

---

[1]   G.D. Fee, 122.

This is followed by an explanation of the charge in two parts.[2] They are considered σαρκικοί first on account of their quarrelling and jealousy (1 Cor 3.3 b, ὅπου γὰρ ἐν ὑμῖν ζῆλος καὶ ἔρις, οὐχὶ σαρκικοί ἐστε). It is precisely the fact that there is ἔρις and ζῆλος amongst them (1 Cor 3.3), which characterises them as worldly in their leadership.[3] Secondly, Paul describes the Corinthians as those who are σαρκικοί because they κατὰ ἄνθρωπον περιπατεῖν; that is, they are behaving in a secular fashion.[4] The accusation is concluded by the analysis, οὐκ ἄνθρωποί ἐστε? (1 Cor 3.4). Paul suggests that it is just such behaviour as this which indicates that they have adopted secular categories. These charges are not merely empty rhetoric, for Paul specifically explains the basis of his accusations.[5]

Paul then expands what he is referring to by this jealousy and quarrelling. It is the divisive party-spirit which brands the Corinthians as secular in leadership. The root of Paul's accusation here in 1 Corinthians 3.3-4 is first outlined in chapter 1 of the epistle: the Corinthians' exclusive loyalty to particular leading figures (1 Corinthians 1.10-17).[6] Paul considers in 1 Corinthians 3.4 that their behaviour is partisan since they are acting merely as men. This enmity involved in the process of establishing one's own patron figure and the divisive nature of secular leadership has been clearly seen in the secular sources of Roman Corinth.[7]

It is these charges that the Corinthian Christians are secular in their behaviour which are foundational to much of Paul's argument in the introductory chapters of 1 Corinthians. Paul's opening criticism of their secular, exclusive allegiance to these leading figures (1 Cor 1.10-18), then provides the starting-point for a much wider examination of their boasting in human wisdom which is characteristic of secular leadership (1 Cor 1.18-3.23).

Following his presentation that the Corinthians' worldliness is displayed in their divisiveness over leading figures, Paul then demonstrates to the Corinthians other aspects of their conduct which suggest the secular nature of their conduct.

The impact of secular society is betrayed in their elevation of the importance of social status for leadership in the church (1 Cor 1.26), and the pursuit of self-exaltation and boasting in order to enhance that status (1 Cor 1.29).[8] The force of Paul's argument in 1 Corinthians 1.18-29 suggests that the

---

[2] Paul's reasons for his accusation are introduced by the ὅπου γάρ and ὅταν γάρ clauses in 1 Cor 3.3-4; ὅπου γὰρ ἐν ὑμῖν ζῆλος καὶ ἔρις, οὐχὶ σαρκικοί ἐστε καὶ κατὰ ἄνθρωπον περιπατεῖτε; ὅταν γὰρ λέγῃ τις, ἐγὼ μέν εἰμι Παύλου, ἕτερος δέ, ἐγὼ Ἀπολλῶ, οὐκ ἄνθρωποί ἐστε?

[3] See the discussion in Chapter Seven regarding the terms ἔρις and ζῆλος.

[4] For Paul's use of the metaphor of walking as significant of the manner in which a person lives see R. Banks, '"Walking" as a metaphor of the Christian Life: The Origins of a significant Pauline Usage', in edd. E.W. Conrad & E.G. Newing, *Perspectives on Language and Text, essays and poems in Honor of Francis I. Andersen's Sixtieth Birthday* (Winona Lake, 1987), 310.

[5] Cf. footnote 2 above.

[6] See the discussion in Chapter Seven regarding loyalty to the 'apostolic' figures.

[7] For specific evidence see the relevant sections in Chapter Three, 31-36.

[8] See also Paul's constant return to this theme of boasting and arrogance in 1 Cor 3.21, 4.7, 4.19, 5.6.

Corinthians have been focusing on the wrong considerations.[9] The wisdom of the world, dear to the Greeks, was being elevated in contrast to the apparent foolishness of the message of the cross. Paul further points out that God has adopted this particular method of the cross, this particular group of people including those of low social status, and this particular message of weakness in order that boasting in one's own abilities, although an important aspect of worldly wisdom, might have no place in the Christian church.[10] It may be seen from the extent that Paul has to concentrate on these matters that they have been overlooked by the Corinthians.

In 1 Corinthians 2, Paul's further concentration on the contrast between worldly and godly wisdom suggests how deeply entrenched in the church is their reliance upon ἡ σοφία τοῦ αἰῶνος τούτου and ἡ σοφία τῶν ἀρχόντων τοῦ αἰῶνος. He alludes again to those in the congregation who pride themselves on being wise "by the standards of the age" in 1 Corinthians 3.18, 21.

In 1 Corinthians 4, Paul returns to their taking pride in one man over against another (1 Cor 4.6, ἵνα μὴ εἷς ὑπὲρ τοῦ ἑνὸς φυσιοῦσθε κατὰ τοῦ ἑτέρου). In a passage of great irony, Paul outlines the criteria which the Corinthians considered significant to leadership, and contrasts these with his own definition of godly leadership: their elevation of wisdom, their strength, and the importance of honour is all contrasted with the experience of the apostles (1 Cor 4.10).

It has been suggested above that, in 1 Corinthians 5, the impact of secular society on the church has led the Corinthians to ignore the sexual immorality of one of their significant patrons.[11] The understanding in Graeco-Roman society that it was often impossible to take a superior to court, and that it was certainly not expedient to criticise a patron on whom one was significantly dependent, may here have influenced the Corinthian church to avoid "expelling the immoral brother".

In 1 Corinthians 6 it is made clear that some leading Christians in Corinthian society were seeking self-advancement by taking fellow Christians to court, much as would have been expected of secular leadership figures in the colony.

It is clear from this brief summary of many of the findings in this study that in the early sections of the epistle Paul is charging the Corinthians with behaving in a secular fashion in the church. This accusation is most directly brought in 1 Corinthians 3.3-4. In each of the instances mentioned above, however, it is consistently the case that Paul's chief concern is that significant members of the Corinthian community have been exercising influence in the church in a way which is characteristic of secular rather than Christian society. These leading figures were bringing with them into the church the principles and practices which would have been expected of them in Graeco-Roman

---

9   See the discussion in Chapter Seven.
10   Cf. 1 Cor 1.27-28. Paul argues forcibly (1 Cor 1.29), that no flesh, therefore, has the right to boast before God.
11   See the argument in Chapter Six.

society. In support of this Munck writes, "I Cor. 1-4 shows us something taken from a Hellenistic *milieu* which has received the Gospel, but which introduces into the Gospel certain elements of that *milieu* which falsify the Gospel".[12]

3. *Paul's Critique of Secular Leadership*

Throughout his discussion of the secular nature of their leadership, Paul defines for the Corinthians the contrasting nature of true Christian leadership. He establishes this definition partly by a critique of the secular leadership which they have introduced into the church, and partly by demonstrating more positively those aspects of leadership which are specifically Christian.

The first criticism is the Corinthians' exclusive attachment to leading figures of the church. Secondly, their adoption of secular wisdom in Christian leadership is highlighted. Next, Paul discusses the situation that secular leaders were responsible for crucifying the Lord of Glory. Fourthly, the failure through the adoption of secular perceptions of status to address the matter of serious immorality within the church is raised. Finally, Paul addresses the situation where Corinthian Christians are taking their minor legal battles to secular courts, rather than solving the differences internally. Each of these points of criticism will be looked at in turn.

i.

Paul's first point of criticism of secular leadership is the exclusive loyalty which each of the Corinthians were showing to particular leading 'patron' figures of the church—Paul, Apollos and Cephas.[13] Paul's disapproval is that their quarrels (ἔριδες, 1 Cor 1.11), displayed a partisanship characteristic of the surrounding society. He urges at the outset of the epistle that they should agree with one another and be united in mind and thought.

It has been demonstrated that one of the principal dynamics within Graeco-Roman society was that of the inequality of relationships: the socially inferior person was aware of his dependence upon the man of wealth and status; correspondingly, the superior man explicitly cultivated a large following of subordinate adherents in order to enhance his own apparent status.[14]

In the Corinthian congregation a similar loyalty of dependence was exercised by some towards the significant, leading figures of Paul, Apollos and Cephas. It was considered important by these people to have been patronised by one of the apostolic figures, and thus to have been able to say, "I belong to ...". Paul outlines in 1 Corinthians 1.13-16 that there existed the danger, with such an attitude towards status, that some might attribute undue

---

[12] J. Munck, *Paul and the Salvation of Mankind* (London, 1959), 152.

[13] 1 Cor 1.12, ἕκαστος ὑμῶν λέγει, ἐγὼ μέν εἰμι Παύλου, ἐγὼ δὲ Ἀπολλῶ, ἐγὼ δὲ Κηφᾶ, ἐγὼ δὲ Χριστοῦ.

[14] See the discussion in Chapters Three and Seven of the present dissertation. Cf. also A.D. Litfin, *St. Paul's Theology of Proclamation: An Investigation of 1 Corinthians 1-4 in the Light of Greco-Roman Rhetoric,* unpublished D.Phil dissertation (Oxford University, 1983).

significance to the fact of having been baptised by one of the leading figures, such as Paul. He, therefore, spells out with a series of rhetorical questions his gratefulness that few can draw significance from the fact that he himself had baptised them (1 Cor 1.13-17).[15]

Such an attitude of patronage, adopted from secular society, towards the relationships between members of the Corinthian congregation and the leading figures such as Paul and Apollos is explicitly discouraged by Paul both in 1 Corinthians 1.10-17 and 3.1-23. In the latter section Paul suggests that this social dynamic has become grounds for ἔρις and ζῆλος, symptomatic of 'worldly' behaviour (being σαρκικός and walking κατὰ ἄνθρωπον). Paul's critique of secular leadership in the church thus includes this aspect of deference to a senior figure as to a patron.

ii.

The second major area of criticism which Paul discusses at some length in the epistle is the wisdom of this age (1 Cor 1.18-3.23). This aspect is again characteristic of secular figures of influence, but is also an identifiable aspect of some within the Corinthian congregation. Indicative of this worldly wisdom is the high significance placed upon social class, and the importance of boasting in the establishment of personal reputation (first alluded to by Paul in 1 Corinthians 1.26 and 29).

Paul's critique rejects the wisdom of the world as inappropriate for Christian leaders, in that it is foolishness in God's sight (1 Cor 3.19, ἡ γὰρ σοφία τοῦ κόσμου τούτου μωρία παρὰ τῷ θεῷ ἐστιν).[16] He bases his critique on the argument that God, in his wisdom, had chosen not to use secular σοφία as a basis for divine election (1 Cor 1.27-28, ἀλλὰ τὰ μωρὰ τοῦ κόσμου ἐξελέξατο ὁ θεὸς ἵνα καταισχύνῃ τοὺς σοφούς, καὶ τὰ ἀσθενῆ τοῦ κόσμου ἐξελέξατο ὁ θεὸς ἵνα καταισχύνῃ τὰ ἰσχυρά, καὶ τὰ ἀγενῆ τοῦ κόσμου καὶ τὰ ἐξουθενημένα ἐξελέξατο ὁ θεός, τὰ μὴ ὄντα, ἵνα τὰ ὄντα καταργήσῃ). The Corinthians, however, have adopted just that wisdom which God had rejected. Furthermore, God's wisdom was specifically chosen to shame (καταισχύνω) that of the world. It should not therefore be used as a tool of self-advancement in the church.[17]

Paul's instruction, which he supports with two quotations from the Old Testament, is that those who are trained in secular wisdom should rather become fools, in order that they might attain 'true' wisdom.[18]

---

[15] Μεμέρισται ὁ Χριστός; μὴ Παῦλος ἐσταυρώθη ὑπὲρ ὑμῶν, ἢ εἰς τὸ ὄνομα Παύλου ἐβαπτίσθητε; 1 Cor 1.13.

[16] The discussion in 1 Cor 1.18-31 which unfavourably compares the wisdom of the world with the foolishness of God is part of Paul's criticism that the adoption of worldly wisdom is inappropriate for leaders in the Christian church.

[17] For more detail see the discussion in Chapter Seven.

[18] 1 Cor 3.18, εἴ τις δοκεῖ σοφὸς εἶναι ἐν ὑμῖν ἐν τῷ αἰῶνι τούτῳ, μωρὸς γενέσθω, ἵνα γένηται σοφός.

iii.

Paul's critique of secular leadership further focuses on the inappropriateness and insufficiency of secular wisdom in 1 Corinthians 2.6-16. This passage provides an important insight into Paul's reaction to secular leadership. He points out that the kind of godly wisdom which he is referring to has already eluded the 'worldly' leaders. Such a wisdom is available only to the leader who has the Spirit.

The particular section in question is 1 Corinthians 2.6-8.[19] The *crux interpretum* here is identifying οἱ ἄρχοντες. The different schools offer three major alternatives; the first is that these authorities are demonic or spiritual powers; the second school suggests that the authorities are purely human; and a further school argues that Paul here is implying both the human and the spiritual powers.

The first of these schools has dominated interpretation of these verses. Morrison refers to Dibelius' reluctance to argue "that Paul, who always seeks the driving forces of redemptive history in the realm of spirits, should here refer to the human cause of Jesus' crucifixion".[20]

The stance which appears between the two extreme positions is that Paul here implies the Jewish perspective of angelology both in 1 Corinthians 2 and Romans 13, and thus assumes that behind the earthly rulers stand effective spiritual authorities.[21]

Cullmann points out that, as a Jew, Paul would have necessarily meant the invisible powers which stand behind all earthly happenings, but he further adds, "it is equally certain that at the same time he is speaking of the effective agents: namely, the earthly rulers, the Roman administrators of Palestine".[22] It is the invisible powers which stood behind Pilate which were ignorant of the

---

[19] The preposition δέ (1 Cor 2.6) opening this section marks the connection with the preceding discussion. The contrast is thus strongly made by Paul between secular wisdom, demonstrated in persuasive words (1 Cor 2.4), and the secret wisdom of God (1 Cor 2.7). Σοφίαν δὲ λαλοῦμεν ἐν τοῖς τελείοις, σοφίαν δὲ οὐ τοῦ αἰῶνος τούτου οὐδὲ τῶν ἀρχόντων τοῦ αἰῶνος τούτου τῶν καταργουμένων· ἀλλὰ λαλοῦμεν θεοῦ σοφίαν ἐν μυστηρίῳ, τὴν ἀποκεκρυμμένην, ἣν προώρισεν ὁ θεὸς πρὸ τῶν αἰώνων εἰς δόξαν ἡμῶν· ἣν οὐδεὶς τῶν ἀρχόντων τοῦ αἰῶνος τούτου ἔγνωκεν, εἰ γὰρ ἔγνωσαν, οὐκ ἂν τὸν κύριον τῆς δόξης ἐσταύρωσαν.

[20] Cf. *The Powers that Be: Earthly Rulers and Demonic Powers in Romans 13:1-7* (London, 1960), 24, and M. Dibelius, *Die Geisterwelt im Glauben des Paulus* (Göttingen, 1909). J. Weiß in his commentary on 1 Corinthians, 53, also suggests, "Freilich darf man heute die ἄρχοντες nicht mehr auf Kaiaphas und Pilatus und auf andre irdische Herrscher oder auch auf die geistigen Weltbeherrscher, die Philosophen deuten, sondern nur auf die wirklichen Beherrscher dieses Aion, d. h. auf dämonische Mächte". Paul's statement appears to Dibelius far too extravagant to refer to the human authorities, an argument which is linked with his doubtful interpretation that Paul is implying the same supernatural authorities in the particular terminology in Romans 13.1-3 (ἐξουσίαι, ἄρχοντες).

[21] C. Morrison *The Powers that Be*, 18, explains, "In its general aspects the spirit world of Judaism was thought to consist of countless radiant beings which adorned the splendour and majesty about the divine throne. They lacked for the most part the personality of names or the individuality of volition". He says of Romans 13, *idem*, 25, "Paul understood that behind the pagan government there were spiritual powers of the same sort that operated in the death of Jesus. The rule of the Roman Empire was the simultaneous integrated endeavour of spiritual and human authorities".

[22] Cf. O. Cullmann, *The State in the New Testament* (London, 1957), 63.

full implication of their actions.[23] It is thus argued that the two words ἐξουσία and ἄρχων in his epistles have double meanings due to Paul's background in both the Greek and Jewish thought worlds.[24]

The views propounded have been dependent on at least one of the following bases: either lexicographical study of the concerned words, or the assumption that uppermost in Paul's mind is the Jewish concept of angelology. The third position adopted by commentators, that Paul is simply referring here to the human authorities,[25] with no necessary implication of supernatural powers, is more often defended by a much closer look at the immediate context of 1 Corinthians 1-4.[26]

Paul's almost interchangeable use of four key phrases sheds much light on the debate—τοῦ αἰῶνος, τοῦ κόσμου, ἀνθρώπων and κατὰ σάρκα.

In 1 Corinthians 1.20 Paul asks the rhetorical question where is the wise man, the scholar and the debater τοῦ αἰῶνος τούτου? He answers, "has not God made ἡ σοφία τοῦ κόσμου seem as foolishness?" This is contrasted with Paul's

---

[23] Cf. O. Cullmann, *The State in the New Testament,* 64. He considers that in "all three Pauline texts which speak of the State there is direct or indirect reference to the angelic powers which stand behind the State. This is particularly clear in 1 Corinthians 2.8 ...", referring to 1 Cor 2.8, Rom 13.1 ff., and 1 Cor 6.1 ff. Cf. *idem,* 65.

[24] G. Delling in 'ἄρχων', *TDNT* I (Grand Rapids, 1965), concedes that the New Testament often denotes Roman and Jewish authorities when using this word, but in the case of 1 Cor 2.6, 8 it is clearly spiritual powers which are implied. W. Wink, in *Naming the Powers, The Language of Power in the New Testament* I (Philadelphia, 1984), approaches the problem from the opposite direction to that of Cullmann. His conclusions, however, are similar. He starts with the statement, "At the very least, then, the *archontes* in 1 Cor 2.6-8 include religious leaders, the military procurator, soldiers, and accomplices ('spies', Lk 20.20), who were the physical agents of Jesus' death". His argument is expanded, however, to include the theories of Dibelius and Günther Dehn and he concludes that Paul is here referring to demonic powers as well as the human authorities which sanctioned the crucifixion. It is interesting to note that Wink considers that both Romans 13 and 1 Peter 2.13-17 both clearly refer to the human rulers. For more discussion see also G.B. Caird, *Principalities and Powers: A Study in Pauline Theology* (Oxford, 1956), 16, 83-4.

[25] There are some important parallels which have often been used in the interpretation of this verse, especially from Luke-Acts. In Luke 23.13, 35 and 24.20 οἱ ἀρχιερεῖς and οἱ ἄρχοντες are used with specific reference to the authorities responsible for the crucifixion of Jesus. Similar terminology is used in Acts 3.17 and 13.27 where the rulers are specifically recorded as having acted in ignorance. These parallels seem to be closely linked with 1 Corinthians 2.6-8, since the context is specifically that of the human authorities responsible for the death of Jesus on the cross. There is also the further link of 'ignorance' in this early kerygma. A parallel is found in 1 Thessalonians 2.14-16 where Paul himself specifically blames the Jews, in their capacity as human authorities, for the death and suffering of Jesus. Paul here suggests that God will hold the Jews themselves responsible for this sin. Cf. W. Carr, 'The Rulers of this Age—1 Corinthians II.6-8', *NTS* 23 (1977), 23, and G. Miller, 'ἀρχόντων τοῦ αἰῶνος τούτου—A New Look at 1 Corinthians 2:6-8', *JBL* 91 (1972), 528.

[26] One of the major defenders of the stance that Paul is here referring to the political powers is J. Schniewind in, *Nachgelassene Reden und Aufsätze* (Berlin, 1952). Regarding the much broader context in 1 Corinthians, he writes, 105, "Dem Gedankenzug von 1. Kor. 1,20-2,16 entspricht nicht die Deutung der Archonten auf Geister, sondern die Deutung auf die Vornehmen, Führenden, Gebildeten unter den Menschen". Cf. also *idem,* 105. We may also note the comments made by Godet in his commentary on this section, "Paul means those who in his time directed the national mind of Israel, those who were the authorities in the Sanhedrim, and perhaps, also, of the Jewish and Gentile representatives of political power in Israel, such as Herod and Pilate. These representatives of human intelligence and politics took part directly or remotely in the execution of the Divine plan, without even suspecting it". F. Godet's explanation for the phrase τῶν καταργουμένων is that as the kingdom of God increases in influence so these human rulers will find their own power proportionately diminishing, cf. *idem,* 135.

own wisdom and the message of the cross referred to in the previous paragraph. Thus it may be seen that the particular comparison which Paul is drawing is between God's wisdom and the wisdom of this age, or of this world—the two terms have been used synonymously. The contrast is between the message of the cross ʹ(1 Cor 1.17-18) and the human figures of stature such as the wise man, the philosopher and the scholar.[27]

This contrast is taken further in 1 Corinthians 1.21 where the wisdom of God is placed in contrast over against that of ὁ κόσμος. In 1 Corinthians 1.25 a further synonym is used where the contrast is again stated—the wisdom and the strength τῶν ἀνθρώπων.

The fourth phrase which Paul uses is κατὰ σάρκα (1 Cor 1.26). Again he is specifically referring to human qualities which were highly regarded in first century society—wisdom, power and good birth; few of the Christians in the community could consider themselves wise, powerful or of noble birth by the standards of the age.

Throughout the first chapter of the epistle the argument has consistently centred on a comparison of God's wisdom in the message of the cross and the wisdom, or standards of recognition, of the world and age in which Paul lived. This essential contrast between human and divine wisdom continues in 1 Corinthians 2 when Paul returns to the subject mentioned in 1 Corinthians 1.17: that is, his own preaching of the cross in the city of Corinth.[28] Paul is deliberately avoiding the use of wisdom and its persuasive argumentation (1 Cor 2.1, 4), and relies rather on the power of God (1 Cor 2.4, 5). In verse 5 it is once again σοφίᾳ ἀνθρώπων which is the contrasting phrase used.

In 1 Corinthians 2.6 the wisdom which has been termed by Paul to be of this age, is further described as being of the rulers of this age. At this point some have argued that Paul now is referring to the spiritual world and its demonic powers, however the line of argument shows no sign of having changed, and instead it more probably continues directly from chapter 1.[29] It is

---

[27] W. Carr, 'The Rulers of this Age—1 Corinthians II.6-8', 25, says of 1 Cor 1.20, "Paul points out that the wisdom of God is refused by the world, and that world is typified by the various callings and types of men—the wise man, the scribe and the debater. Such wisdom is no abstraction or hypostasized being. It is tied to the world of real men whose attitudes are reflected in their activities as wise man, scribe or debater".

[28] This is a point brought out by G. Miller in 'ἀρχόντων τοῦ αἰῶνος τούτου—A New Look at 1 Corinthians 2:6-8', 525, where he says, "The contrast throughout is between the 'wisdom of God' and 'human wisdom', and not between the 'wisdom of God' and that of some opposing spiritual power. The condemnation of the 'rulers of this age' is that, failing to know and acknowledge God through their human wisdom upon which they depended, they ignorantly crucified the 'Lord of glory'".

[29] J.B. Lightfoot in his *Notes on epistles of St. Paul from Unpublished Commentaries* (London, 1904), writes of 1 Cor 2.6 and 8 that it refers to "the great men of this world, as the whole context seems imperatively to demand; the princes whether in intellect or in power or in rank, so that οἱ ἄρχοντες κ.τ.λ. would include the σοφοί, δυνατοί, εὐγενεῖς of 1.26. ...'the princes of this world' are to be understood as great men according to the world's estimate of greatness". "As types and representatives of the princes of this world, Saint Paul takes the Jewish and heathen rulers who crucified the Lord (comp. Acts iv:27)".

also the case that the wisdom which stems from God was ordained before the present aeon came about (1 Cor 2.7).

It is consistent with the interpretation suggested that Paul contrasts the spirit of the world with the Spirit which is of God in 1 Corinthians 2.12-13. The former is taught by humans (not by supernatural revelation), and the latter is taught only by God. The human, as opposed to superhuman, context for this wisdom is further argued in verse 14 where it is linked with the ψυχικός man. 1 Corinthians 3.18-19 confirms this comparison which Paul is drawing between the human and the godly forms of wisdom, which is concluded by quotations from the Old Testament in support of his case.[30]

Paul's contention is that secular wisdom is being defended by some in the church. In contrast, Paul is pressing for the leaders in the Christian community to adopt God's wisdom. He demonstrates by historic reference to those leaders who were responsible for the crucifixion of the Lord of Glory, that the world's wisdom of leadership is insufficient for the Christian.

Thus, Paul's own definition of the nature of Christian leadership is partly demonstrated by his critique of the secular authorities—Christian leadership is to be different from secular leadership on the grounds that secular leadership is καταργουμένων and it was just those secular authorities who were responsible for crucifying the Lord of Glory (1 Cor 2.6, 8).

Paul's discussion of the inappropriateness of secular wisdom is continued to the end of 1 Corinthians 2. He explains that just as only the spirit of a man may know the thoughts of that man, so it is only by the Spirit of God that the thoughts of God are to be discerned.[31] Since they have received the Spirit of God, it is to spiritual wisdom that the Corinthians should turn.[32]

iv.

A fourth instance where Paul defines Christian leadership by criticising secular aspects of leadership is in 1 Corinthians 5. It has been noted that there remains the possibility here that those in the Corinthian congregation have conformed to the secular practices of endorsing patrons to the extent that they have ignored the serious sexual misconduct of one of their patrons. The depth of Paul's criticism is seen in his suggestion that the actions being tolerated in the church are of such a nature that it is not even heard of among gentiles.[33] In some instances the Corinthians adopt secular practices in the church; in this particular situation, they have gone even further than pagans!

Paul spells out clearly that he is not suggesting that they cut themselves off from the world (1 Cor 5.9-10). The heart of his criticism is that secular influences are allowed to have an impact on the church; μὴ συναναμίγνυσθαι

---

[30] Job 5.12; Ps 93.11.
[31] Cf. 1 Cor 2.11.
[32] 1 Cor 2.11-13.
[33] Paul's horror at the situation is seen in his use of the adverb ὅλως, 'it is actually reported'. Cf. G.D. Fee, 199, where he argues on the basis of Paul's use of the adverb in 1 Cor 6.7 and 15.29 that the sense has to be "it is actually reported" rather than, "it is universally reported."

πόρνοις, οὐ πάντως τοῖς πόρνοις τοῦ κόσμου τούτου ἢ τοῖς πλεονέκταις καὶ ἅρπαξιν ἢ εἰδωλολάτραις, ἐπεὶ ὠφείλετε ἄρα ἐκ τοῦ κόσμου ἐξελθεῖν. νῦν δὲ ἔγραψα ὑμῖν μὴ συναναμίγνυσθαι ἐάν τις ἀδελφὸς ὀνομαζόμενος ἢ πόρνος ἢ πλεονέκτης ἢ εἰδωλολάτρης ἢ λοίδορος ἢ μέθυσος ἢ ἅρπαξ, τῷ τοιούτῳ μηδὲ συνεσθίειν.[34]

v.

The situation exists in 1 Corinthians 6.1-8 where members of the Christian congregation with high status have been involved in legal battles with fellow Christians—a practice widely exercised in Graeco-Roman society for encouraging enmity and self-advancement. Paul's critical response is again one of outrage, intended to shame, πρὸς ἐντροπὴν ὑμῖν λέγω. Three times he asks them rhetorically οὐκ οἴδατε; he appeals to them that even some of the despised (ἐξουθενημένοι) in the church could handle these matters; he questions them as to whether there is any 'wise' enough in the church to handle such matters; and his use of the verb τολμάω (1 Cor 6.1) is deliberately to shame.

From this survey of 1 Corinthians 1-6 it is seen that Paul has given a firm critique of secular influences in the community. It has also been seen that Paul urges the Corinthians that their view of Christian leadership should differ from the expectations of leadership in secular Corinth. Paul opposes their adoption of a party-spirit of loyalty to specific patron figures; their elevation of the importance of status in the Christian church; their boasting in men; their affinity with the wisdom of secular leaders; their turning a blind eye to the sexual immorality of influential members of the Christian community; and also, their exercising influence by taking fellow Christians to court. Paul's critique of secular leadership is sustained throughout these chapters. It is not only by means of criticism that his definition of Christian leadership is given. Paul also develops his argument by contrasting his own way of demonstrating leadership with that of the Corinthian Christians and the surrounding society of which he is a part.

4. Paul's Parameters of Christian Leadership

Paul lays parameters for Christian leadership for the Corinthians in two further ways: his deliberate use of non-status leadership vocabulary, and his urge that they follow specific examples of Christian leadership.[35] Paul's choice of language and imagery—agricultural, artisan and household imagery, as well as the rôle of irony and covert allusion in his redefinition of Christian leadership—will be considered before turning to the examples of good leadership given by Paul in the epistle.

---

[34] This is also the thrust of verse 12. It is not Paul's concern to judge secular influences in the secular world. The problem arises for him when those influences come within the church.

[35] This contrasts with their secular understanding of what it is to follow a leader (1 Cor 1.12).

a. *Agricultural and Artisan Language*

In 1 Corinthians 3, Paul adopts two images which are applied to both Apollos and himself: one from agriculture, and the other from building. It is significant that in both of these images, the rôles assigned to the apostolic figures are necessarily menial.

Paul introduces the first image in 1 Corinthians 3.5 by stating that both he and Apollos are διάκονοι under God's jurisdiction (διάκονοι δι' ὧν ἐπιστεύσατε, καὶ ἑκάστῳ ὡς ὁ κύριος ἔδωκεν). The use of the particle τί, as opposed to the more personal τίς, emphasises further the impact that Paul is making; rather than "who are Paul and Apollos", the accent is on "what is Paul", and "what is Apollos"; the particular rôle, rather than the person, is emphasised.[36] In this way, Paul's language, and thus also his understanding of Christian leadership, are seen to be task-orientated. Paul deliberately plays down the rôle which the apostles fulfil: first, these leaders are to be considered no more than servants who function under the Lord; and secondly, the focus is not on who they are, but rather on what their task is.

This task-orientated perception of leadership is clearly to be contrasted with the way in which the Corinthians had been viewing their leadership figures. The discussion in both 1 Corinthians 1.10-17 and 3.1-4 shows how the Corinthians were focusing their attention on the personalities of the apostles, and taking pride in them as men.[37] Paul, rather, concentrates on the particular task each leader is accomplishing.

It is further to be noticed that in this agricultural image the key rôle is assigned to God. Apollos and Paul are both allotted the menial tasks of the one who plants and the one who waters; to God is attributed the growth of the plant (1 Cor 3.6, ἐγὼ ἐφύτευσα, Ἀπολλῶς ἐπότισεν, ἀλλὰ ὁ θεὸς ηὔξανεν). The focus of Paul's image on the importance of God rather than the human leaders is made all the clearer when he reminds the Corinthians that neither the one involved in the watering, nor the one involved in the planting has any importance—only God, who is credited with the growth of the plant (1 Cor 3.7, ὥστε οὔτε ὁ φυτεύων ἐστίν τι οὔτε ὁ ποτίζων, ἀλλ' ὁ αὐξάνων θεός).

Paul's understanding of his own rôle is contrasted with the description of the Corinthians given in 1 Corinthians 3.3-4. The one focuses on the importance of the man, whereas the other, deliberately juxtaposed, diminishes any importance that the man might have. Paul insists that both he and Apollos should not be regarded as anything more than servants. The significance of this lies in the fact that Paul had deliberately inverted the Graeco-Roman scale

---

[36] Cf. A. Dittberner, "'Who is Apollos and who is Paul?'—I Cor. 3:5', *The Bible Today* 71 (1974), 1549-52. Paul does not see Apollos as a rival apostle, responsible for the divisions in the church.

[37] Paul demonstrates in 1 Cor 1.15-17 that he had avoided baptising many of the Corinthian congregation in order that they might not attach loyalty to him in person. Instead, he had concentrated on the particular task which Christ had sent him to accomplish, οὐ γὰρ ἀπέστειλέν με Χριστὸς βαπτίζειν ἀλλὰ εὐαγγελίζεσθαι, οὐκ ἐν σοφίᾳ λόγου, ἵνα μὴ κενωθῇ ὁ σταυρὸς τοῦ Χριστοῦ.

of values: those who are being looked up to as patron figures, he is describing rather as their διάκονοι (1 Cor 3.5).[38]

The second functional image used by Paul is that of building (1 Cor 3.9-15).[39] In this image it is again manual work which is referred to. Such a metaphor in itself would have been significant to the status-conscious Corinthians. Where manual labour was frowned upon by those of high status in the Graeco-Roman world, Paul deliberately applies it to those leaders whom the Corinthians are wrongly elevating.[40] Plutarch uses a number of images to describe significant leaders, but they are metaphors which themselves have status. Indeed he says of the aristocracy that they like the work of the artisan, but not the artisan himself.[41]

The significance of these images is considerable in that Paul, by using them, specifically disparages any self-exaltation.[42] The emphasis throughout avoids elevating personal status, and instead concentrates on the function of the apostles. Paul's focus is on the particular tasks which had been allotted to himself and Apollos; in the agricultural metaphor the one was doing the planting, whilst the other was responsible for the watering—God causes the plant to grow (1 Cor 3.6-9); in the building metaphor, the one lays the foundation, whilst the other builds upon it—Jesus Christ himself is the foundation (1 Cor 3.10-13).

In the context of personality divisions within the Corinthian congregation, Paul's careful side-by-side use of both himself and Apollos as examples which should be imitated is most powerful. This is particularly so since the

---

[38] Dio Chrysostom writes of the attitude commonly held towards slaves, in *Orationes* 14.1, "Men desire above all things to be free and say that freedom is the greatest of blessings, while slavery is the most shameful and wretched of states"; see also *Orationes* 74.9, "Nobody trusts slaves when they make an agreement, for the reason that they are not their own masters".

[39] J. Shanor, 'Paul as master builder: construction terms in First Corinthians', *NTS* 34 (1988), 461-71, has drawn links between Paul's language here and construction terminology derived from epigraphic sources.

[40] Elsewhere, Paul also refers to manual labour; 1 Cor 4.12; 1 Thess 2.9; 2 Thess 3.6-16; see B.W. Winter, "'If a man does not wish to work …'": A Cultural and Historical Setting for 2 Thessalonians 3:6-16', *Tyndale Bulletin* 40 (1989), 303-15. Cf. also B. Fiore, '"Covert Allusion" in 1 Corinthians 1-4', *The Catholic Biblical Quarterly* 47 (1985), 94, "the laborers' analogy, which presents the community's teachers in harmonious service of God and thereby undercuts the elevation of one over another".

[41] Plutarch, *Pericles*, 1.4-2.1, writes, "while we delight in the work, we despise the workman, as, for instance, in the case of perfumes and dyes; we take a delight in them, but dyers and perfumers we regard as illiberal and vulgar folk. … Labour with one's own hands on lowly tasks gives witness, in the toil thus expended on useless things, to one's own indifference to higher things. … For it does not of necessity follow that if the work delights you with its grace, the one who wrought it is worthy of your esteem". See also Philo, *Quod deterius potiori insidiari solet* 33-4, who contrasts the established of society with those who work with their hands and are without status: "Those who take care of themselves are men of mark and wealth, holding leading positions, praised on all hands, recipients of honours, portly, healthy and robust, revelling in luxurious and riotous living, knowing nothing of labour (πόνον οὐκ εἰδότες), conversant with pleasures which carry the sweets of life to the all-welcoming soul by every channel of sense". Cf. also B.W. Winter, "'If a man does not wish to work…'" A Cultural and Historical Setting for 2 Thessalonians 3.6-16', 303-15.

[42] R.F. Hock, 'Paul's Tentmaking and the Problem of his Social Class', *JBL* 97 (1978), 555-64, argues that Paul, in doing manual labour, deliberately suffers a loss of status.

Corinthians have been making unfavourable contrasts between the two apostles.[43]

In the world of secular leadership, the testing of a man's success in the political world was carried out by the assessment of the public. If he had a clear following and support, he was then recognised as a successful leading figure in the secular ἐκκλησία of Corinth. Paul points out, however, that it is not the judgment of men which will see the establishment of the Christian leader.[44] It will rather be God's testing by fire (1 Cor 3.13, ἑκάστου τὸ ἔργον φανερὸν γενήσεται, ἡ γὰρ ἡμέρα δηλώσει· ὅτι ἐν πυρὶ ἀποκαλύπτεται, καὶ ἑκάστου τὸ ἔργον ὁποῖόν ἐστιν τὸ πῦρ [αὐτὸ] δοκιμάσει).

b. *Household Images*

In addition to the artisan images of 1 Corinthians 3.5-15, Paul also uses household images with reference to leadership. Following his statement that the Corinthians should view their leaders as belonging to them, and not that they belong to their leaders (1 Cor 3.21-23), Paul summarises his argument by saying in 1 Corinthians 4.1-2, οὕτως ἡμᾶς λογιζέσθω ἄνθρωπος ὡς ὑπηρέτας Χριστοῦ καὶ οἰκονόμους μυστηρίων θεοῦ.[45] This reinforces Paul's reasoning that the Corinthians should have their perception of leadership in the church turned upside-down. These leaders whom they are exalting should be perceived as household servants of God.

Regarding the difference between the διάκονος and the ὑπηρέτης, Rengstorf writes,

> In the case of the διάκονος the accent is on the objective advantage his service brings to the one to whom it is rendered ... The special feature of ὑπηρέτης, however, is that he willingly learns his task and goal from another who is over him in an organic order but without prejudice to his personal dignity and worth.[46]

With reference to 1 Corinthians 4.1, however, Rengstorf has missed the impact of Paul's argument when he suggests that the meaning of ὑπηρέτης comes close to the sense of ἀπόστολος.[47]

As Paul's discussion unfolds, the διάκονος of 1 Corinthians 3.5 is replaced in 1 Corinthians 4.1 by a term which more specifically refers to a household

---

[43] Paul is aware in 1 Cor 4.3-5 that he is being judged by the Corinthians, and that he is being compared with Apollos (1 Cor 4.6-7).

[44] This would have been the case in the *ordo decurionum* (βουλή) of the Corinthian colony. Cf. the discussion in Chapter Two.

[45] For ὑπηρέτης see K.H. Rengstorf, *TDNT* VIII, 542; and for a religious background to οἰκονόμος see J. Reumann, 'Servants of God—Pre-Christian Religious Application of OIKONOMOS in Greek', *JBL* 77 (1958), 339-49; and also 'οἰκονομία-Terms in Paul in Comparison with Lucan *Heilsgeschichte*', *NTS* 13 (1966/7), 147-67.

[46] K.H. Rengstorf, 'ὑπηρέτης', 533. This distinction may be too strong; Barrett, 99, suggests that there may in fact be very little difference in meaning. He argues, "The *servant* in any case has no significance of his own; the work done is not his but his master's; apostolic ministry is marked by the fact that it makes no claims for itself, but points from itself to Christ".

[47] K.H. Rengstorf, 'ὑπηρέτης', 542.

steward, οἰκονόμος. His use of this term serves to focus Paul's argument once again not on the person but on his task. If both Apollos and Paul are to be regarded as οἰκονόμοι, the question remains as to what they are stewards of, or what responsibility is entrusted to them by the master of the house.[48] The argument returns to the fact that Paul and Apollos are not aiming to receive their assessment from men,[49] as in the decurional council, but that they have a responsibility to God. They are employees of God, and not of the Corinthian congregation.

c. *Paul's Use of Covert Allusion and Irony*

1 Corinthians 4 may also be seen as highly significant in Paul's defining of Christian leadership. In this section the Corinthians' perception of leadership is dramatically inverted by Paul. In 1 Corinthians 4.8-13 Paul employs colourful imagery to demonstrate that the apostles, who had been the figure-heads of the Corinthian party divisions, are in effect placed at the end of the line in terms of secular status.[50]

In 1 Corinthians 4, Paul deliberately uses covert allusion as a device with which to confront the Corinthians that their leadership is inappropriate for the church of God.[51] Fiore argues that Paul's motivation for using covert allusion is as a tool appropriate to the perceived social status of those in the Corinthian congregation.[52] He writes that,

> If the rhetorical device hits the mark, then the factionalists will reevaluate their attitude toward the teachers in light of the image of their harmony in 3.5-15. They will also reestimate their wisdom and judgment in the light of their own initial acceptance of the *kerygma* of the cross (1.26-31) and with respect to the

---

[48] O. Michel, 'οἰκονόμος', *TDNT* V (Grand Rapids, 1987), 150, where he wrongly suggests that Paul's use of οἰκονόμος here has no concern with social standing.

[49] 1 Cor 4.3-4, ἐμοὶ δὲ εἰς ἐλάχιστόν ἐστιν ἵνα ὑφ' ὑμῶν ἀνακριθῶ ἢ ὑπὸ ἀνθρωπίνης ἡμέρας· ἀλλ' οὐδὲ ἐμαυτὸν ἀνακρίνω· οὐδὲν γὰρ ἐμαυτῷ σύνοιδα, ἀλλ' οὐκ ἐν τούτῳ δεδικαίωμαι, ὁ δὲ ἀνακρίνων με κύριός ἐστιν. This recalls the point made by Paul that each man's work will be judged by fire (1 Cor 3.12-15).

[50] 1 Cor 4.9, δοκῶ γάρ, ὁ θεὸς ἡμᾶς τοὺς ἀποστόλους ἐσχάτους ἀπέδειξεν ὡς ἐπιθανατίους, ὅτι θέατρον ἐγενήθημεν τῷ κόσμῳ καὶ ἀγγέλοις καὶ ἀνθρώποις.

[51] Paul uses covert allusion to stress the humiliation of the apostolic rôle. This picture, shunning status and reputation, is consonant with the nature of the message which is being preached, and the subject of that message: Christ crucified (1 Cor 1.17-18, 23). Paul adjusted his own *modus operandi* whilst in Corinth in order to fit the particular message he was proclaiming (1 Cor 2.1-5).

[52] B. Fiore, '"Covert Allusion" in 1 Corinthians 1-4', 95: "Theissen's analysis of the social stratification within the Corinthian community ... suggests the importance of the small but influential group of upper class Christians for the organization and continuation of the community's life in faith. Judge's description of the early Christians as 'scholastic community' suggests the interest of at least the Christian patrons to resemble those of other groups around sophists and professional rhetoricians. If, then, it was these same highly placed Christians who were guilty of lionizing one teacher over another (1.10; 3.4), of vaunting their own knowledge (3.1; 6.12; 8.1-13), of making distinctions in the community rooted in pride (4.7; 5.2), or of slighting the poor at the assemblies (11.17-34), then Paul would have to proceed with caution, both for the good of the church and for the improvement of those at fault. ... Then, too, are not these people the ones who would appreciate the elegance and variety of the figured language used by Paul?"

apostolic example both in the *kerygma* (1.18-25) and in the *didaskalia* (2.6-16).[53]

What is particularly unusual about Paul's use of covert allusion is that he makes plain to the Corinthians that he is in fact using this device by announcing in 1 Corinthians 4.6 that this figurative language is being applied to himself and Apollos.[54] He thus undermines any sense of covertness.

Paul outlines for the Corinthians the secular nature of their own leadership; he contrasts that secular leadership with the Christian leadership characterized by Apollos and himself; and he closes the section of irony by depicting in detail the very different nature of his own leadership.

Paul firstly describes the Corinthian leadership in 1 Corinthians 4.8 in terms of its secular success and self-sufficiency. Already they have had their fill (κορέννυμι, be satiated or glutted); already they have become rich; and already they have become kings. The three images are descriptive of thoroughly secularised leadership.

Paul then explains in 1 Corinthians 4.9 that the apostolic leaders have metaphorically been given the contrastingly shameful place at the end of the procession. Instead of a position of honour, they have been made a public spectacle (θέατρον ἐγενήθημεν τῷ κόσμῳ καὶ ἀγγέλοις καὶ ἀνθρώποις). Paul further emphasises that it was God who has displayed the apostles (in whom the Corinthians had been taking pride), at the end of the procession.

In 1 Corinthians 4.10, by juxtaposing the contrasts between the two types of leadership, Paul dramatically exposes the differences:

ὑμεῖς ... φρόνιμοι ἐν Χριστῷ	ἡμεῖς μωροὶ διὰ Χριστόν
ὑμεῖς ... ἰσχυροί	ἡμεῖς ἀσθενεῖς
ὑμεῖς ἔνδοξοι	ἡμεῖς ... ἄτιμοι

In a catalogue of deprivations, Paul brings a climax to his passage of irony. Where he began by listing the secular success of the Corinthians' leadership, he closes by showing how dishonourable his own leadership was in those terms: ἄχρι τῆς ἄρτι ὥρας καὶ πεινῶμεν καὶ διψῶμεν καὶ γυμνιτεύομεν καὶ κολαφιζόμεθα καὶ ἀστατοῦμεν καὶ κοπιῶμεν ἐργαζόμενοι ταῖς ἰδίαις χερσίν· λοιδορούμενοι εὐλογοῦμεν, διωκόμενοι ἀνεχόμεθα, δυσφημούμενοι παρακαλοῦμεν· ὡς περικαθάρματα τοῦ κόσμου ἐγενήθημεν, πάντων περίψημα, ἕως ἄρτι (1 Cor 4.11-13). Contrary to the secular practices of leadership, Paul argues that the apostles are treated as the περικαθάρματα of the earth: they go hungry

---

53 B. Fiore, '"Covert Allusion" in 1 Corinthians 1-4', 95.

54 B. Fiore, '"Covert Allusion" in 1 Corinthians 1-4', 95-96, "The glaring discrepancy with the rhetorical models of this device is Paul's exposure of what should be a covert allusion. In fact, he not only lays bare the fact that he is using a *logos eschematismenos* (4.6) but also makes explicit censures and lessons which he wishes the community to apply to itself (4.6 and 2.5; 3.1-4, 18, 21; 4.1-3). Then too whatever good is to be gained through oblique references would seem to be lost in the ironical characterization of the Corinthians in 4.7-8 and in the contrast of their security with the apostolic trials and with their own former condition (4.9-13). Furthermore, while the covert allusion is to the example of Paul and Apollos together, the personal application by Paul to himself intrudes regularly (2.1-5; 3.1-5; 4.3-5) until it supplants that of the joint laborers (4.14-21), and that right after the impassioned description of the common apostolic toils (4.9-13)".

and thirsty, are homeless and poorly clothed, they are cursed, slandered and persecuted.[55] This portrayal points out all the more sharply the wrongness of the Corinthians' quarrelling and boasting over their apostolic leaders as if they were figures of status.

5. *Paradigms of Christian Leadership*

In addition to his choice of leadership terminology, Paul's definition of Christian leadership is also detailed for the Corinthians by his selection of leadership examples which they should imitate.[56] The principal example they are asked to follow is that of Paul himself.[57] A contrast is thus built up between those secular models which the Corinthians have been following, and the examples Paul commends in 1 Corinthians.

Paul explicitly contrasts his own *modus operandi* used during his first visit to Corinth in 1 Corinthians 2.1-5 with that of the Graeco-Roman expectations of leadership. The one method employs persuasive oratory (ὑπεροχὴν λόγου ἢ σοφίας, 1 Cor 2.1) whilst the other is a picture of fear and trembling (ἐν ἀσθενείᾳ καὶ ἐν φόβῳ καὶ ἐν τρόμῳ πολλῷ, 1 Cor 2.3).[58]

The paradigm of himself is continued in 1 Corinthians 2.6-16. Paul maintains that he *does* speak a wisdom, although one that contrasts with that of this age, and he points out to the Corinthians that his particular wisdom is taught, not by humans, but by the spirit of God.[59] Paul makes clear, therefore, that he has deliberately chosen in his own ministry to avoid fulfilling the expectations of the wisdom of the world. He defines a more appropriate practice of leadership by reminding the Corinthians of his own *modus operandi* whilst in their own city of Corinth, and of his initial aim to avoid their faith being dependent on human wisdom (1 Cor 2.5).

More positively in 1 Corinthians 3.5-9, Paul describes the nature of leadership in terms of servanthood. He points out, using both Apollos and himself as examples, that their leadership is characterised by their service—an exceptional contrast to a worldly manner of leadership.

Paul reverses the pattern of seniority. Rather than the apostolic leaders being elevated by the Corinthians to a status which is not theirs, Paul points

---

[55] 1 Cor 4.11-13.

[56] Imitation is a theme which Paul returns to at a number of points. There are other instances in the Pauline corpus where imitation of himself, or other Christians, or indeed God, is commended: 1 Cor 11.1; Eph 5.1; 1 Thess 1.6, 2.14; 2 Thess 3.7, 9.

[57] See the helpful article on this subject, B. Sanders, 'Imitating Paul: 1 Cor 4:16', *HTR* 74 (1981), 353-63.

[58] This is discussed in detail by B.W. Winter in *Philo and Paul among the Sophists: A Hellenistic Jewish and a Christian Response,* unpublished PhD dissertation (Macquarie University, 1988), 151-68, where it is demonstrated that Paul deliberately contrasts his own practice with those practices expected of a sophistic rhetor as he arrived in a city. L. Hartman, 'Some Remarks on 1 Cor. 2:1-5', *Svensk Exegetisk Årsbok* 39 (1974), 118-19, speaks of Paul as the anti-rhetor in this passage; cf. also T.H. Lim, '"Not in Persuasive Words of Wisdom, but in the Demonstration of the Spirit and power" (1 Cor. 2:4)', *Novum Testamentum* 29 (1987), 146-7.

[59] 1 Cor 2.6, 13.

out in fact that it is the leaders who belong to the congregation. In 1 Corinthians 3.21-23, Paul urges that instead of saying "I belong to …", the Corinthians should understand that these elevated apostolic figures are only there to serve. It is the apostolic leaders who in fact belong to them, and not vice-versa (ὥστε μηδεὶς καυχάσθω ἐν ἀνθρώποις πάντα γὰρ ὑμῶν ἐστιν, εἴτε Παῦλος εἴτε Ἀπολλῶς εἴτε Κηφᾶς εἴτε κόσμος εἴτε ζωὴ εἴτε θάνατος εἴτε ἐνεστῶτα εἴτε μέλλοντα, πάντα ὑμῶν, ὑμεῖς δὲ Χριστοῦ, Χριστὸς δὲ θεοῦ). In this way, Paul's example of leadership starkly contrasts with secular perceptions adopted by the Corinthians.

Paul models a paradigm of leadership which he urges the Corinthians to imitate. This is specifically made clear in 1 Corinthians 4.16, παρακαλῶ οὖν ὑμᾶς, μιμηταί μου γίνεσθε. In distinction to the secular categories of leadership which had been so readily adopted, Paul defines the Christian practice of leadership for them: they are not to rely on boasting or social status to create reputation, not to establish a popular following by recourse to the law-courts, and not to rely on a reputation carved out by oratorical prowess or patronal respect. This constitutes an inverting of the world's views of leadership.[60]

It is clear that, throughout the letter, Paul's concern to define for the Corinthians a Christian view of leadership is achieved by continuous reference to his own example of leadership amongst them. Paul, however, does not only draw their attention to his own example and that of Apollos. Other figures who are good examples of Christian leadership are also pointed out as paradigms. In contrast to the Corinthians who do not model Paul's understanding of Christian leadership, he draws their attention to two leaders who have faithfully imitated Paul. The first example is of one of Paul's fellow-workers, and the second is of a leader who himself is in the church at Corinth.

Paul uses these examples as part of his intention to correct the Corinthian view of legitimation. In order to aid the Corinthians in their imitation of the absent Paul, he decides to send to them his fellow-worker Timothy.

---

[60] In 1 Corinthians 9 Paul outlines further still the nature of Christian leadership by reference to his own practice whilst amongst them. In response to the Corinthians' questioning of Paul's apostolic status, he lists his credentials; he is free; he has seen Jesus; and he has fathered the church in Corinth. One further credential Paul concentrates on—the right to subsistence support from the community. It would appear that this is a major criticism levelled at Paul by the Corinthians—he does not accept their support and therefore cannot be an apostle. Paul, on the surface, endorses the Corinthian argumentation that a man should be supported for the work that he does, and he cites the soldier, the farmer and the shepherd as examples. This defence is further established by reference to the Torah, and later also Temple practice and even the Lord's command. Since Paul is at work in the community, he has the right to be supported by them and may be considered an apostle to that community. The defence of his apostleship, however, is not the stress which Paul leaves with the Corinthians. In 1 Corinthians 9.12 he changes the thrust of his argument with the word ἀλλὰ and then momentarily returns with yet more credentials in 1 Cor 9.13-14, before emphatically altering the direction of his argument back to a correction of their view of legitimation in v. 15 with ἐγὼ δὲ. It is this last and longest section of the chapter which Paul wants to leave with the Corinthians. It is of vital importance to Paul that he does not receive their material support, for he stresses that his work is inspired by an irresistible compulsion. It is a self-legitimating work since it provides its own reward. Paul is at one and the same time ἐλεύθερος and δοῦλος, and his motivation is the gospel itself. Paul is the servant leader, who considers first the needs of his congregation and not his own rights.

Timothy has so faithfully imitated Paul in his leadership that he will be able
to remind the Corinthians of Paul's way of life (1 Cor 4.17, ἔπεμψα ὑμῖν
Τιμόθεον, ὅς ἐστίν μου τέκνον ἀγαπητὸν καὶ πιστὸν ἐν κυρίῳ, ὅς ὑμᾶς ἀναμνή-
σει τὰς ὁδούς μου τὰς ἐν Χριστῷ ['Ιησοῦ], καθὼς πανταχοῦ ἐν πάσῃ ἐκκλησίᾳ
διδάσκω). In 1 Corinthians 16.10-11, Paul refers the community again to the
fact that Timothy may well arrive. Timothy is to be warmly accepted since he
is working for the Lord in a way which imitates that of Paul.

The second example Paul draws their attention to in order to make plain his
definition of Christian leadership regards Stephanas in 1 Corinthians 16.15-16.
It is clear from this passage that Stephanas is being singled out as one who
gave himself to the service of the saints, εἰς διακονίαν τοῖς ἁγίοις ἔταξαν
ἑαυτούς. This labouring on behalf of the saints is regarded by Paul as a significant criterion which legitimates Christian leadership. It may be seen also here
that where Graeco-Roman society would focus on status and rank, Paul
elevates Christian leaders on the grounds of their function.

These good examples of leadership, such as Stephanas and those like him,
Paul warmly recommends. It is these who deserve recognition in the community. They should be submitted to and others should follow their example. Paul
emphasises this aspect by highly commending everyone else who "joins in the
work and labours at it".[61] All in the Christian church should receive their reputation, not by status, but by their function. Paul offers the specific grounds by
which men deserve recognition—they must do the Lord's work. Furthermore,
in 1 Corinthians 15.58 Paul urges *all* to abound in their labour for the Lord,
knowing that such labour is not in vain.[62] This basis of legitimation is thus
contrary to that of the surrounding Graeco-Roman society.

6. *Conclusions*

One of Paul's chief concerns with the Corinthians in 1 Corinthians 1-6 is to
deal with the issue of leadership within the Christian community. This
question is addressed directly at a number of points in the early chapters of the
epistle, and it has become clear that Paul's own assessment of the situation is
that within the church are those who have derived their view of leadership
from the surrounding Graeco-Roman society.

Paul confronts this situation on two fronts: he demonstrates the inappropriateness of secular leadership models within the Christian church; and
secondly, he presents his own definition of true Christian leadership.

In redefining for the Corinthians the true nature of Christian leadership,
Paul's careful use of language is of considerable importance. He adopts

---

[61] 1 Cor 16.16.

[62] A.L. Chapple, *Local Leadership in the Pauline Churches: theological and social factors in its
development: a study based on 1 Thessalonians, 1 Corinthians and Philippians,* unpublished PhD
Thesis (Durham University, 1984), 398-429, has an extensive discussion of this section of
1 Corinthians.

images of leadership which erode the secular perception of how leaders should view themselves, and he *patently* uses the rhetorical device of covert allusion, itself a device of secular leaders, in order to make plain to the Corinthians the nature of their leading.

Paul also refers the Corinthians to the good examples of Christian leadership which they have encountered. Principally he reminds them of his own behaviour whilst working amongst them. Also, he recommends the examples both of Timothy, who is to visit them, and Stephanas, who himself is in the Corinthian congregation.

Much of the material drawn upon in this chapter occurred in the first six chapters of 1 Corinthians; it has been possible to demonstrate briefly, however, that Paul's concern that the Corinthians should display Christian, and not secular, leadership practices is consistently displayed throughout the epistle.

CHAPTER NINE

CONCLUSIONS

1. *Summary*

By comparing secular leadership in Corinthian society with leadership in the Corinthian church, it has been argued from 1 Corinthians 1-6 that one of Paul's major concerns with the church in Corinth is the extent to which significant members in the church were employing secular categories and perceptions of leadership in the Christian community.

It was suggested in the Introduction that studies of Pauline church leadership this century often suffer from one of two imbalances: either they are too narrowly constructed on the theological ideals of the Pauline material; or they are too strongly dictated by modern social theory without taking sufficient cognizance of the socio-historical context. The first method, whilst importantly concentrating on the Pauline text, has a limited picture of the socio-historical situation. The result is an improbable reconstruction of local leadership based on the supposed theological ideals of Paul. In order to overcome this weakness a number of studies using the second method have supplemented Paul's theological assessments with insights from Weberian social theory. This method, however, also often fails to set the Pauline material sufficiently within the first century Graeco-Roman context.

The more appropriate method, adopted here with regard to leadership practices in 1 Corinthians 1-6, has been to assess the socio-historical situation as a background for considering the New Testament material. Relevant sections of 1 Corinthians 1-6 have been interpreted in the light of leadership attitudes and practices prevalent in the surrounding Graeco-Roman society.

By studying the epigraphic, numismatic and literary sources, Graeco-Roman leadership profiles and practices in the first century colony of Corinth have been defined. Chapter Two of the study appraised this non-literary material of Corinth and outlined the administrative and leadership posts in the Roman colony. This synopsis is supplemented in Appendix A by specific prosopographical information on the honorary offices held by a considerable number of individuals compiled from this period.

The third chapter considered in greater detail specific characteristics of these Graeco-Roman leaders. The ways in which social élites jostled for position and popularity in Graeco-Roman city life was described from this comprehensive catalogue of first century Corinthian leaders. It was seen how status, patronage and benefaction, political enmity and oratory were crucial to a successful profile of secular, political leadership.

Chapter Four turned to the text of 1 Corinthians 1-6, examining evidence which demonstrated that within the Christian community there were some members from the Corinthian social élite. Discussion of the key terms σοφός, δυνατός and εὐγενής showed that Paul's comment in 1 Corinthians 1.26 presupposed the existence in the church of Corinth of at least some from the ruling class of the city. It was these characteristics of wisdom, influence and noble birth which were widely used to describe those of the established classes. The figure of Erastus, termed οἰκονόμος τῆς πόλεως in Romans 16.23, also offered the possibility of an identified civic leader being a significant member of the Corinthian church. Whether the interesting identification can be fully established or not, it is now clear that the Erastus of Romans 16.23 at the least was a man of significant means in the Christian community.

Having established that there were in the Pauline community those from the social élite of Corinthian society, it was then demonstrated in Chapters Five to Seven, from the text of 1 Corinthians 1-6, that certain secular practices of leadership were also being adopted in the church. Paul understood that there were those in the church who were responsible for an erosion of the Christian principles of leadership. Two instances, dealt with in greater detail in Chapters Five and Six, demonstrated particular practices in the church which mirrored secular society and contrasted with the Christian practices which the church should have adopted.

First, Chapter Five considered the situation described by Paul in 1 Corinthians 6.1-8 where Christians from élite society were taking their fellow Christians to the secular law courts. It was seen that legal proceedings were undertaken by those of high social standing in order to elevate further their own status and reputation—a practice highly beneficial to those in positions of leadership in society. Litigation spawned much enmity and Paul strongly argued that those in the community should not resort to the secular courts and its practices. Rather, such matters should be dealt with in the community, where even the 'despised' of society were qualified—'wise' enough—to handle such disputes.

Secondly, Chapter Six argued that the congregation's toleration of gross sexual immorality within the church in 1 Corinthians 5 may have arisen for reasons of expediency. If the guilty brother were a significant patron figure of the church, one of the members of the élite class, then it would have been certainly difficult, perhaps impossible, to confront him on the matter. Paul took the church to task because their assessment of the status of the incestuous man—their 'pride' in him—had caused them to overlook their need to confront him on the matter of sexual immorality.

Further aspects of secular leadership evident in the Corinthian church were assessed in Chapter Seven. It was demonstrated that there were in the community those who elevated the place of worldly wisdom, boasted about status, created divisions over personal loyalties and encouraged leadership reliant on persuasive oratory. Here again, Paul specifically addressed those who adopted within the Christian church such aspects of leadership which were entirely secular.

In the light of this intrusion of secular perceptions of leadership into the Corinthian church, Paul redefined for the Corinthians the nature of Christian leadership. This was shown in Chapter Eight by outlining Paul's decisive critique of secular leadership and his commendation of paradigm leaders whom they should imitate. Paul's own example demonstrated an avoidance of persuasive oratory and secular boasting and a refusal to give particular esteem to those in the community with high secular status.

Paul's criticism arose from his identification of aspects of secular leadership in the church. This consistently emerged throughout the early chapters of the epistle, beginning with his evaluation of their boasting in men, continuing with his discussion of the Corinthians' reliance on human wisdom and ending with his instructions regarding those who brought secular practices into the church. In addition to this identification and criticism of secular leadership in the church, Paul constructed for the Corinthians different parameters of leadership. This positive definition offered a stark contrast to the secular patterns of leadership. Paul deliberately focused not on status, but on task; the terminology used was specifically that of function; and the individuals whom he referred to as examples of good Christian leadership were specifically chosen for their commitment to service and not status.

2. *Implications and Significance*

In addition to the conclusions which directly arise from the study and which are included in the summary above, a number of further conclusions may be drawn from the work taken as a whole.

First, it may be concluded, on a general level, that the multi-disciplinary approach which combines social history and New Testament exegesis offers insights which are inaccessible to either a purely exegetical study or a Weberian analysis. Geertz's suggestion that by turning to the 'classical' sociologists only predictable results would be achieved was pointed out in the Introduction. He argues that the use of, for example, historical research may avoid this narrow 'academicism'. In this study it has been shown that historical research produces very different results regarding an understanding of the nature of local leadership in 1 Corinthians.

The consensus view, following Sohm, drew the conclusion that there was no leadership in the Corinthian community. Weberian analysis, derived via Sohm from 1 Corinthians, produces the predictable results that the church in 1 Corinthians demonstrates the beginning of the process of institutionalising leadership.[1] This study which analyses 1 Corinthians within its socio-historical

---

[1]   Cf. B. Holmberg, *Paul and Power: The structure of authority in the primitive Church as reflected in the Pauline epistles* (Lund, 1978), 158 f.; K. Giles, 'Demystifying Ordination with the

context, however, suggests that Sohm was wrong to conclude that there was no hierarchical leadership in the community; and that those who impose Weberian models of analysis on the text, without undertaking the necessary proto-sociological work, are basing their conclusions on limited historical data.

Within this study it has been possible to clarify the nature of leadership within the Corinthian congregation and demonstrate that this matter was of considerable importance for Paul. This conclusion has only been reached by setting the Pauline material against its original backdrop of the dynamics of leadership in Roman Corinth. The assumption that few references to offices in 1 Corinthians necessarily means no leadership in the community is inappropriate for Graeco-Roman society of the first century. It has been shown clearly that, rather than an absence of leadership in the Corinthian church, Paul is deeply concerned with the nature of the leadership which did exist in the community.

This study raises implications regarding the use of Weberian social theory for Pauline ecclesiology in 1 Corinthians. By using Weberian models of leadership, scholars have reached a conclusion, contrary to that of Sohm, that local leadership did exist in the church. This conclusion has only been inferred, however, from a few selected verses. The present study, using the broader social context, has been able to demonstrate not only that there was leadership in the community, but that this was a key theme and concern of Paul's throughout the epistle and notably in chapters 1-6.

This study has shown that research into Graeco-Roman social history produces a wealth of information unavailable either to the purely theological study or analysis based only on Weberian social theory. The validity of using either method to understand the Pauline leadership situation in the church of Corinth is pulled sharply into question when insufficient cognizance is taken of the socio-historical situation.

3. Further Study

Leadership is dealt with by Paul at such length in 1 Corinthians that it has been necessary to limit the focus of the study to detailed analysis of 1 Corinthians 1-6 alone. The consistency of Paul's analysis and criticism of secular leadership practices in the church, however, may be seen throughout the epistle and this does suggest areas which can be further pursued.

---

help of Max Weber', *Tyndale Paper* 32 (July, 1987); M.Y. MacDonald, *The Pauline Churches. A Socio-historical Study of Institutionalization in the Pauline and Deutero-Pauline Writings* (Cambridge, 1988), 55-60.

1 Corinthians 8 includes Paul's discussion of how the Corinthians should handle the matter of food sacrificed to idols.[2] This is also of some social significance for those of the élite classes, as demonstrated by recent literature on the subject.

1 Corinthians 9 concerns the rights and privileges of position which Paul chooses to deny himself with regard to the Corinthians. Again here Paul contrasts himself with the way leaders exercised their own rights in secular society. Paul's vocabulary of voluntary slavery and weakness is distinguished from what would have been expected of secular leaders.[3] He counters the way in which the Corinthians determine who is an apostle and, instead, he gives his own grounds for legitimating his leadership.

There may be in 1 Corinthians 11.2-16 aspects of social norms in the wearing of head coverings and the relationship between men and women.[4] 1 Corinthians 11.17-34 may thus be highly relevant to the tensions between the social classes in the Corinthian church.[5]

1 Corinthians 12-14 appears to be concerned partly with the ways in which people gifted in the spectacular gifts of oratory conduct themselves within the congregation. Paul stresses in these chapters that ἀγάπη and οἰκοδομή are to characterise the actions of all such people with gifts.

1 Corinthians 16 has a significant section on the person of Stephanas and the way in which Paul endorses this model of leadership. Stephanas is praised for his devoted service and labour, and not for his status.

It would seem that the issue of leadership casts its shadow over almost every chapter of 1 Corinthians. These areas suggest grounds for further study to develop the thesis throughout 1 Corinthians. The Graeco-Roman background has recently been used to study a number of aspects of 2 Corinthians.[6] The church's view of leadership in 2 Corinthians could also be assessed in the light of the Roman Corinthian background.

---

[2] See B.W. Winter, 'In Public and in Private: Early Christian Interactions with Religious Pluralism', in edd. A.D. Clarke & B.W. Winter, *One God, One Lord in a World of Religious Pluralism* (Cambridge, 1991), 132.

[3] Cf. 1 Cor 9.19, 22.

[4] Cf. D.W.J. Gill, 'The Importance of Roman Portraiture for Head Coverings in 1 Corinthians 11.2-16', *Tyndale Bulletin* 41 (1990), 245-60; see esp. 260 regarding these verses, "It seems to reflect the jostling for power and authority amongst the leading families within the church at Corinth … It reflects the love of ambition usually met within an urban community of the Roman world such as a colony".

[5] See B.W. Winter, 'The Lord's Supper at Corinth: An Alternative Reconstruction', *Reformed Theological Review* 37 (1978), 73-82; R.A. Campbell, 'Does Paul Acquiesce in Divisions at the Lord's Supper?', *Novum Testamentum* 33 (1991), 61-70; and G. Theissen, *The Social Setting of Pauline Christianity: essays on Corinth* (Edinburgh, 1982), 145-74.

[6] Cf. the recent work by T.B. Savage on Paul's understanding of ministry in 2 Corinthians within its Graeco-Roman context, *Power through Weakness: An Historical and Exegetical Examination of Paul's Understanding of the ministry in 2 Corinthians,* unpublished PhD dissertation (Cambridge University, 1986); also Peter Marshall's, *Enmity in Corinth: Social Conventions in Paul's Relations with the Corinthians* (Tübingen, 1987); and B.W. Winter's assessment of the sophistic background to 2 Corinthians 10-13 in *Philo and Paul among the Sophists: A Hellenistic Jewish and a Christian Response,* unpublished PhD dissertation (Macquarie University, 1988).

It has been argued in the study that the Graeco-Roman context has been the principal background against which to elucidate the social dynamics of leadership in the Corinthian church. It has been pointed out in the Introduction that Jewish and Old Testament influences in the community may provide additional data with which to understand the local Christian leadership.

This study, whilst focusing simply on the early chapters of 1 Corinthians, does carry implications for the wider study of Pauline and New Testament ecclesiology. It will not, of course, be possible to carry over into other epistles or situations all the conclusions which have been drawn here—a mistake that has been made before. These conclusions are drawn from Corinthian, biblical and extra-biblical, sources and will not necessarily apply to Ephesus, Philippi or Thessalonica. It does suggest, however, that similar studies could be undertaken for these other situations which might open up again the debate regarding Pauline ecclesiology. It may be asked whether these other communities had a similar representation of the élite classes; and whether they were as strongly influenced by aspects of secular society.

Further implications may be drawn for Ancient History. Although it has been said that the New Testament, by itself, offers too little data for extensive social reconstruction, it must be said that in some areas it supplements some of the Ancient Historical sources. Too often, the New Testament is considered poor source material, but this misunderstanding is changing.[7]

It is clear that, whilst this study offers helpful insights regarding the nature of leadership in 1 Corinthians, there remains considerable scope for the development of this central New Testament issue.

---

[7]   See, for example, D. Engels' discussion of the church in his volume *Roman Corinth: An Alternative Model for the Classical City* (Chicago, 1990), 107-116; and a lecture delivered to The Society for Early Christianity, Macquarie University (December, 1989) by B.W. Winter entitled 'The New Testament as Commentator on the Cultural Setting of First Century Roman Corinth'.

APPENDIX A

Appendix A is a compilation in tabular form of prosopographical information of Roman Corinthian leading figures derived from epigraphic and numismatic primary sources. Much of this material can be gleaned from the secondary literature cited below.

Abbreviations

agon	agonothete
q iivir	quinquennial duovir
iivir	duovir
cur ann	curator annonæ
praef	praefectus iure dicundo
aed	aedile

A	Amandry, M., 'Le Monnayage des duovirs corinthiens', *Bulletin de Correspondance Hellénique, Supplément* XV (1988).
E	Edwards, K.M., *Corinth, Coins 1896-1929,* VI (Cambridge, Massachusetts, 1933).
K	Kent, J.H., *Corinth—Inscriptions 1926-1950 Corinth: Results,* viii, Part III (Princeton, 1966).
M	Meritt, B.D., *Corinth—Greek Inscriptions 1896-1927 Corinth: Results,* viii, Part I (Cambridge, Massachusetts, 1931).
W	West, A.B., *Corinth—Latin Inscriptions 1896-1920 Corinth: Results,* viii, Part II (Cambridge, Massachusetts, 1931).

#	Name	agon	q iivir	iivir	cur ann	praef	aed	Additional Information	Date	Ref	Lang
1	-gha-		•	•				Duovir in reign of Domitian. (Found in central Agora, North of Bema).	Domitian	K # 172	Latin
2	-thus, ...			•				Granted the *ornamenta* of Duovir in the reign of Trajan. Inscription erected *decurionum decreto*. (Found in S Stoa).	Trajan	K # 167	Latin
3	Accius, Marcus, Candidus			•				Duovir with C Fulvius Flaccus in c. AD 59-66 (A p 24, suggests 54/55 or 55/56).	c. AD 59-66	E # 54-55	Latin
4	Aebutius, Publius, Sp f ...		•	•				Duovir with C Heius Pamphilus in c. 1 BC - AD 3 (A p 141, 17/16 BC); and Quinqennial Duovir with C Julius Heraclanus in AD 7/8? and 12/13? (A p 148, AD 1/2).	AD 12/13	E # 32-33	Latin
5	Aebutius, Publius, ...			•				Duovir with C Pinnius ... in 37/36 BC?. Quinquennial Duovir in 29/28 BC with M Antonius Theophilus (A p 138, 30 BC).	37/36 BC?	E # 20-21	Latin
6	Aeficius, Lucius, Certus			•				Duovir in 43/42 BC? with C Julius (A p 120, 44/43 BC) The name of the coin is reversed, thus Certus Aeficius, and the name Lucius is omitted.	Duovir in 43/42 BC?	E # 16	Latin
7	Aeficius, Publius, Firmus Statianus						•	Of the tribe Aemilia. Granted the *ornamenta* of Aedile during Hadrian's reign. (Found South of the Bema).	Hadrian	K # 237	Latin
8	Aelius, Publius, Sospinus							Rhetor, grandson of Antonius Sospis, 'for upright character and general excellence' (ἀνδραγαθίας, ἀρετή). Inscription erected *decurionum decreto*. (Found in S Basilica and S Stoa).	Hadrian	K # 226	Greek
9	Andreas						?	Οἰκονόμος—the only reference to this title in Corinth, besides Romans 16.23 and the Vitellius inscription. A Christian gravestone. (Found in a cavern at Lerna).	AD 267-268	K # 558	Greek
10	anon							Pyrophor to Agonothete, Isagogeus. The inscription was part of the victor's wreath. (Found in S Stoa and S Basilica).		K # 214	Latin
11	anon							'-mus revetted the colonnade and [built at his own expense] the walls of the *exedrae* and their columns [- - -]'. (Found near fountain of Peirene).		K # 337	Latin

Name	agon	q iivir	iivir	cur ann	praef	aed	Additional Information	Date	Ref	Lang
12 anon	•						Possibly of the tribe Aemilia. *Sodalis Augustalis* (which suggests he was a freedman). Isagogeus of the Caesarean Sebasteion and Agonothete of the Caesarean games. (Found in S Stoa and S Basilica).	late C1, early C2 AD	K # 213	Latin
13 anon						•	Granted the *ornamenta* of Decurion and Aedile. (Found near the Isthmian Gate).	C1 AD	K # 233	Latin
14 anon	•		•			•	(Found in SE Agora).		K # 171	Latin
15 anon	•				•		Theocolus. (Found in SE Agora).		K # 203	Latin
16 anon	•			•			(Found in NW Agora).		K # 227	Latin
17 anon							Military Tribune Legion XII Fulminata (which suggests equestrian rank), Procurator in charge of fiscus in Egypt under Trajan, Iuridicus of Egypt. Erected by Ti. Claudius Speratus to his friend. Inscription erected *decurionum decreto*.	Trajan	K # 136	Greek
18 anon				•			Praefectus Fabrorum. (Found East of Theatre).		K # 234	Latin
19 anon			•				Ptolemaios dedicated this inscription to his anonymous friend and Procurator of Achaea. Inscription erected *decurionum decreto*. (Found in S Basilica, S Stoa and SE Agora).	c. mid C2 AD	K # 146	Greek
20 anon				•			(Found near shops along Lechaion Road).		K # 169	Latin
21 anon			•				Monument erected at public expense, and *decurionum decreto* which is very rare and suggests that he was a man of some prominence. Two Duoviri were in charge of the construction of the monument. (Found North of Theatre).	From Nero to Hadrian	K # 165	Latin
22 anon	•		•			•	*Sodalis Augustalis* (which suggests that he was a freeman). He was granted the *ornamenta* of Aedile, Duovir and Agonothete. Inscription erected *decurionum decreto*. (Found in Central Shops).	2nd 1/4 C2 AD	K # 219	Latin

	Name	agon	q iivir	iivir	cur ann	praef	aed	Additional Information	Date	Ref	Lang
23	anon		•	•			•	Isagogeus of Cornelius Pulcher. He was granted the *ornamenta* of Aedile, Duovir and Duovir Quinquennalis. The inscription was erected *post obitum* by his wife. (Found in SE Agora).	c. AD 43.	K # 173	Latin
24	anon		•	•				Erected *sua pecunia*. (Found near Bema).	Augustus	K # 157	Latin
25	anon							Legate of Hadrian, Propraetor of Cappadocia, and maybe known as a philosopher. 'Because of generosity'. Erected by L Gellius Justus and L Gellius Menander. Of senatorial rank. (Found in S Stoa and S Basilica).	Hadrian	K # 124	Greek
26	anon			•				'He revetted the Bema and paid personally the expense of making all its marble'. (Found North of Bema).	Mid C1 AD	K # 322	Latin
27	anon	•		•				Agonothete of the Isthmian games. (Found in S Stoa).		K # 178	Latin
28	anon		•	•			•	NB the order of the *cursus honorum* on the inscription is Aedile, Duovir, Agonothete, Duovir Quinquennalis. He was granted the *ornamenta* of these offices. Inscription erected *decurionum decreto*. (Found in Julian Basilica).		K # 166	Latin
29	anon	•		•				Granted the *ornamenta* of Agonothete and Duovir. Inscription erected *decurionum decreto*. (Found in NE Agora).		K # 180	Latin
30	anon							Dedicated by Marcus Antonius Promachus to his friend and patron (φίλον καὶ προστάτεν), 'for fine character and trustworthiness'. (Found in Central Agora, near Bema).	Mid C2	K # 265	Greek
31	anon				•			'For the monthly grain supply and every display of his good will' (εὐνοίᾳ and ἀρετή). Inscription erected *decurionum decreto* and by the people. (Found in Agora and Central Shops).		K # 267	Greek

Name	agon	q iivir	iivir	cur ann	praef	aed	Additional Information	Date	Ref	Lang
32 anon				•			He was probably the provincial Censor of Achaea, and either Curator or Praefectus Annonae, and also the Curator of either public works or taxes. (στεφανηφόρος, στρατηγός). (Found in S Stoa, NW Agora and Theatre).	Late C2 AD	K # 127	Greek
33 anon						?	Argyrotamias (or Curator Kalendarii, the Greek title in a Latin inscription is a sign of the hellenization process towards the end of the first century). Quaestor, IIII vir (no other instance of this division in Corinth). (Found in Julian Basilica).	Late C1 or early C2 AD	W # 104a, 104 b	Latin
34 anon	•						Agonothete of the Caesarean Nervanea Trajanea games, of the Isthmian and the Caesarean games. (Found in S Basilica).		K # 218	Latin
35 anon					•	•	Theocolus of Jupiter Capitolinus, Irenarches of Janus, *ob iustitiam*. Inscription erected *decurionum decreto*. (Found in Temple E).	end of C1 AD	K # 195	Latin
36 Antonius, Lucius, Julianus			•				Latest reference to a Corinthian Duovir - in Pius' reign. Duovir with Titus Flavius Pompeianus. Erected by the two Duoviri to Faustinus, the wife of Pius. Public expense. Inscription erected *decurionum decreto*.	Pius	K # 107	Latin
37 Antonius, Lucius, L f Priscus		•	•	•	•	•	Of the tribe Meninia. Aedile during Hadrian's reign. Granted the *ornamenta* of Praefectus iure dicundo. Duovir and Duovir Quinquennalis during the reign of Hadrian. Inscription erected *decurionum decreto* with money from the will; the work of his family. (Found in Central S Stoa).	Hadrian ?	K # 177	Latin

Name	agon	q iivir	iivir	cur ann	praef	aed	Additional Information	Date	Ref	Lang
38 Antonius, Marcus, Achaicus	•	•	•	•	•	•	Unusually prominent. Of the tribe Aemilia. Aedile during Nero's reign. Praefectus iure dicundo, Curator annonae and Duovir in Vespasian's reign and once Quinquennial Duovir in Domitian's reign. Agonothete during Domitian's reign of the Nervanea Trajanea, the Isthmian and Caesarean games. Inscription erected *decurionum decreto*, and also dedicated to Prifernius Paetus in Argos. (Found in NE Agora).	AD 70-100	K # 164, 224	Latin
39 Antonius, Marcus, Hipparchus			•				Duovir with C Servilius C f Primus in 2/1 BC (cf. A p 144. Cf. Plutarch, Antony 67.7). Also Duovir with M Novius Bassus in 10/9 - 5/4 BC (cf. A p 142).	27-18 BC	E # 28-31	Latin
40 Antonius, Marcus, Orestes		•					Quinquennial Duovir with Cn Publicius ... in 19-18 BC (A p 41, 40 BC).	19-18 BC	E # 27	Latin
41 Antonius, Marcus, Theophilus		?	?				Quinquennial Duovir with P Aebutius ... in ? 29/28 BC (A p 138, 30 BC). (Found near Lechaion Road).	29/28 BC	E # 22-24	Latin
42 Arrius, Aulus, Proclus			•			•	Monument erected by the Hieromnemones of the Caesarea. Of the tribe Aemilia. Augur. Praefectus Fabrorum. Aedile during the reign of Tiberius. Imperial Priest of Neptune. Isagogeus of the Tiberea and Caesarea. Duovir in c. AD 14-16. Agonothete of the Isthmian and Caesarean games in AD 39. (Found in central Agora, North of the Bema).	c. AD 39	K # 156	Latin
43 Arrius, Lucius, Peregrinus			•				Duovir with L Furius Labeo in c. AD 29 (A p 168, AD 32/33).	c. AD 29	E # 39-43	Latin
44 Atticus, Herodes							Very flowery epitaph to Herodes' wife, extolling the virtues of Herodes himself. Inscription erected by Boule. (Found in Temple F, and Peirene).	early C2 AD	K # 128, M # 86	Greek
45 Aurelius, Eutychianus							Ex-Praetor. The monument was set up to Ptolemaeus with the approval of the Boule. (Found in W Shops).	mid C4 AD	K # 502	Greek

	Name	agon	q iivir	iivir	cur ann	praef	aed	Additional Information	Date	Ref	Lang
46	Babbius, Gnaeus, Philinus			•			•	Aedile during Augustus' reign. A Pontifex who dedicated to Neptune, possibly connected closely with the worship of Poseidon. Erected *sua pecunia*. Duovir in c. AD 9-11. This name occurs more frequently than any other in the Corinthian inscriptions. Babbius' inscriptions have been found on four buildings and it may be assumed that he was a significant benefactor of Corinth and in return was made both Pontifex and Duovir. His father's name is nowhere mentioned, and it may therefore be that he was a freedman. The cognomen betrays Greek origin. (Found beside the Babbius monument, Lechaion Road, East of Agora, Agora and North of the Propylaea).	AD 9-11	K # 155, W # 2, 3, 98-101, 132	Latin
47	Babbius, Marcus, ...	•	•	•		•	•	*Sodalis Augustalis*—originally a very select group of Romans promoting the Imperial cult, but later it was less confined simply to the aristocracy, and other leading citizens were eligible to be included. Granted the *ornamenta* of Aedile, Duovir, Duovir Quinquennalis and Agonothete during the reign of Pius. A senator at Rome. (Found in central area of S Stoa).	Pius	K # 185	Latin
48	Barbatius, Marcus, M f Celer		•	•		•	•	Aedile during the reign of Tiberius. Of the tribe Aemilia. Quinquennial Duovir (Praef.) with C Julius C f Laco in AD 17/18? Duovir with Manius Acilius in c. AD 19-21 (for problems regarding provenance see A p 25). The order of the *cursus honorum* is notable. Provincial Quaestor in 41 BC.	AD 21	W # 80	Latin
49	Barbatius, Quintus, Celer							Praefectus pro Duovir in c. AD 19-21.	AD 19-21	W p 63	Latin
50	Bassus, ...	•						Agonothete in AD 61. Referred to by Barrett in his commentary, 131.	AD 61	Philostratus, Vita Apoll. 4.26	Greek
51	Bellius, Marcus, Proculus			•				Duovir with P Vipsanius Agrippa in AD 38/39 (A p 181, AD 37/38).	AD 38/39	E # 47-49	Latin

Name	agon	q iivir	iivir	cur ann	praef	aed	Additional Information	Date	Ref	Lang
52 Caecilius, Quintus, Niger			•				Duovir with C Heius Pamphilus in 7-4 BC (A p 133, 34-31 BC).	7-4 BC	E # 25-26	Latin
53 Calpurnius, Lucius, Proclus							Curator of Trajanic roads, Proconsul of Achaea, governor of Belgica, Praetor, candidate for Tribune of plebs under Hadrian, candidate for Quaestor under Trajan, Legatus of Legio I Minerva, member of board charged with minting coins, Hadrian's nominee for Tribune and possibly also for Praetor (and therefore highly honoured). Erected by Menander and Justus *o b iustitiam*. Military Tribune of Legio I Minerva and Legio III Gemina. Also inscriptions at Ancyra and Pisidian Antioch. Of senatorial rank. (Found in SE Agora, NW Stoa, and middle of S Stoa).	Trajan and Hadrian	K # 125	Latin
54 Calpurnius, Publius, Crotonensis							Procurator of Achaea. (Found in SE Agora).		K # 147	Latin
55 Caminius, Lucius, Agrippa			•				Duovir in AD 68-69.	AD 68-69	E # 65-73	Latin
56 Caminius, Publius, Agrippa,		•					Procurator of Achaea possibly late in Augustus' reign. Quinquennial Duovir with L Castricius Regulus in AD 22/23 (A p 165, AD 21/22). The Caninii were an important first century Corinthian family, and it appears that Agrippa's father, Alexiades, was an enfranchised Greek. Naming the father may suggest that although Agrippa was a citizen, his father may not have been one. The tribe was either Cornelia or Collina.	AD 22/23	E # 44, W # 65, 66	Latin
57 Caristanius, Caius, Julianus							Proconsul of Achaea under Trajan, *adlectio inter tribunicios* (and therefore of Senatorial rank). Possibly military Tribune of Legio XII Fulminata. Belonged to a family from Pisidian Antioch. Other inscriptions to this man have been found at Delphi and Athens.	Trajan	W # 55	Latin

	Name	agon	q iivir	iivir	cur ann	praef	aed	Additional Information	Date	Ref	Lang
58	Cas, Lucius, ...	•	•	•				Duovir with M Insteius L f Tectus (A p 124,42 or 41 BC).	42/41 BC	E # 18-19	Latin
59	Castricius, Lucius, Regulus			•		•	•	Amandry appears to miss out Regulus' post as Aedile, p 11. Quinquennial Duovir with P Caninius Agrippa in AD 22/23 (A p 165, AD 21/22). Agonothete in 2 BC? and AD 23 ?—the Tiberea Caesarea Sebastea, the Isthmian and the Caesarean games. Built and restored buildings, first to preside over Isthmian games in New Corinth, very rich and prominent in Corinth, expanded the programme of the games and restored the buildings in the sanctuary. Gave a banquet in honour of all the inhabitants of the colony. Prefect in 7-4 BC. Very prominent and probably one of the richest people in Corinth during the reign of Tiberius. Inscription erected *decurionum decreto*. (Found in central Agora South of Bema).	AD 22/23	E # 44, K # 153	Latin
60	Ce-, [S]pur[ius]			•	•		•	Of the tribe Aemilia. Aedile and Duovir in Pius' reign. (Found in S Stoa).	Pius	K # 188	Latin
61	Cerialis, Gaius							Procurator of Achaea for Hadrian, officer in charge of Imperial Marble quarries at Karystos. (Found in the Bouleuterion).	Hadrian	K # 137	Latin
62	Cestianus, Peducaeus							Orator of Apollonia. Nothing more is known about this non-Corinthian. Apollonia was originally a Corinthian colony. Inscription erected *de-curionum decreto*. (Found in E Agora).	Later than Aurelius	K # 269	Greek
63	Cispuleius, Quintus, Q f Theophilus						•	Probably of the tribe Aemilia. Granted the *orna-menta* of Decurion and Aedile during the reign of Tiberius. Inscription erected *decurionum de-creto*. A freedman. (Found near the Lechaion Road).	Tiberius	W # 107	Latin

Name	agon	q iivir	iivir	cur ann	praef	aed	Additional Information	Date	Ref	Lang
64 Claudius, Tiberius, Anaxilaus	•	•	•				Proquaestor, immediate successor to Gallio. Duovir with P Ventidius Fronto in AD 55/56? (A p 24, suggests 67/68); and Quinquennial Duovir with Tiberius Claudius Dinippus in 57/58 or possibly 52/53. Agonothete in Vespasian's reign. Proquaestors were usually appointed from ex-quaestors whenever the number of Quaestors was insufficient. (Found East of Peirene).	c. AD 50-60	E # 54-55, K # 212, W # 54	Latin
65 Claudius, Tiberius, Dinippus	•	•	•				Of the tribe Fabia. Quinquennial Duovir with Tiberius Claudius Anaxilaus in AD 57/58. Sacerdos of Britannic Victory, military Tribune of Legion VI Hispanensis, Praefectus Fabrorum. Curator annonae three times. Agonothete of the Neronea Caesarea and of the Isthmian and Caesarean games in AD 67. Of equestrian rank. (Found in S Stoa, SE Agora, Julian Basilica, and NE Agora).	c. AD 67	K # 158-163, W # 87-92	Latin
66 Claudius, Tiberius, Hermoxenus		•	•		•		Duovir in Hadrian's reign; also granted the *ornamenta* of Duovir during the reign of Pius. (Found in S Stoa).	Hadrian ?	K # 184	Latin
67 Claudius, Tiberius, Optatus			•	•			Duovir with C Julius Polyaenus in c. AD 59-66 (A p 24, suggests 57/58 or 58/59). Also magistrate at Sicyon (A p 26).	c. AD 59-66	E # 61-64	Latin
68 Claudius, Tiberius, Primigenius							Son of freedman, outstanding member of collegium. Cf. also Titus Flavius Antiochus. Erected by the two freedmen by decision of the Association of Lares of the Imperial House. The Collegium would seem to have consisted largely of men of servile origin. (Found in SW Agora).	Hadrian	K # 62	Latin
69 Claudius, Tiberius, ...	•						Agonothete in AD 181 of the Isthmian games. (Found in Peirene and Peribolos of Apollo).	AD 181	M # 16	Greek

Name	agon	q iivir	iivir	cur ann	praef	aed	Additional Information	Date	Ref	Lang
70 Cornelius, Caius, Martialis							Prefect of cohort I Raetorum, military Tribune of Legion XIII Gemina, awarded the dona militaria by Trajan, looked after supplies in Dacia expedition, Procurator of Achaea and of Iron mines. Probably honoured at the moment of promotion. Of the tribe Oufentina (restricted to Italians and therefore he was probably not a Corinthian). Inscription set up by L. Gellius Menander. Of equestrian rank. (Found in SE Agora).	c. AD 114	K # 135	Latin
71 Cornelius, Gnaeus, Speratus							Recognised *ob iustitiam*. Monument dedicated to Augustus. (Found in SE Agora and S Basilica).		K # 52	Latin
72 Cornelius, Maecianus							Possibly an equestrian (κράτιστον); monument dedicated to him by the city of the Lyttians. It is unusual that the Lyttians should have set this monument to him in the city of Corinth, for he was still probably a native of Corinth. The Cornelius family had been prominent in Corinthian affairs from the early days of the colony. (Found in Julian Basilica, and Theatre).	early C2 AD	K # 248	Greek
73 Cornelius, Publius, Crescens							Deputy chief collector of the imperial manumissions tax for Achaea and Syria. Crescens set up the monument in honour of Trajan. (Found in SE Agora).	AD 114-116	K # 100	Latin
74 Cornelius, Quintus, Secundus						•	Built the meatmarket and fishmarket. Of the tribe of Aemilia. (Found in S Basilica).	Augustus	K # 321	Latin
75 Curtius, Caius, C f Lesbicus	•	?	?			•	Of the tribe Clustumia. Aedile during Trajan's reign, Theocolus of Jupiter Capitolinus, Priest, Agonothete of the Isthmian and Caesarean games during Hadrian's reign, Duovir or Quinquennial Duovir during Hadrian's reign. Unusual order unless Duovir should read Quinquennial Duovir (in the inscription there is a gap after IIVIR, which may suggest a Quinquennial Duovir). (Found in SE Agora).	Hadrian ?	K # 198	Latin

	Name	agon	q iivir	iivir	cur ann	praef	aed	Additional Information	Date	Ref	Lang
76	Erastus						•	Cf. Romans 16.23. Aedile during Nero's reign. The letters were of metal, of which two small pieces still remain. (Found *in situ* East of stage building of Theatre).	c. AD 50	K # 232	Latin
77	Fabius, Quintus, Carpetanus							Curator of Nomentanum road, military Tribune of Legion X Gemina, Prefect of cavalry, Procurator of Achaea for Augustus. The family name Carpetani suggests the possibility of Spanish origin.	Augustus	K # 132	Latin
78	Felix, ...	•	•	•			•	Granted the *ornamenta* of Aedile, Duovir, Quinquennial Duovir and Agonothete during the reign of Ant. Pius. (Found in NE Agora).	Pius	K # 182	Latin
79	Flavius, Hermogenes							Most distinguished governor, benefactor, builder of harbour. (Proconsul of Achaea AD 353-358). Erected by city council and citizens. (Found at Lechaion).	AD 358	K # 503	Greek
80	Flavius, Titus, -clanus							Most distinguished governor under the emperors Flavius Valentinian and Flavius Valens— Λαμπρό-τατος ἀνθύπατος. (Found in W Shops and S Stoa).	Mid C4 AD	K # 504, 505	Greek
81	Flavius, Titus, Antiochus							Outstanding member of collegium—probably a private patriotic club, freedman of the Emperor, an official imperial cult. The membership of the club may largely have been servile. Cf. Tiberius Claudius Primigenius. Erected by decision of the Association of Lares of the Imperial House. (Found in SW Agora).	Hadrian	K # 62	Latin
82	Flavius, Titus, Pompeianus			•				Latest reference to a Corinthian Duovir - in Pius' reign. Duovir with Lucius Antonius Julianus. The two Duoviri erected the monument to Faustina the wife of the emperor Pius. Inscription erected *decurionum decreto* with public money.	Pius	K # 107	Latin
83	Fulvius, Caius, Flaccus			•				Duovir with M Accius Candidus in c. AD 59-66 (A p 24, suggests 54/55 or 55/56).	c. AD 59-66	E # 54-55	Latin

	Name	agon	q iivir	iivir	cur ann	praef	aed	Additional Information	Date	Ref	Lang
84	Fulvius, Quintus, Nobilior							Honoured with *ornamenta*; Nobilior was a very influential family. Of the tribe Oufentina (which was restricted to Italians, and therefore he was probably not a Corinthian). Of senatorial rank. (Found in Julian Basilica and NE Agora).		K # 120	Latin
85	Furius, Lucius, Labeo			•				Duovir with L Arrius Peregrinus in c. AD 29 (A p 168, AD 32/33).	c. AD 29	E # 39-43	Latin
86	Fuscus, ...			•				Duovir in Pius' reign. (Found in Central Agora)	Pius	K # 189	Latin
87	Gellius, Lucius, L f Justus	•		•			•	Son of Lucius Gellius Menander. Aedile, Duovir and Agonothete during Hadrian's reign. Inscription was dedicated *ob iustitiam* to an anonymous Legatus of Hadrian and Propraetor of Cappadocia, who was possibly also termed a philosopher. The Gellii were a prominent second century Corinthian family. Menander was a Roman citizen of Greek birth, probably Corinthian, or admitted to Corinthian citizenship. (Found in S Basilica, SW Agora and East of Agora).	Hadrian	K # 124 W # 93, 94	Greek
88	Gellius, Lucius, Mysticus	•						Agonothete during Pius' reign. A list of officials and victors at the Isthmian games. The Gellii were a prominent family.	Pius	K # 223	Greek
89	Granius, Quintus, Bassus							Procurator of Achaea, Praefectus Fabrorum. Cf. Tacitus Annals 4.21. Erected *sua pecunia*, in honour of the Corinthian colony. Inscription erected *decurionum decreto*. (Found in S Stoa).	c. AD 20	K # 130, 131	Latin
90	Heius, Caius, Aristo		•	?			•	Freedman. Aedile during Augustus' reign. Duovir in ?14/3 BC, and Quinquennial Duovir in ?9/8 BC. It is unclear where Kent finds evidence for the post of Duovir. Erected by the colonists. Inscription erected *decurionum decreto*. (Found in Agora, North of Bema).	AD 3-15	K # 151	Latin
91	Heius, Caius, Pollio			•				Duovir with C Heius Pamphilus in c. 1 BC - AD 4 (A p 133, 34-31 BC), and with C Mussius Priscus in AD 4/5.	1 BC - AD 4/5	E # 34, 36-39	Latin

Name	agon	q iivir	iivir	cur ann	praef	aed	Additional Information	Date	Ref	Lang
92 Heius, Gaius, Pamphilus	•					•	Agonothete of the Isthmian and Caesarean games in AD 7? Was appointed Duovir twice. Duovir with Q Caecilius Niger in c. 7-4 BC (A p 133, 34-31 BC); and with C Heius Pollio in AD 4/5. Prefect pro Duovir twice, once with P Aebutius Sp f (A p 141, 17/16 BC); (first by decree of council and vote of colony, secondly by command of the emperor Augustus). Possibly a freedman (the cognomen Philinus was largely confined to slaves and freedmen—cf. also no mention of father or tribe); Pamphilus' *cursus honorum* appears to go in reverse order. (Found near Julian Basilica, West of Lechaion Road and SE Agora).	25 BC-AD 10	E # 25-26, 33, 34, K # 150	Latin
93 Insteius, Marcus, C f Tectus		•	•				Duovir and Quinquennial Duovir in 34/33 BC. One of the earliest Duoviri of the colony. Co-commander of Mark Antony's centre line at Actium, Cf. Plutarch Antony 65.1. Duovir with L Cas-... (A p 124, 42 or 41 BC). (Found in the Julian Basilica, NE Agora, beside Lechaion Road).	34/33 BC	E # 18-19, K # 149, 345	Latin
94 Julius, Caius, C f Laco	•	•					Procurator of Claudius in the Imperial system. Augur. Agonothete of the Isthmian and Caesarean games in AD 19? Quinquennial Duovir in AD 17/18? with M Barbatius M f Celer. Associated with the Imperial cult. A distinguished Spartan family but with many connections with Corinth. They probably owed their citizenship to the emperor Augustus, and were held in high acclaim throughout the province of Achaea. (Found in NW shops).	Claudius	W # 67	Latin
95 Julius, Caius, Hera[clanus]		•					Quinquennial Duovir with P Aebutius Sp f ... in AD 7/8? and 12/13? (A p 148, AD 1/2).	AD 7/8?, 12/13?	E # 32	Latin
96 Julius, Caius, Nicephorus			•				Duovir with P Tadius Chilo in 43/42 BC (cf. A p 123).	43/42 BC	E # 17	Latin
97 Julius, Caius, Polyaenus			•				Duovir with Tiberius Claudius Optatus in c. AD 59-66 (A p 24, suggests 57/58 or 58/59).	c. AD 59-66	E # 61-64	Latin

#	Name	agon	q iivir	iivir	cur ann	praef	aed	Additional Information	Date	Ref	Lang
98	Julius, Caius, Severus							Proconsul of Achaea, Legatus of IV Scythica under Trajan. A wealthy Gallo-Greek from Ancyra. Family probably received citizenship under Augustus. Of the tribe Fabia. Very prominent in Galatia. While Severus was resident in Corinth he became patron and curia of the tribe Maneia. Of senatorial rank. (Found in the region of the Lechaion Road).	c. AD 134	K # 126, W # 56, 57	Latin
99	Julius, Caius, ...			●				Duovir in 43/42 BC? with L Aeficius Certus (A p 120, 44/43 BC).	43/42 BC?	E # 16	Latin
100	Juventius, ..., Proclus	●						Agonothete in AD 41?	AD 41?	Syll, 802; CP 1928, 258ff.	Greek
101	Laconis, Caius, Julius f, Spartiaticus	●	●					Procurator, military Tribune, granted equestrian rank by Claudius, son of Laco. Priest. Quinquennial Duovir in AD 47/48? and 52/53? Agonothete in AD 47 of the Isthmian and Caesarean games. A non-Corinthian. Prominent not only in Corinth, but also in Athens. His family had become very prominent in Greece. (Found in S Basilica, on Lechaion Road).	Claudius	M # 70, W # 68	Latin
102	Licinus, ...			●				Duovir with Octavius ... in c. AD 41-46.	c. AD 41-46	E # 50	Latin
103	Maecius, Lucius, Faustinus			●				Duovir, member of Panhellion, orator (ῥήτορα ἀγαθόν), in honour of upright character (καλοκαγαθία). Erected by vote of the city council. (Found in SE Agora, S Stoa and S Basilica).	mid C2 AD	K # 264	Greek
104	Manius, Acilius			●				Duovir with M Barbatius M f Celer in c. AD 19-21. For the problems of provenance and names (Acilius or Accius) see A p 25.	c. AD 19-21	W # 80	Latin

	Name	agon	q iivir	iivir	cur ann	praef	aed	Additional Information	Date	Ref	Lang
105	Manlius, Titus, T f Juvencus	•				•	•	Juvencus was of the tribe Collina. Aedile during Augustus' reign. Praefectus iure dicundo possibly for the emperor Tiberius in AD 32/33 and Duovir in c. 34-37. Pontifex. Agonothete of the Isthmian and Caesarean games in AD 15? First to schedule Caesarean games ahead of Isthmian. The inscription was erected by members of the tribe Agrippia. (Found in S Stoa and NW shops).	AD 32/33?	K # 154, W # 81,86	Latin
106	Maximus, …			•				Duovir in M Aurelius' reign. (Found in SW Agora).	Aurelius	K # 191	Latin
107	Memmius, Publius, Cleander		•					Quinquennial Duovir with L Rutilius Piso in AD 67/68 (A p 24, suggests 66/67). (Found East of Agora).	AD 67/68	BMC Cor # 569-571, W # 169	Latin
108	Memmius, Publius, Regulus		•					Propraetor of Achaea from AD 35-44, *Sodalis Augustalis*. The governor of Moesia, Macedonia and Achaea under Tiberius, Caligula and Claudius. Many inscriptions have been found to him throughout Achaea, which suggests great popularity. (Found in propylaea).	AD 35 - 44	W # 53	Latin
109	Munatius, Lucius, Gallus			•				Proconsul of Achaea in c. AD 98/99. (Found in S Basilica).	c. AD 98/99	K # 122	Latin
110	Mussius, Caius, Priscus		•					Duovir with C Heius Pollio in AD 4/5.	AD 4/5	E # 36-39, A p 151	Latin
111	Novius, Marcus, Bassus			•				Duovir with M Antonius Hipparchus (A p 142, 10/9 - 5/4 BC).	27-18 BC	E # 30-31	Latin
112	Octavius, …			•				Duovir in c. AD 41-46 twice; once with … Licinus.	c. AD 41-46	E # 50	Latin

Name	agon	q iivir	iivir	cur ann	praef	aed	Additional Information	Date	Ref	Lang
113 Olius, Sextus, Secundus	•	•	•			•	Of the tribe Aemilia. Praefectus Fabrorum, Theocolus of Jupiter Capitolinus, an outstanding citizen of the colony; granted the *ornamenta* of Aedile, Duovir and Quinquennial Duovir and Agonothete during Augustus' reign. Of the tribe Aemilia. Inscription erected *decurionum decreto*. This inscription dates more accurately the return of the Isthmian games from Sicyon to Corinth—between the years 7 BC - AD 3. (Found in SE area of Agora).	Augustus	K # 152	Latin
114 Orfidius, Caius, Benignus Juventianus							Theocolus of Jupiter Capitolinus, priest. Cf. Tacitus, Historia 2.43; Plutarch, Otho 12.4—Legatus of first legion Adiutrix under Otho. Slain in battle at Bedriacum in AD 69. Of senatorial rank. (Found in SE Agora).	AD 69	K # 196	Latin
115 Paccianus, ...	•						Agonothete of the Isthmian games in AD 137. (Found near Gymnasium).	AD 137	M # 15	Greek
116 Paconius, Lucius, Flam[ininus?]			•				Duovir with Cn Publicius Regulus in AD 50/51.	AD 50/51	E # 51-53	Latin
117 Pacuvius, Marcus, ...		•	•			•	Of the tribe Aemilia. Was granted the *ornamenta* of Aedile, Duovir and Duovir Quinquennalis during the reign of Hadrian. (Found in SW Agora and S Stoa).	Hadrian ?	K # 175	Latin
118 Papius, Lucius, L f Lupercus	•	•	•			•	Of the tribe Falerna, was granted the *ornamenta* of Aedile during Tiberius' reign, Duovir, Agonothete during Trajan's reign? and Duovir Quinquennalis. Inscription erected *decurionum decreto*. The extensive list of *ornamenta* suggests he was a very generous benefactor. The tribe Falerna was not a Corinthian tribe which probably means Lupercus was a non-Corinthian and might explain why he was granted *ornamenta* of these posts. (Found North of Propylaea).	Trajan ?	W # 105	Latin

Name	agon	q iivir	iivir	cur ann	praef	aed	Additional Information	Date	Ref	Lang
119 Papius, Lucius, Venereus	•						Of the tribe Aemilia. Isagogeus to Tiberius Claudius Anaxilaus, Pyrophorus of the Isthmian sanctuary, Coagonothete with L. Vibullius Pius during Domitian's reign in the Isthmian games, victor at Nemean games, priest of Mars Augustus. A sort of priestly *cursus honorum*. (Found in the Hellenistic Stoa South of Temple Hill, SE Agora).	AD 90	K # 212	Latin
120 Philerus							Freedman, Procurator of the vicesium hereditatium of Achaea, treasurer (tabularius) of Emperor and province. Inscription erected *decurionum decreto*. Dedicated to the genius of the emperor. (Found in floor of Bouleuterion and S Stoa).	mid C3 AD	K # 67	Latin
121 Pinnius, Caius, ...			•				Duovir with P Aebutius ... in ? 37/36 BC.	37/36 BC?	E # 20-21	Latin
122 Polyaena							Priestess of victory, highly accorded, set up by Archiereus Publius Licinus Priscus Iuventianus. Inscription erected *decurionum decreto*.	mid C2 AD	K # 199	Latin
123 Polyaenus, Tiberius, ...			•				Duovir with ... Sosthenes in Trajan's reign. The two Duoviri erected the monument together to an anonymous person using public money at the decree of the decuriones. (Found North of Theatre).	Trajan ?	K # 165	Latin
124 Pontius, Memmius, Ptolemaius							*Vir clarissimus*, patron of Corinth, also named Parnasius. A Parnasius, native of Patras, served in Egypt. Set up by Aurelius Eutychianus, an ex-Praetor and possibly also Consul, with the approval of the city council. (Found in front of the W Shops).	AD 357	K # 502	Greek
125 Poseidonius							Priest, rhetor, helladarch (maybe the obscure author mentioned by Athenaeus 1.13.b).	end C2 AD	K # 307	Greek

Name	agon	q iivir	iivir	cur ann	praef	aed	Additional Information	Date	Ref	Lang
126 Prifernius, Titus, Paetus							Military Tribune of Legion X Fretensis, Prefect of cohort I Miliaria, Prefect of squadron II Flavia, honoured with military gifts by Trajan, imperial Procurator of Achaea. (Cf duplicate inscription at Argos). Of the tribe Quirinus. Erected by M Antonius Achaicus *sua pecunia*.	c. AD 102-114	K # 134	Latin
127 Priscus, P Licinius, Juventianus						●	Probably a High Priest in the imperial cult, a liberal benefactor of Isthmian sanctuary (φιλοτιμία). Aedile during M Aurelius' reign. Cf. election promises, K # 300—1 denarius given to the citizens, free accommodation for athletes during the games. Dedicated to Polyaena, priestess of victory. Inscription erected *decurionum decreto*. He was possibly the Lucanius referred to by Plutarch in Quaest. Conviv. 5.3.1—an Archiereus who entertained Plutarch at Corinth. (Found in S Stoa).	mid C2 AD	K # 199-201, 306, W # 70	Latin
128 Ptolemaios							Advocatus fisci (a post created by Hadrian). To an anonymous friend who was also the Procurator of Achaea. (Found in S Basilica, S Stoa and SE Agora).	Hadrian	K # 146	Greek
129 Pu-, M	●						Of the tribe Aemilia. Isagogeus of the Caesarea Neronea. Agonothete in AD 59? when Rufus was Agonothete. (Found in SE Agora).	AD 59?	K # 208	Latin
130 Publicius, Gnaeus, M f Rusticus	●	●	●				Of the tribe Aemilia. Granted the *ornamenta* of Duovir, Quinquennial Duovir, and the *ornamenta* of Agonothete during Hadrian's reign. Son and daughter in law (who was from the Babbius family, also very prominent) erected the monument. Inscription erected *decurionum decreto*. Publicii were probably very prominent in Corinth. (Found in S Stoa).	Hadrian ?	K # 176	Latin
131 Publicius, Gnaeus, Regulus			●				Duovir with L Paconius Flamininus in AD 50/51.	AD 50/51	E # 51-53	Latin

Name	agon	q iivir	iivir	cur ann	praef	aed	Additional Information	Date	Ref	Lang
132 Publicius, Gnaeus, ...		•					Quinquennial Duovir with M Antonius Orestes in 19/18 BC (A p 41, 40 BC). Amandry gives him the final name 'Regulus', p. 12.	19/18 BC	E # 27	Latin
133 Pulcher, -alenus			•		•	•	Prefect in Hadrian's reign and Duovir in Pius' reign. (Found in S Basilica and S Stoa).	Hadrian and Pius	K # 187	Latin
134 Pulcher, Cornelius	•						Agonothete of the Isthmia and the Caesarea Sebastea in AD 43. (Found in SE Agora).	AD 43	K # 173	Latin
135 Puticius, Publicius, Rufus							Isagogeus to Agonothete M Pu- in ?AD 59. (Found in SE Agora).	? AD 59.	K # 208-209	Latin
136 Puticius, Publius, M f Jullus			•				Of the tribe of Aemilia or Fabia (Fabia was a Corinthian tribe). Granted ornamenta of Aedile and of Duovir during the reign of Trajan. Inscription erected decurionum decreto. (Found in Peribolos of Apollo).	Trajan ?	W # 106	Latin
137 Rutilius, Lucius, L f Fuscus	•						Of the tribe Aemilia. Isagogeus of the Tiberea Claudia Caesarea Sebasteion to his father, L Rutilius. Agonothete in AD 51 of the Isthmian games. The Rutilii were an important family in Corinth. (Found in East side of Lechaion road and W Shops).	AD 51	W # 82, 84	Latin
138 Rutilius, Lucius, Piso		•					Quinquennial Duovir with P Memmius Cleander in AD 67/68 (A p 24, suggests 66/67).	AD 67/68	BMC Cor # 569-571	Latin
139 Rutilius, Lucius, Plancus			•				Duovir with A Vatronius Labeo in AD 39/40 (A p 156, AD 12/13 - 15/16).	AD 39/40	E # 43-46	Latin
140 Secundius, Caius, Dinippus	•						Agonothete in AD 3.	AD 3	SEG XII, 61, 6-7	Greek
141 Secundus							Imperial freedman who erected a statue of Hygeia. (Found West of Odeion).	Early C2	K # 64	Greek
142 Servilius, Caius, C f Primus			•				Duovir with M Antonius Hipparchus in c. 28-19 BC (A p 144, 2/1 BC). Cf Plutarch Ant 67.6.	28-19 BC	E # 28-29	Latin

Name	agon	q iivir	iivir	cur ann	praef	aed	Additional Information	Date	Ref	Lang
143 Sospes, Antonius	•		•	•			Quaestor. Military Tribune of Legion III Augusta. Curator annonae. Commander of Legion II Adiutrix. Agonothete. Duovir in Trajan's reign. Cf Plutarch Quaest Conv 8.4.1-4; 9.5.1-2. Agonothete three times (Trajan's and Hadrian's reign). Inscription 170 in Latin; inscription 226 in Greek. (Found in Peirene, Peribolos of Apollo, beside Temple A, SE Agora, Shops East of Lechaion Road, NE Agora).	Trajan and Hadrian	K # 170, 226	Latin Greek
144 Sosthenes, …			•				Duovir with Tiberius … Polyaenus in Trajan's reign? The two Duoviri erected the monument together to an anonymous person using public money at the decree of the Decuriones. (Found North of the Theatre).	Trajan ?	K # 165	Latin
145 Tadius, Publius, Chilo			•				Duovir with C Julius Nicephorus in 43/42 BC, cf. A p 33, 123.	43/42 BC	E # 17	Latin
146 Tiberius, Gnaeus, Cornelius, f Pulcher	•	•		•	•		Son of Tiberius Cornelius Pulcher of the tribe of Fabia and perhaps a native of Epidauros where he served as Agonothete of the Asklepiaia. Gnaeus Cornelius Pulcher possibly made Corinth his home and certainly was a patron of the city. Praefectus iure dicundo in Trajan's reign. Curator annonae. Duovir Quinquennalis in Hadrian's reign. Agonothete of the Trajanea and Isthmian games. Military Tribune of Legio IV Scythica, Procurator of Epirus, Iuridicus of Egypt and Alexandria, Helladarch of Achaean league, priest of Hadrian Panhellenius and Panhellenic Archon. He provided Ateleia which was freedom from taxation—it could be that he was honoured for this reason. In M # 76 the agonothesia appears before the duovirate. (Found in the Julian Basilica, central area of Agora, South of the Bema, North of the Peribolos of Apollo, beside the Lechaion Road, SE Agora, E Agora, SW Basilica, Propylaea).	Trajan and Hadrian	K # 138-143, M # 76, 80-83, W # 71	Greek Latin

Name	agon	q iivir	iivir	cur ann	praef	aed	Additional Information	Date	Ref	Lang
147 Valerianus, Claudius, ...						•	Possible granted the *ornamenta* of Aedile. (Found in the NW Shops, Agora South of the Bema).		K # 244	Latin
148 Valerius, Marcus, Taurinus							Philosopher, good orator, fine character (ἀγαθός, ἀρετή). Inscription erected *decurionum decreto*. (Found in SE Agora, S Basilica, and S Stoa).	late C2	K # 268	Greek
149 Vatronius, A, Labeo			•				Duovir with L Rutilius Plancus in AD 39/40 (A p 156, AD 12/13 - 15/16).	AD 39/40	E # 43-46	Latin
150 Ventidius, Publius, Fronto			•				Duovir with Tiberius Claudius Anaxilaus in AD 55/56? (A p 24, suggests 67/68).	AD 55/56?	E # 54-55	Latin
151 Vibius, Gaius, Euelpistus							Physician, priest of Asklepios. Honoured by the city of Corinth. (Found West of Asklepieion).	end C2 AD	K # 206	Greek
152 Vibullius, Lucius, Pius	•						Was Coagonothete with L Papius Venereus during Domitian's reign in the Isthmian games. Priest of Mars Augusta which was linked with an Imperial cult. (Found in SE Agora and the Hellenistic Stoa of Temple hill).	Domitian	K # 212, W # 95	
153 Vipsanius, Publius, Agrippa			•				Duovir with M Bellius Proculus in AD 38/39 (A p 181, AD 37/38).	AD 38/39	E # 47-49	Latin
154 ..., Caius ...	•						Dedication by one of the Corinthian tribes. Agonothete of the Caearean Vespasanean Sebasteon and the Isthmian and Caesarean games. (Found in S Basilica and S Stoa).	Vespasian	K # 210	Latin
155 ..., Cocceius							Quaestor. Apparently an early inscription from the colony. Possibly L Cocceius Nerva, special envoy in 37 BC, cf. Horace, Sat, 1.5.27; Appian BC, 5.60. (Found in the S Central area of the Agora).	?39 BC	K # 119	Latin
156 ..., Delm					•		Decurion and Praefect. A bilingual inscription. A dedication made at the cost of 2,000 sesterces in the will of a freedwoman, Theodora. (Found at village of Solomo).		K # 276	Latin Greek

Name	agon	q iivir	iivir	cur ann	praef	aed	Additional Information	Date	Ref	Lang
157 ..., Lucius	•	•	•			•	Of the tribe Aemilia. Imperial Quaestor, and granted the *ornamenta* of Aedile, Duovir, Duovir Quinquennalis and Agonothete. Inscription erected *decurionum decreto*. (Found in Central S Stoa).		K # 168	Latin
158 ..., Q C- ...	•						Agonothete of the Isthmian and Caearean games during Hadrian's reign. Possibly of the tribe Vatinia. (Found in S Basilica and S Stoa).	Hadrian	K # 222	Latin
159 ..., ..., Cornelius	•						Most worthy, most excellent (κράτιστον suggests equestrian rank). Agonothete during Gordian's reign of the Caesarean and Augustan games, and the Asklepieia, the Isthmian and the Caesarean games. (Found in SE Agora).	Gordian	K # 230	Greek
160 ..., ..., Hicesius						•	Founded the theatre at own expense. Aedile during the reign of Augustus). Inscription erected *decurionum decreto*. (Found at Theatre).	Augustus	K # 231	Latin

THE GOOD AND THE JUST IN THE CITY AND ROMANS 5.7

1. *Introduction*

In Romans 5.6-8 Paul contrasts the greatest acts of human heroism on behalf of a good or righteous man with the far greater act of self-sacrifice which was made by Jesus Christ on behalf of us sinners. The thrust of Paul's argument highlights God's action in his Son. So clear is this thrust that a number of commentators have tended to skip over the possible difficulties of verse 7, to concentrate on the impact of verses 6 and 8.[2]

In fact, the argument of verse 7 has appeared to many somewhat incongruous, and has led interpreters to adopt a number of quite different stances. The verse can be divided into two clauses—7a, "for scarcely will anyone die for a δίκαιος" and 7b, "though for ὁ ἀγαθός someone might possibly dare to die".

2. *Romans 5.7 in Recent Interpretation*

The main problem in this verse has been determining whether a contrast is being drawn between δίκαιος and ὁ ἀγαθός, or whether, in essence, these two nouns are synonymous. There are six principal lines of interpretation commonly adopted.

The majority of commentators argue that the nouns are essentially synonymous, with some arguing for complete identity between the two types of people.[3] Thus verse 7b simply allows for the outside possibility that such a sacrificial act of heroism might just happen. In this sense, we may paraphrase

---

[1]   An earlier version of this paper appeared as Andrew D. Clarke, 'The Good and the Just in Romans 5:7', *Tyndale Bulletin* 41 (1990), 128-142.

[2]   Y. Landau, 'Martyrdom in Paul's Religious Ethics: An Exegetical Commentary on Romans 5.7', *Immanuel* 15 (1982-83), 25, points out that since the intended comparison in vv. 6-8 is clear, the exegetical difficulties of v. 7 are often overlooked. W.G. Kümmel, *Exegetical Method: A Student Handbook* (ET: New York, 1981), 63, suggests that no real certainty regarding the meaning of Romans 5.7, despite it being the *crux interpretum,* can be attained; F.F. Bruce, *The Letter of Paul to the Romans* (Leicester, 1985), 117, offers little discussion of the clause concerning δίκαιος. C.K. Barrett, *The Epistle to the Romans* (London, 1984), 106, suggests that the details of v. 7 are insignificant, and moves quickly on to v. 8.

[3]   Amongst these are some of the older commentators, including Calvin. More recently H.A.W. Meyer, *Critical and Exegetical Handbook to the Epistle to the Romans* (ET: Edinburgh, 1879), 232; F.F. Bruce, *The Letter of Paul to the Romans,* 117, who suggests that there is really very little distinction in this passage between the two qualities; and J. Murray, *The Epistle to the Romans* I (Grand Rapids, 1959), 167-8, who goes so far as to argue that the same person is being characterized here as possessing the qualities of both justice and goodness.

Paul: "Rarely will anyone die for a just or good man, although someone may possibly do it".

A modification of this view suggests a distinction in meaning between δίκαιος and ὁ ἀγαθός. The latter is a stronger description. A 'just' man would describe the person who, before the letter of the law, is unimpeachable. Although such a person may well be admirable, he is somewhat without compassion. It is the person who is 'good' that attracts more sentiment. One who is ἀγαθός is prepared to go beyond the call of duty, and is, therefore, a more compelling cause for heroism.[4] Paul makes a valid point at the outset, and modifies it later with a slight concession. In this sense, he might be saying: "No one is really prepared to die for the man who is merely law-abiding; although it does occasionally happen that a man might lay down his life for the kind and generous friend". One clear argument for this stance has been put forward by Landau who suggests that the,

> pre-Christian ideal of righteousness, especially proclaimed by the Pharisaic opponents of Paul's embryonic religion, is rejected by the apostle along with any attachment to the outmoded Law which dispensed death. Any man who claimed to be righteous according to the old, Judaic standard was, in Paul's post-conversion view, a deluded moralist at best, and a hypocritical legalist at worst. This unflattering image would not evoke great sympathy, much less heroic altruism, on the part of another who might be in a position to sacrifice his life for this dikaios.[5]

A third position, which is also common, is to suggest that Paul, having made the statement in verse 7a, immediately realises that it is both rash and untrue. His reaction is to withdraw it hastily, although somewhat clumsily, with a correction in the second part of the verse.[6] On this reading, no particular

---

[4]   Cf. C.H. Dodd, *The Epistle of Paul to the Romans* (London, 1947), 75; L. Morris, *The Epistle to the Romans* (Leicester, 1988), 223-4; F.J. Leenhardt, *L'Épître de Saint Paul aux Romains* (Geneva, 1981), 79 n.5; W. Sanday & A.C. Headlam, *A Critical and Exegetical Commentary on the Epistle to the Romans* (Edinburgh, 1920), 128; J.B. Lightfoot, *Notes on Epistles of St Paul from Unpublished Commentaries* (London, 1904), 287; E.H. Gifford, *The Epistle of St. Paul to the Romans* (London, 1886), 113; J.A. Ziesler, *The Meaning of Righteousness in Paul: A linguistic and theological enquiry* (Cambridge, 1972), 197; and H. Cremer, *Biblico-Theological Lexicon of New Testament Greek* (ET: Edinburgh, 1883), 3.

[5]   Y. Landau, 'Martyrdom in Paul's Religious Ethics: An Exegetical Commentary on Romans 5.7', 31. *Agathos* is contrastingly seen as a "more human, generally attainable and respectable virtue than the more lofty and suspect ideal of 'Judaic' righteousness", *idem,* 33.

[6]   Cf. F.J. Leenhardt, *The Epistle to the Romans* (ET: London, 1961), 136; H. Lietzmann, *Einführung in die Textgeschichte der Paulusbriefe an die Römer* (Tübingen, 1983), 59; M.-J. Lagrange, *Saint Paul Épître aux Romains* (Paris, 1950), 103; H. Schlier, *Der Römerbrief* (Freiburg, Basel, Wien, 1977), 153; O. Kuss, *Der Römerbrief* (Regensburg, 1963); U. Wilckens, *Der Brief an die Römer* I (Zürich, 1978). E. Käsemann, *Commentary on Romans* (ET: Grand Rapids, 1980), 137, comments on v. 7b, "the apostle remembers that sacrificial deaths are common enough. He thus concedes quite tortuously this possibility as regards the good"; and C.K. Barrett, *The Epistle to the Romans,* 105, offers the possibility that Paul intended to retract his initial, inappropriate comment and replace it with the second clause. His *amanuensis,* Tertius (Rom. 16.22), however, failed to delete the first statement, and thus it remains. A modification of this general stance is taken by G. Bornkamm, 'Paulinische Anakoluthe im Römerbrief', in *Das Ende des Gesetzes* (München, 1966), 78, where Rom 5.6-8 is taken to be "einen mühsamen Versuch des Paulus, der Sprache die zutreffende Formulierung seines Gedankens abzuzwingen".

distinction in meaning between δίκαιος and ἀγαθός is supported. Quite simply, Paul has made a considerable overstatement, which he immediately retracts.

A fourth possible interpretation relies on the suggestion that the article preceding ἀγαθός provides a deliberate distinction from the anarthrous δίκαιος. τοῦ ἀγαθοῦ is taken to be neuter—"the good cause"—where δίκαιος is still understood as a masculine noun, "a just man". In this case, it is argued that it is extremely rare that anyone might die simply on behalf of another fellow human-being, but it is more common to witness someone consumed by a good cause to such an extent that he is prepared to lay down his life for it.[7]

A fifth line of interpretation, but recently much less common, must be mentioned. Cranfield, maintaining that τοῦ ἀγαθοῦ is masculine, argues that it may be taken in a quite different sense from the general "a good man". It deliberately refers to a more specific "the good man", namely one's benefactor. After a discussion of other possible interpretations, Cranfield finally offers this solution, but it is neither expanded nor substantiated in much detail.[8]

---

[7] A major exponent of this view is F. Godet, *Commentary on St. Paul's Epistle to the Romans* I (Edinburgh, 1895), 327. The neuter is firmly denied by many commentators including M.-J. Lagrange, *Saint Paul Épître aux Romains*, 103; R.C.H. Lenski, *The Interpretation of St. Paul's Epistle to the Romans* (Columbus, 1936), 351; and E. Käsemann, *Commentary on Romans*, 137. The principal objection to this reading is that the surrounding context entirely concerns people (cf. ἀσθενῶν, ἀσεβῶν v. 6, and ἁμαρτωλῶν v. 8), and the introduction of an impersonal cause at this point is unnatural, cf. F. Wisse, 'The Righteous Man and the Good Man in Romans V.7', *NTS* 19 (1972-3), 92. C.E.B. Cranfield, *A Critical and Exegetical Commentary on the Epistle of Paul to the Romans* I (Edinburgh, 1979), 264, argues that if the neuter is intended in the second clause, then it is a serious understatement, bearing in mind the considerable numbers who had died in battle for their country. C.F.D. Moule, *An Idiom Book of New Testament Greek* (Cambridge, 1959), 111, argues that the article is not demonstrative but deictic (pointing to some familiar type or genus); cf. also A.T. Robertson, *Grammar of the Greek New Testament in the Light of Historical Research* (Nashville, 1923), 763, a generic article.

[8] A similar suggestion was made by F.A.G. Tholuck, *Exposition of St. Paul's epistle to the Romans* I (Edinburgh, 1833), 262, "Perhaps also the article before ἀγαθός is here significant, and stands for the pronoun, quasi, *his* benefactor". (This interpretation of the use of the article is commonly adopted by those who see ἀγαθός as a reference to one's benefactor). See also O. Michel, *Der Brief an die Römer* (Göttingen, 1978), 182. J.A. Ziesler, *Paul's Letter to the Romans* (London, 1989), 140-1, hesitates between the two possibilities of 'the good cause' (neuter), or 'the benefactor' (masculine). Cranfield is followed by B.W. Winter, 'The Public Honouring of Christian Benefactors, Romans 13.3-4 and 1 Peter 2.14-15', *JSNT* 34 (1988), 93. Quoted by a number of commentators (including C.E.B. Cranfield, *A Critical and Exegetical Commentary on the Epistle of Paul to the Romans* I, 265, O. Michel, *op. cit.*, 181 n. 20, and J.D.G. Dunn, *Romans 1-8* (Dallas, 1988), 256), is the papyrological excerpt brought to light by A. Deissmann, *Light from the Ancient East* (ET: London, 1927), 118, Herculaneum Vita Philonidis 1044, "[For] (?) the most beloved of his relatives or friends he would readily stake his neck". It is interesting to note that this interpretation of the ἀγαθός as one's benefactor received much greater support in the last century and earlier part of this century. Further commentators adopting a similar stance who have not been widely referred to should be brought to light at this point. D.J.G. Rosenmüller, *Scholia in Novum Testamentum* III (Norimberg, 1829), 605, suggests that δίκαιος here carries the sense of *bonus*, and ἀγαθός carries the sense of *vir beneficus*. His paraphrase of Rom 5.7b is, *Pro viro benefico (qui magnis nos ornavit beneficiis) forsitan quis animum induxerit oppetere mortem*. F.A. Philippi, *Commentary on St Paul's Epistle to the Romans* (ET: Edinburgh, 1878), 240-243, who has a careful discussion of the classical usage of ἀγαθός and δίκαιος, from which is drawn the conclu-

Finally, there is the group of commentators who solve the anomalies by suggesting textual emendations, variations or glosses.[9]

There are thus six principal interpretations of the relationship between δίκαιος and ἀγαθός in Romans 5.7: (i) there is no intended distinction between δίκαιος and ἀγαθός. Rare occurrences of personal self-sacrifice on behalf of the good and righteous man are possible; (ii) ἀγαθός is a stronger term than δίκαιος, and it depicts a warmer and more genial character than the merely law-abiding citizen; (iii) the two terms are virtually synonymous; Paul has overstated his case, and retracts it in verse 7b; (iv) τοῦ ἀγαθοῦ is taken in the neuter sense of a "good cause"—a more compelling ground for self-sacrifice than to die on behalf of a fellow human-being; (v) τοῦ ἀγαθοῦ is taken in the technical sense of a patron or benefactor to whom one has greater obligations; and (vi) the text of Romans 5.7 is in some way not original.

---

sion that there is some gradation in sense between the two terms, Philippi suggests, "Thus, doubtless, ὁ ἀγαθός comes very near to the meaning of ὁ εὐεργέτης, yet without quite coinciding with it; ὁ εὐεργέτης, implying more another's relation to myself in respect of conduct; ὁ ἀγαθός, more a description of another's character in itself". H.A.W. Meyer, *Critical and Exegetical Handbook to the Epistle to the Romans*, 232-235, although disagreeing with the association with the benefactor, offers a long list of commentators who do adopt this position. In a later edition of the Meyer series, B. Weiß, *Kritisch exegetisches Handbuch über den Brief des Paulus an die Römer* (Göttingen, 1886), 248, suggests the possibility of the benefactor is not ruled out of account entirely. P.C. Boylan, *St. Paul's Epistle to the Romans* (Dublin, 1934), 79, "As the context speaks of persons rather than of things, it is better to take δικαίου and ἀγαθοῦ as masculines—meaning a just man, and a benefactor respectively. The article in τοῦ ἀγαθοῦ is practically equivalent to 'his'. One will scarcely die for a just man, though, possibly, a man may decide to die for his benefactor". Also A. Nygren, *Commentary on Romans* (ET: London, 1952), 200 f., "Paul does not deny that human love may lead one to die for another. But it would require a strong motivation. ... One would be most likely to make the sacrifice for a relative or a benefactor. But for whom did Christ lay down his life? Not for benefactors, but for enemies; not for the righteous, but for sinners and the ungodly. This is truly 'unmotivated' love".

[9]   Cf. L.E. Keck, 'The Post-Pauline Interpretation of Jesus' Death in Rom 5,6-7', in edd. C. Andresen & G. Klein, *Theologica Crucis—Signum Crucis, Festschrift für Erich Dinkler* (Tübingen, 1979), 237-248, who argues that the cumulative evidence of the text-critical problems of Rom 5.6; the apparent redundance of vv. 6-7 if retracted from the paragraph; and the repetition of the content of v. 6 in v. 8 suggest that we are dealing here with a post-Pauline addition to the text. H. Sahlin, 'Einige Textemendationen zum Römerbrief', *Theologische Zeitschrift* 9 (1953), 96 f., argues that there is the fumbled correction of a copyist's mistake; v. 7 is a secondary addition containing two apparently contradictory glosses. Cf. also W. Schmithals, *Der Römerbrief, Ein Kommentar* (Gütersloh, 1988), 198-9, and A. Jülicher, *Der Brief an die Römer* II (Göttingen, 1917), who are cited and refuted by Käsemann and Dunn. Jülicher's argument that the gloss was added in order to take account of Christian martyrs is adopted by J.C. O'Neill, *Paul's Letter to the Romans* (Harmondsworth, 1975), 94. We may also note here the lack of textual support for v. 7 amongst some of the Fathers. J.S. Semler, *Paraphrasis epistolae ad Romanos* (Magdeburg, 1769), 57, U. Wilckens, *Der Brief an die Römer* I, 295 n. 975, and J.D.G. Dunn, *Romans 1-8*, 245, notice the omission of the verse in Irenaeus. Semler concludes this to be suggestive that the verse was not originally Pauline; but it may simply be that only 5.6, 8-10 served the writer's purpose. Marcion also appears not to refer to this verse, although it would seem that it might suit his thesis of the good and the just Gods admirably, cf. A. von Harnack, *Marcion: Das Evangelium vom fremden Gott* (Leipzig, 1924), 105. The possible gnostic link was pointed out by W. Sanday and A.C. Headlam, *A Critical and Exegetical Commentary on the Epistle to the Romans*, 128, and A. Pallis, *To the Romans* (Liverpool, 1920), 77.

To clarify the relationship between the two nouns, a number of questions must be asked. Godet has perceptively articulated these. Why does Paul substitute ὁ ἀγαθός for δίκαιος in the second half of the verse? Why is there a distinction between the two nouns in the presence or absence of the article? Why is τοῦ ἀγαθοῦ placed first in the second clause, thus creating a marked contrast?[10] Why does Paul use καὶ in verse 7b, implying some gradation?[11]

From a syntactical point of view, these are objections to the interpretation that the nouns are approximately synonymous. It may also be noted that a number of commentators affirm a distinction in meaning in Greek literature between ἀγαθός and δίκαιος.[12]

It is almost universally accepted that Paul is using a secular analogy in Romans 5.7.[13] For this reason, it is the normal secular usage of the two nouns which should be addressed.[14]

3. Ἀγαθός and Δίκαιος in Classical and Hellenistic Greek

Although it may be noted that these two nouns are normally thought of as qualities which go together to describe a person, often a ruler, this merely shows that the two qualities are commended and not necessarily incompatible.[15] Liddell and Scott shows that δίκαιος is understood as observant of custom or rule, and of duty to the gods. In many contexts, ἀγαθός is seen more as a comment on social standing. The first meaning given is that of well-born, and the fourth meaning is closer to our idea of 'good' in its moral sense.

In a study of traditional Greek values, Adkins demonstrates the development of the word ἀγαθός.[16] It was amongst the most valued words of praise that could be attributed to a man in Greek society from Homeric days

---

[10] Cf. also F.A.G. Tholuck, *Exposition of St. Paul's epistle to the Romans* I (Edinburgh, 1833), 258.

[11] F. Godet, *Commentary on St. Paul's Epistle to the Romans* I, 325.

[12] Cf. F.A.G. Tholuck, *Exposition of St. Paul's epistle to the Romans* I, 258; J.B. Lightfoot, *Notes on Epistles of St Paul*, 286-7; and E.H. Gifford, *The Epistle of St. Paul to the Romans*, 123.

[13] We may contrast Paul's 'theological' use of ἀγαθός in Romans 7.18-19. In Romans 5.7, he is simply talking of what is commonly recognised in Graeco-Roman society as good.

[14] Cf. E. Käsemann, *Perspectives on Paul* (ET: London, 1971), 45. J.D.G. Dunn, *Romans 1-8*, 256, follows Wilckens in pointing out that Paul does not use ἀγαθός in this sense anywhere else. For further discussion of Paul's use of analogy see H.M. Gale, *The Use of Analogy in the Letters of Paul* (Philadelphia, 1964), esp. 175-7, 223-31.

[15] Cf. Dio, *Orationes* 1.16, "For it is impossible that the δίκαιος and ἀγαθός han'jr should repose greater confidence in any other being than in the δίκαιοι and ἄριστοι—the gods"; 32.26, "Among these over-lords, then, are included kings ... real guardians and χρηστοὶ and δίκαιοι leaders of the people, gladly dispensing the ἀγαθά ..."

[16] A.W.H. Adkins, *Merit and Responsibility, A Study in Greek Values* (Oxford, 1960); *Moral Values and Political Behaviour in Ancient Greece, From Homer to the End of the Fifth Century* (London, 1972).

onwards.[17] It described one who was valued because he was of considerable benefit to his immediate society.[18] At one time, this was the person who was heroic and successful in war, through his courage and physical abilities.[19] He was considered ἀγαθός because he could offer valuable protection to his family and dependants. Thus it was the ἀγαθός man who, by virtue of his wealth, possessed armour and therefore could offer protection to his city. ἀγαθός thus became associated with the possession of wealth.

Later, the "good man" was so-called because of his value to the city in the political realm. By virtue of his wealth he could afford the leisure to become involved in the political life of his city. ἀγαθός, in time, denoted a particular social class, namely the wealthy and ruling élite. We may note a similar distinction between a moral quality and a social class definition in our English words 'gentle' (gentleman), and 'noble' (nobleman, nobility).[20] ἀγαθός particularly carried this sense of social class when combined in the phrase καλός κἀγαθός.[21]

It is significant also for the present context that ἀγαθός, as a social qualification, took precedence over some of the other moral values, such as, for example, δικαιοσύνη. Adkins writes,

> To be agathos had always been more important than merely to be dikaios, and one's injustice did not traditionally ... impair one's arete. Again, to be agathos

---

[17] Adkins, *Merit and Responsibility*, 30-1.

[18] Cf. J. Gerlach, ΑΝΗΡ ΑΓΑΘΟΣ, doctoral dissertation Ludwig-Maximilians-Universität (München, 1932), 14, "ἀγαθός, vom Manne gesagt, ist in der Sprache der Inschriften nirgends weder an irgeneinem Ort noch zu irgendeiner Zeit ein individualethischer Begriff zur Bezeichnung immanenter Qualitäten, immer ist es vielmehr die Anerkennung des Staates oder einer Gemeinschaft für wertvolle Leistungen im Interesse der Gemeinschaft. Die Verdienste selbst mögen verschiedenster Art sein, immer ist es der Staat, der seinen Wohltäter durch Zuerkennung jener Bezeichnung ehrt. Wertendes Subjekt ist also die Gemeinschaft, bewertetes Objekt sind die Leistungen (einzelne oder mehrere), die Relation der Wertung ist ebenfalls die Gemeinschaft".

[19] Cf. Liddell and Scott, sv ἀγαθός, where the meaning is given of 'brave' and 'valiant' "since courage was attributed to chiefs and nobles"; also the sense of 'good' and 'capable' with reference to abilities. P.J. Rhodes, *The Greek City States, A source book* (London, 1986), 19, refers to Aristotle, *Politics,* 4.10.10, "The earliest constitution among the Greeks, after the kingships, consisted of those who were actually soldiers, the original form consisting of the cavalry (for war had its strength and its pre-eminence in cavalry, since without orderly formation heavy-armed infantry is useless, and the sciences and systems dealing with tactics did not exist among the men of old times, so that their strength lay in their cavalry)".

[20] Cf. 'gentle' and 'noble' in the *OED*.

[21] For ἀγαθός as a description of the propertied classes see also A.W. Gomme, 'The Interpretation of ΚΑΛΟΙ ΚΑΓΑΘΟΙ in Thucydides 4.40.2', *Classical Quarterly* 47, ns. 3 (1953), 65-8, who suggests that the term was very flattering, and normally appropriated to themselves by the upper classes—used by the well-to-do of themselves, and not necessarily used by others to describe the well-to-do. G.E.M. de Ste. Croix, 'Additional note on KALOS, KALOKAGATHIA', *The Origins of the Peloponnesian War* (London, 1972), 371-6, draws similar conclusions. The original meaning of the phrase was of denoting excellence and distinction; he then points out, "Then, in the late fifth century and the fourth, while the expression *kalos kagathos* continues to be used on occasion as a general term of commendation, two specialized uses become prominent: one essentially social-political, which develops first and can be seen clearly in Aristophanes and Thucydides, and the other primarily moral, emerging rather later, from Xenophon onwards—it is often thought to be largely a product of the Socratic circles".

was to be a specimen of the human being at his best, making to society the contribution that society valued most; and the poorer citizens could not deny this, nor yet that they were not agathoi themselves. In accepting arete as more important than dikaiosune they were of course not letting their hearts run away with their heads, but treating the well-being of the city as more important than the injustice of an individual: a calculation of advantages.[22]

Thus, in certain contexts, the primary meaning of ἀγαθός was a technical description for the wealthy upper classes, and, in these instances, it did not carry strong moral overtones. It would be incorrect to understand, in contrast to this, however, that δίκαιος was a negative term.[23] Frequently both terms would appear together as a laudatory description of some leading figure. It may be accepted, therefore, that these two nouns had different nuances in classical Greek, although both are commendable and desirable qualities. It remains to be shown that Hellenistic Greek retained these meanings, and consequently that it would have been reasonably used by someone with Paul's Hellenistic background.

During the Principate, the essential philosophy that value was to be given to those who offered the greatest benefits to their society was still highly conspicuous.[24] Political security was more important than justice, and consequently political and military acumen, both requiring much capital outlay, were more highly prized qualities than δικαιοσύνη.[25] Wealth, family background and rank still attracted greater recognition than the quieter moral values. This can be clearly seen in the legal privileges which were accorded to those who were high-born and wealthy.[26] A man could not easily bring a case against his social superior, except for certain crimes; those of high rank could not be executed for capital crimes; and if a rich man found a legal case going against him, he might draw the attention of the jury to some of the benefactions which he had given out of his 'generosity' to the city, and thus demonstrate his rectitude of character.[27] Dio Chrysostom tries to counter this direct link between value and social status by suggesting that ἀρετή (excellence), as a moral quality, should be attributed to those who are virtuous in their actions, and not simply to those who are well-born.[28]

---

[22] Adkins, *Moral Values,* 124; cf. also 126-7; *Merit and Responsibility,* 70, 156.

[23] *Contra* for example Y. Landau, 'Martyrdom in Paul's Religious Ethics: An Exegetical Commentary on Romans 5.7', 32-34; and the slightly negative tone in C.H. Dodd, *The Epistle of Paul to the Romans,* 75.

[24] Cf. Cremer, sv ἀγαθός, esp. 4, 7 where Rom 5.7 is alluded to.

[25] The ἀγαθός would be expected to secure the advancement of his city at all costs, even that of δικαιοσύνη.

[26] Cf. the thorough argument of P. Garnsey in *Social Status and Legal Privilege in the Roman Empire* (Oxford, 1970). "In law, as in other aspects of Roman society, the principal benefits and rewards were available to those groups most advantageously placed in the stratification system by reason of their greater property, power and prestige", *idem,* 280.

[27] Cf. Plutarch, *Moralia* 817.D; also S.C. Mott, 'The Power of Giving and Receiving: Reciprocity in Hellenistic Benevolence', in ed. G.F. Hawthorne, *Current Issues in Biblical and Patristic Interpretation* (Grand Rapids, 1975), 69.

[28] Cf. Dio, *Orationes* 15.31, "And so when a man is well-born in respect to virtue, it is right to call him 'noble', even if no one knows his parents or his ancestors either".

4. *Benefaction*

Once it is established that there can be this distinction between δίκαιος and ἀγαθός, it may already be seen how a man's debt to the ἀγαθός is greater than to the merely δίκαιος. The former has been of some specific, probably financial and political, benefit to the immediate society and perhaps also to himself.

A deeply established social hierarchy, dominated by the wealthy and well-born, was continuously being reinforced during the period of the late Republic and early Empire. This was partly achieved by a convention of patronage which exploited the power inherent in giving gifts.[29] The power of the wealthy was such that a high proportion of society was immediately dependent upon them. Influential men would have large staffs of slaves, whose whole livelihoods would be secured by their masters. A freedman would be under legal obligation and social pressure to continue to attend his master in business or politics long after being given liberty. Many freedmen might be dependent on the social élite for their daily finance. A young man starting out in public life would owe his initial reputation to a senior patron whose advice and support had been received.

In Rome, social hierarchy was reinforced daily through the convention whereby socially inferior men would arrive each morning at the residences of their superiors for some form of dôle. This practice was part of the relationship of *patronus* and *cliens;* the attendance of the client was *officium;* and the dôle given to the dependant was called *beneficium*.[30] The recipient of a *beneficium* was immediately under an obligation to his benefactor, and necessarily in his debt. The strength of the obligation was considerable, and social pressure to acknowledge and respond to the *beneficium* extreme. Social standing and reputation were linked to a complex network of relationships and obligations. To break an obligation was considered an offensive move which engendered enmity between the two parties.[31]

The advantage to the benefactor of this relationship was that it enhanced his own status and public recognition. For this reason, it is clear that benefaction was not normally a disinterested action, but a necessity by which the donor could maintain his security and public standing.[32]

---

[29] Cf. S.C. Mott, 'The Power of Giving and Receiving: Reciprocity in Hellenistic Benevolence', 60. H. Stephanus, *Thesaurus Graecae Linguae* I (Paris, 1831), sv ἀγαθός, gives the sense of 'euergeta, beneficus'.

[30] Seneca writes at length about this convention in his essays entitled *De Beneficiis*.

[31] Cf. A.R. Hands, *Charities and Social Aid in Greece and Rome* (London, 1968), 26.

[32] P. Marshall, *Enmity in Corinth, Social Conventions in Paul's relations with the Corinthians* (Tübingen, 1987), 2.

5. *The Benefactor as* ὁ ἀγαθος

Godet questions why, if 'benefactor' is intended, Paul does not use the perfectly adequate Greek words of ἀγαθοποιός or εὐεργέτης?[33] This may be simply explained by the natural reluctance to use the words *patronus* and *cliens* in direct address. Saller draws the conclusion,

> Patently, the Romans applied the language of patronage to a range of relationships, with both humble dependants and their junior aristocratic colleagues labelled *clientes:* usage was more fluid than usually supposed, and the connotations of *amicus, cliens* and *patronus* were subtly and variously manipulated in different circumstances. It must be admitted, however, that the typical word for a junior aristocratic associate and others further down the social ladder was *amicus.*[34]

In some instances, where social comparisons of status were less obvious, the term would happily be used. The parallel usage in Dio's *Orationes* of the nouns ἀγαθός and εὐεργέτης may be noted.[35] Time and again, in polemic, Dio refers to both the benefactors of the city and the good men of society in the same breath, clearly as the same group of people. In one famous oration against the citizens of Rhodes, there are a number of such parallels,

It is in regard to these matters, men of Rhodes, that I ask you to believe that the situation here among you is very bad and unworthy of your state, your treatment, I mean, of your εὐεργέται and of the honours given to your ἀγαθοί ἄνδρες ..."; "But to commit an outrage against ἄνδρες ἀγαθοί who have been the εὐεργέται of the state, to annul the honours given them and to

---

[33] F. Godet, *Commentary on St. Paul's Epistle to the Romans* I, 326. Cf. also H.A.W. Meyer, *Critical and Exegetical Handbook to the Epistle to the Romans,* 234.

[34] R.P. Saller, 'Patronage and Friendship', in ed. A. Wallace-Hadrill, *Patronage in Ancient Society* (London, 1989), 57; cf. also Saller, *Personal Patronage under the Early Empire* (Cambridge, 1982), 9, "The reason for the infrequent appearance of *patronus* and *cliens* in literature lies in the social inferiority and degradation implied by the words".

[35] Cf. Dio, *Orationes* 46.2-3, "Now with reference to my father, there is no need for me to tell whether he was an ἀγαθός, for you are always singing his praises, both collectively and individually, whenever you refer to him, as being no ordinary citizen ... Again, no one could say of my grandfather either that he disgraced the city or that he spent nothing on it out of his own means. For he spent on public benefactions all that he had from his father and his grandfather, so that he had nothing left at all". Cf. also Plutarch, *Moralia* 218.A, where an ἀγαθός king is described as one who is benefactor to his friends; and 851.D, "Laches, son of Demochares, of Leuconoë, asks from the senate and people of the Athenians for Demochares, son of Laches, of Leuconoë, a grant of a bronze statue in the market-place, and maintenance in the Prytaneum for him and the eldest of his descendants in perpetuity, and the privilege of a front seat at all spectacles, because he proved himself a εὐεργέτης and an ἀγαθός counsellor to the people of the Athenians and benefited the people ..." F.A. Philippi, *Commentary on St Paul's Epistle to the Romans,* 240, includes the citation from Xenophon, *Cyrop.* 3.3.4, κῦρον ἀνακαλοῦντες τὸν εὐεργέτην, τὸν ἄνδρα τὸν ἀγαθόν. In Seneca, *De Beneficiis,* there is much evidence to show a connection between the 'good man' and the one who is benefactor. Cf. 2.17.7, "The best man is he who gives readily, never demands any return, rejoices if a return is made, who in all sincerity forgets what he has bestowed, and accepts a return in the spirit of one accepting a benefit"; 7.17.2, "To a good man I shall hand back his benefit, to a bad one I shall fling it back; to the former, because I am indebted to him, to the latter, in order that I may no longer be indebted to him"; 7.19.3, "to a good man I shall make return when it is convenient; to a bad man, when he asks for it".

blot out their remembrance, I for my part do not see how that could be otherwise termed"; "The one act, namely, means being ungrateful to your εὐεργέται, but the other means insulting them; the one is a case of not honouring the ἄνδρες ἀγαθοί, the other, of dishonouring them"; "How very much worse it is to rob ἀγαθοί of honours bestowed than to rob anybody else, and to injure your εὐεργέται than to injure any chance person, is something that nobody fails to see".[36]

Epigraphic evidence also usefully shows this direct link between the benefactor and the good man. With regard to a benefactor, the Athenians determined, "... to praise him because he is ἀνὴρ ἀγαθός καὶ ποιεῖ ὅτι δύναται ἀγαθὸν for the people of Athens ... it is resolved that Menelaos be considered a benefactor".[37]

There, is therefore a definite connection in Hellenistic Greek between the ἀγαθός and the benefactor. It is a connection that is seen both in literary and epigraphic sources.

6. *Conclusions*

If Cranfield and others are correct to draw a link between ἀγαθός and "the benefactor" in Romans 5.7, this may explain the gradation in 7b, thus answering the questions raised by Godet above.[38] It may then be asked if Paul elsewhere talks in these secular terms. The contrasting instance in Romans 7, where Paul is clearly using ἀγαθός in its moral sense instead, has already been noted. As in Romans 5.7, Winter argues that the use of τὸ ἀγαθὸν ἐργόν and τὸ ἀγαθόν in Romans 13.3-4 is secular benefaction terminology. A similar usage may be seen in the verbs τὸ ἀγαθὸν ποιεῖν (Romans 13.3), and ἀγαθοποιεῖν (1 Peter 2.14).[39] A further possible parallel has been suggested in Galatians 6.10.[40]

---

[36] Dio, *Orationes* 31.8; 31.14; 31.27; 31.65.

[37] W. Dittenberger, *Sylloge Inscriptionum Graecarum* I-IV (Leipzig, 1918-24), 174. Cf. also *Sammlung der griechischen Dialekt-Inschriften,* ed. H. Collitz *et al.* (Göttingen, 1884-1915), 5366, 5464, 5698 and *SIG* 127, 167 (all cited by B.W. Winter, 'The Public Honouring of Christian Benefactors', 100, n. 32). From the first and early second century period may be added *SIG* 704, 800, 805, 1019. J. Gerlach, ANHP ΑΓΑΘΟΣ, 7-14, gives further epigraphic evidence for the use of the term ἀνὴρ ἀγαθός.

[38] See p. 163 above.

[39] B.W. Winter, 'The Public Honouring of Christian Benefactors', 92-3, against C.E.B. Cranfield, *A Critical and Exegetical Commentary on the Epistle of Paul to the Romans* II, 664 n. 5. Cranfield suggests that, in Romans 13.3, the sense of ἀγαθός is naturally to be taken as moral.

[40] Cf. Bauer/Arndt/Gingrich sv. τό ἀγαθόν, where the sense of benefaction is given. Cf. also E.D.W. Burton, *A Critical and Exegetical Commentary on the epistle to the Galatians* (Edinburgh, 1921), 346, "The expression is not quite identical with τό καλόν, v. 9, signifying, rather, what is beneficial to another than what is morally right". H.A.W. Meyer, *Critical and Exegetical Commentary on the New Testament* VII *The Epistle to the Galatians* (ET: Edinburgh, 1884), 335 f., on the contrary does not see this as a reference to beneficence, although he does list a number of commentators who do adopt this stance.

Romans 5.7 has proven problematic to a number of commentators, because the adjectives 'good' and 'just' in the twentieth century carry connotations which differ from the first century. It has been seen that a frequent meaning of ἀγαθός in first century cultural usage would have been to the social élite; and a widely adopted extension of this was to see ἀγαθός as a reference to the benefactor of a city or individual.

If 'benefactor' is the implied meaning in Romans 5.7, it may then clearly be seen why, "very rarely will anyone die for a righteous man, though for a good man someone might possibly dare to die". The obligations which were owed to one's benefactor were socially binding, and it would not have been unthinkable for a man to lay down his life for such an honourable person. There is a similar resonance in Dio Chrysostom:

> for, whereas in the cause of justice and virtue and ancestral rights and laws, a noble soul, one that does not cling to life, will, if need be, suffer, and even die for a good king; yet if a man hangs himself for a chorus-girl, a low-born outcast, not fit to live, what depths of disgrace does that betoken![41]

Given this use of the term ἀγαθός, Paul's argument in Romans 5.6-8 comes very sharply into focus. While it is almost inconceivable that someone would give up their life merely for an upright citizen, it is not unthinkable in the first century that someone—because of the ties of patronage—would give up their life for their benefactor, ὁ ἀγαθός. Yet Christ gave up *his* life *for us*—when we were yet sinners without any claim on him.[42]

It has been shown that support for this interpretation is by no means lacking. Indeed a survey of the commentators would suggest that it received widespread acceptance during the nineteenth century. More recently the interpretation has increased once again in favour, although it has not been defended with the same conviction which it once enjoyed. The present discussion, whilst bringing to light some of the older support, also seeks to provide additional evidence which firmly endorses the revived viewpoint.

---

[41] *Orationes* 32.50. M. Hengel, *The Atonement, The Origins of the Doctrine in the New Testament* (ET: Philadelphia, 1981), 9-14, gives a discussion of instances in Greek literature of people prepared to die on behalf of their native city, friends or family. However, he does not draw the obvious Pauline parallel of human self-sacrifice in Romans 5.7.

[42] C.E.B. Cranfield, *A Critical and Exegetical Commentary on the Epistle of Paul to the Romans* I (Edinburgh, 1979), 264, notes that 'benefactor' and ἀγαθός as references to God are not uncommon descriptions in the Old Testament, and most especially in the Psalms. It is clear that Jesus' death, however, is here being treated by Paul in dialectical contrast to the benefaction concept. It is the one, elsewhere termed benefactor, who is dying for his clients.

SELECT BIBLIOGRAPHY

Aalders, G.J.D., 'Plutarch's Political Thought', *Verhandeligen der koninklijke Nederlandse Akademie van Wetenschappen* (Amsterdam, 1982).

Abbott, F.F. & Johnson, A.C., *Municipal Administration in the Roman Empire* (New York, 1968).

Adkins, A.W.H., *Merit and Responsibility, A Study in Greek Values* (Oxford, 1960).

——, *Moral Values and Political Behaviour in Ancient Greece, From Homer to the end of the Fifth Century* (London, 1972).

Allo, E. -B., *Saint Paul Première Épître aux Corinthiens* (ed 2: Paris, 1956).

Amandry, M., 'Le monnayage des duovirs corinthiens', *Bulletin de Correspondance Hellénique, Supplément* XV (1988).

Apuleius, L., *Metamorphoses*, Loeb Classical Library (Cambridge, Massachusetts, 1989)

Aristotle, *The Art of Rhetoric*, Loeb Classical Library (Cambridge, Massachusetts, 1982).

——, *Politics*, Loeb Classical Library (Cambridge, Massachusetts, 1990).

Bagdikian, A., *The Civic Officials of Roman Corinth*, unpublished MA dissertation (University of Vermont, 1953).

Bagnall, R.S., *The Administration of Ptolemaic possessions outside Egypt* (Leiden, 1976).

Balsdon, J.P.V.D., *Roman Women: Their History and Habits* (London, 1977).

Bammel, E., 'The Trial before Pilate', in edd. E. Bammel & C.F.D. Moule, *Jesus and the Politics of His Day* (Cambridge, 1984), 415-451.

Banks, R., *Paul's Idea of Community: The Early House Churches in their Historical Setting* (Exeter, 1980).

——, '"Walking" as a metaphor of the Christian Life: The Origins of a significant Pauline Usage', in edd. E.W. Conrad & E.G. Newing, *Perspectives on Language and Text, essays and poems in Honor of Francis I. Andersen's Sixtieth Birthday* (Winona Lake, 1987), 303-13.

Barclay, J.M.G., 'Mirror-reading a polemical letter: Galatians as a test case', *Journal for the Study of the New Testament* 31 (1987), 73-93.

Barrett, C.K., *A Commentary on The First Epistle to the Corinthians* (ed 2: London, 1983).

——, *Essays on Paul* (London, 1982).

——, *The Epistle to the Romans* (London, 1984).

——, *Church, Ministry, and Sacraments in the New Testament* (Exeter, 1985).

——, 'Boasting (καυχᾶσθαι, κτλ.) in the Pauline Epistles', in ed. A. Vanhoye, *L'Apôtre Paul—Personnalité, Style et Conception du Ministère* (Leuven, 1986), 363-368.

——, *The New Testament Background: Selected Documents* (ed 2: London, 1987).

Barrow, R.H., *Plutarch and his Times* (London, 1967).

——, *Slavery in the Roman Empire* (London, 1928).

Barth, K., *The Resurrection of the Dead* (ET: London, 1933).

Baur, F.C., *Paulus, der Apostel Jesu Christi, sein Leben und Wirken, seine Briefe und seine Lehre* I (ed 2: Leipzig, 1866).

——, *The Church History of the First Three Centuries* I (London, 1878).

——, *Paul, The Apostle of Jesus Christ* I (London, 1873).

Baur, W.A., *A Greek-English Lexicon of the New Testament and Other Early Christian Literature* (ed 2: Chicago, 1979).

Bernard, J.H., 'The Connexion Between the Fifth and Sixth Chapters of 1 Corinthians', *The Expositor*, Series 7, Vol 3 (1907), 433-443.

Best, T.F., 'The Sociological Study of the New Testament: Promise and peril of a new discipline', *Scottish Journal of Theology* 36 (1983), 181-194.

Betz, H.D., *Plutarch's Ethical Writings and Early Christian Literature* (Leiden, 1978).

Blass, F. & Debrunner, A., *A Greek Grammar of the New Testament and Other Early Christian Literature* (Cambridge, 1961).

Bornkamm, G., *Das Ende des Gesetzes* (München, 1966).

Bosch, J.S., '"Gloriarse" segun San Pablo, Sentido y teología de καυχάομαι', *Analecta Biblica* 40 (Rome, 1970).

Bowersock, G.W., *Augustus and the Greek World* (Oxford, 1965).

——, *Greek Sophists in the Roman Empire* (Oxford, 1969).

Bowie, E.L., 'The Importance of Sophists', *Yale Classical Studies* 27 (1982).

Bowyer, W., *Critical Conjectures and Observations on the New Testament* (ed 3: London, 1782).

Boylan, P.C., *St. Paul's Epistle to the Romans* (Dublin, 1934).

Braund, D., *The Administration of the Roman Empire—(241 BC-AD 143)* (University of Exeter, 1988).

Broneer, O., 'Corinth, Center of St Paul's missionary work in Greece', *Biblical Archaeologist* 14 (1951), 78-96.

Bruce, F.F., *1 and 2 Corinthians* (London, 1971).

——, *The Epistle of Paul to the Galatians* (Exeter, 1982).

——, *The Letter of Paul to the Romans* (Leicester, 1985).

Brunt, P.A., *Social Conflicts in the Roman Republic* (London, 1971).

——, 'The Romanization of the Local Ruling Classes in the Roman Empire', in ed. D.M. Pippidi, *Assimilation et résistance à la culture greco-romaine dans le monde ancien* (Paris, 1976), 161-173.

Bultmann, R., *Theology of the New Testament* II (ET: London, 1955).

——, 'καυχάομαι, καύχημα, καύχησις', *TDNT* III (Grand Rapids, 1989), 645-654.

Burrows, M., *The Dead Sea Scrolls* (London 1956).

Burton, E. de W., *A Critical and Exegetical Commentary on the Epistle to the Galatians* (Edinburgh, 1921).

Cadbury, H.J., 'Erastus of Corinth', *Journal of Biblical Literature* 50 (1931), 42-58.

Caird, G.B., *Principalities and Powers: A Study in Pauline Theology* (Oxford, 1956).

Campbell, R.A., 'Does Paul Acquiesce in Divisions at the Lord's Supper?', *Novum Testamentum* 33 (1991), 61-70.

Campenhausen, H. von, *Ecclesiastical Authority and Spiritual Power in the Church of the First Three Centuries* (ET: London, 1969).

Carr, W., 'The Rulers of this Age—1 Corinthians II.6-8', *New Testament Studies* 23 (1977), 20-35.

Cartledge, P., & Spawforth, A., *Hellenistic and Roman Sparta* (London, 1989).

Cassius, Dio, *Roman History* 6, 7, Loeb Classical Library 2 vols (London, 1968, 1980).

Chapple, A.L., *Local Leadership in the Pauline Churches: theological and social factors in its development: a study based on 1 Thessalonians, 1 Corinthians and Philippians,* unpublished PhD dissertation (Durham University, 1984).

Chrysostom, Dio, *Discourses,* Loeb Classical Library 1-5 (London, 1932-).

Chrysostom, J., 'Homilies on the Epistles of Paul to the Corinthians', in ed. P. Schaff, *A Select Library of the Nicene and Post-Nicene Fathers of the Christian Church* 21 (Grand Rapids, 1969).

Cicero, *Pro Caecina,* Loeb Classical Library (London, 1959).

——, *De inventione,* Loeb Classical Library (Cambridge, Massachusetts, 1968).

——, *Pro Murena,* Loeb Classical Library (Cambridge, Massachusetts, 1977).

——, *Epistulae ad Familiares,* Loeb Classical Library (Cambridge, Massachusetts, 1954).

——, *Pro Cluentio,* Loeb Classical Library (London, 1959).

Clarke, A.D. & Winter, B.W. edd., *One God, One Lord in a World of Religious Pluralism* (Cambridge, 1991).

Clarke, A.D., 'The Good and the Just in Romans 5:7', *Tyndale Bulletin* 41 (1990), 128-142.

——, 'Another Corinthian Erastus Inscription', *Tyndale Bulletin* 42 (1991), 146-151.

Collitz, H., *et al., Sammlung der griechischen Dialekt-Inschriften* (Göttingen, 1884-1915).

Conzelmann, H., 'Korinth und die Mädchen der Aphrodite: Zur Religionsgeschichte der Stadt Korinth', *Nachrichten von der Akademie der Wissenschaften in Göttingen* 8 (1967-8), 247-61.

——, *1 Corinthians* (ET: Philadelphia, 1975).

Corbett, P.E., *The Roman Law of Marriage* (Oxford, 1969).

Cranfield, C.E.B., *A Critical and Exegetical Commentary on the Epistle of Paul to the Romans* I, II (Edinburgh, 1979).

Cremer, H., *Biblico-theological Lexicon of New Testament Greek* (ET: Edinburgh, 1883).

Crook, J.A., *Law and Life of Rome* (London, 1967).

Csillag, P., *The Augustan Laws on Family Relations* (Budapest, 1976).

Cullmann, O., *The State in the New Testament* (London, 1957).

Dahl, N.A., 'Paul and the Church at Corinth according to 1 Corinthians 1:10-4:21', edd. W.R. Farmer, C.F.D. Moule, R.R. Niebuhr, *Christian History and Interpretation: Studies Presented to John Knox* (Cambridge, 1967), 313-335.

Daube, D., '"Ne quid infamandi causa fiat": The Roman law of defamation', *Atti del Congresso Internazionale di Diritto Romano e di Storia del Diritto, Verona 1948,* (Milan, 1951), 413-50.

——, *The New Testament and Rabbinic Judaism* (London, 1956).

——, 'Pauline Contributions to a Pluralistic Culture: Re-creation and beyond', in edd. D.G. Miller & D.Y. Hadidian, *Jesus and Man's Hope* II, (Pittsburgh, 1971), 223-245.

——, 'Biblical Landmarks in the Struggle for Women's Rights', *Juridical Review* 90, n.s. 23 (1978), 177-97.

——, 'Historical Aspects of Informal Marriage', *Revue Internationale de Droits de L'Antiquité* 25 (1978), 95-107.

——, *Ancient Jewish Law: Three Inaugural Lectures* (Leiden, 1981).

——, 'Onesimos', in edd. G.W.E. Nickelsburg & G.W. MacRae, *Christians among Jews and Gentiles, Essays in Honor of Krister Stendahl* (Philadelphia, 1986), 40-3.

——, *Appeasement or Resistance and other essays on New Testament Judaism* (London, 1987).

Davis, J.A., *Wisdom and Spirit: An Investigation of 1 Corinthians 1.18-3.20 Against the Background of Jewish Sapiential Traditions in the Greco-Roman Period* (Lanham, 1984).

Deissmann A., *Paulus: Eine kultur- und religionsgeschichtliche Skizze* (Tübingen, 1911).

——, *Paul: A Study in Social and Religious History* (ET: ed 2: London, 1926).

——, *Light from the Ancient East* (ET: London, 1927).

Delcor, M., 'The courts of the Church of Corinth and the courts of Qumran', in ed. J. Murphy-O'Connor, *Paul and Qumran, Studies in New Testament Exegesis* (London, 1968), 69-84.

Delling, G., 'ἄρχων', *TDNT* I (Grand Rapids, 1965).

Derrett, J.D.M., 'Midrash, The Composition of Gospels, and Discipline', in *Studies in the New Testament* IV (Leiden, 1986).

Dibelius, M., *Die Geisterwelt im Glauben des Paulus* (Göttingen, 1909).

Diogenes Laertius, *Lives of the Sophists,* Loeb Classical Library, (Cambridge, Massachusetts, 1959, 1963).

Dittberner, A., '"Who is Apollos and who is Paul?"—I Cor. 3:5', *The Bible Today* 71 (1974), 1549-52.

Dittenberger, W., *Sylloge Inscriptionum Graecarum* I-IV (ed 3: Leipzig, 1915-24).

Dixon, S., *The Roman Mother* (London, 1988).

Dodd, C.H., *The Epistle of Paul to the Romans* (London, 1947).

Dowdy, B.A., *The Meaning of KAUCHASTHAI in the New Testament,* unpublished PhD dissertation (Vanderbilt University, 1955).

Duff, A.M., *Freedmen in the Early Roman Empire* (Cambridge, 1958).

Duncan-Jones, R., 'Costs, Outlays and *summae honorariae* from Roman Africa', *Papers of the British School at Rome* 30 (1962), 47-115.

Dunn, J.D.G., *Unity and Diversity in the New Testament* (London, 1977).

——, *Romans 1-8, 9-16* (Waco, 1988).

Earl, D.C., *The Moral and Political Tradition of Rome* (London, 1967).

——, *The Political Thought of Sallust* (Cambridge, 1961).

Edwards, K.M., *Corinth, Coins 1896-1929,* VI (Cambridge, Massachusetts, 1933).

Ellicott, C.J., *St Paul's First Epistle to the Corinthians with a critical and grammatical commentary* (London, 1887).

Ellis, E.E., 'How the New Testament uses the Old', in ed. I.H. Marshall, *New Testament Interpretation—Essays on Principles and Methods* (Exeter, 1977), 199-219.

Engels, D., *Roman Corinth: An Alternative Model for the Classical City* (Chicago, 1990).
Epstein, D.F., *Personal Enmity in Roman Politics—218 - 43 BC* (London, 1987).

Fascher, E., *Der erste Brief des Paulus an die Korinther* I (Berlin, 1975).
Fee, G.D., *The First Epistle to the Corinthians* (Grand Rapids, 1987).
Feuillet, A., 'Les "Chefs de ce siècle" et la sagesse divine d'après 1 Cor 2:6-8', *Studiorum Paulinorum Congressus Internationalis Catholicus* I (1961), 383-393.
Fiebiger, 'Decurio', *Pauly's Real-Encyclopädie* IV (Stuttgart, 1901).
Fiore, B., '"Covert Allusion" in 1 Corinthians 1-4', *The Catholic Biblical Quarterly* 47 (1985), 85-102.
Fitch, W.O., 'Paul, Apollos, Cephas, Christ, Studies in Texts: 1 Corinthians 1:12', *Theology* 74 (1971), 18-24.
Forbes, C., 'Comparison, self-praise and irony: Paul's boasting and the conventions of Hellenistic rhetoric', *New Testament Studies* 32 (1986), 1-30.
Frank, R.I., 'Augustus' Legislation on Marriage and Children', *California Studies in Classical Antiquity* 8 (1975), 41-52.
Friedländer, L., *Roman Life and Manners under the Early Empire* I (ET: ed 7: London, 1909)
Fuller, R.H., 'First Corinthians 6:1-11: An Exegetical Paper', *Ex Auditu* 2 (1986), 96-104.
Furnish, V.P., 'Corinth in Paul's time. What can Archaeology tell us?', *Biblical Archaeology Review* 15 (1988), 14-27.

Gager, J. G., 'Shall We Marry our Enemies?—Sociology and the New Testament', *Interpretation* 36 (1982).
Gaius, *The Institutes of Gaius and Rules of Ulpian* (ET: Edinburgh, 1880).
Gale, H.M., *The Use of Analogy in the Letters of Paul* (Philadelphia, 1964).
Gardner, J.F., *Leadership and the Cult of the Personality* (London, 1974).
——, 'The Recovery of Dowry in Roman Law', *Classical Quarterly* 35 (1985), 449-53.
——, *Women in Roman Law and Society* (London, 1986).
Garnsey, P. & Saller, R., *The Early Principate, Augustus to Trajan* (Oxford, 1982).
——, *The Roman Empire—Economy, Society and Culture* (London, 1987).
Garnsey, P., '*Taxatio* and *pollicitatio* in Roman Africa', *Journal of Roman Studies* 61 (1971), 116-29.
——, 'Aspects of the Decline of the Urban Aristocracy in the Roman Empire', *ANRW* II.1 (Berlin, 1974), 229-252.
——, 'Descendants of Freedmen in Local Politics: some Criteria', in ed. B. Levick, *The Ancient Historian and his Materials* (Westmead, 1975), 167-180.
——, 'Honorarium Decurionatus', *Historia* 20 (1971), 309-325.
——, 'Legal Privilege in the Roman Empire', in ed. M.I. Finley, *Studies in Ancient Society, Past and Present Series* (London, 1974), 141-165.
——, 'Non-Slave Labour in the Roman World', in ed. P. Garnsey, *Non-Slave Labour in the Greco-Roman World, Cambridge Philological Society* supplement 6 (1980), 34-47.
——, *Social Status and Legal Privilege in the Roman Empire* (Oxford, 1970).
Geagan, D.J., 'Notes on the Agonistic Institutions of Roman Corinth', *Greek, Roman and Byzantine Studies* IV (1968), 69-80.
Geertz, C., 'Religion as a Cultural System', in ed. M. Banton, *Anthropological Approaches to the Study of Religion* (London, 1966), 1-46.
Gelzer, M., *The Roman Nobility* (ET: Oxford, 1969).
Gerlach, J., ΑΝΗΡ ΑΓΑΘΟΣ, Doctoral dissertation Ludwig-Maximilians-Universität (München, 1932).
Gifford, E.H., *The Epistle of St. Paul to the Romans* (London, 1886).
Giles, K., 'Demystifying ordination with the help of Max Weber', *Tyndale Paper* 32 no. 3 (1987).
Gill, D.W.J., 'Erastus the Aedile', *Tyndale Bulletin* 40 (1989), 293-301.
——, 'The Importance of Roman Portraiture for Head Coverings in 1 Corinthians 11.2-16', *Tyndale Bulletin* 41 (1990), 245-60.
Godet, F., *Commentary on St. Paul's First Epistle to the Corinthians* I (Edinburgh, 1886, 1887).
——, *Commentary on St. Paul's Epistle to the Romans* I (Edinburgh, 1895).

Gomme, A.W., 'The Interpretation of ΚΑΛΟΙ ΚΑΓΑΘΟΙ in Thucydides 4.40.2', *Classical Quarterly* 47 ns 3 (1953), 65-8.

Gordon, M.L., 'The Freedman's Son in Municipal Life', *Journal of Roman Studies* 21 (1931), 65-77.

——, 'The Nationality of Slaves under the Early Roman Empire', in ed. M.I. Finley, *Slavery in Classical Antiquity, Views and Controversies* (Cambridge, 1960), 171-189.

Griffiths, J.G., *Apuleius of Madaurus, The Isis-Book (Metamorphoses XI)* (Leiden, 1975).

Grotius, H., *Annotationum in Novum Testamentum* II (Paris, 1746).

Haley, P., 'Rudolph Sohm on Charisma', *The Journal of Religion* 60 (1980), 185-97.

Hammond, H., *A Paraphrase and Annotations upon all the Books of the New Testament briefly explaining all the difficult places thereof* (ed 7: London, 1702).

Hands, A.R., *Charities and Social Aid in Greece and Rome* (London, 1968).

Hardy, E.G., *Three Spanish Charters and other documents* (Oxford, 1912).

Harnack, A. von, *Marcion: Das Evangelium vom fremden Gott* (Leipzig, 1924).

Harrison, P.N., *Paulines and Pastorals* (London, 1964).

Hartman, L., 'Some Remarks on 1 Cor. 2:1-5', *Svensk Exegetisk Årsbok* 39 (1974), 109-20.

Heinrici, K.F.G., *Das erste Sendschreiben des Apostels Paulus an die Korinthier* (Berlin, 1880).

Hemer, C.J., *The Book of Acts in the Setting of Hellenistic History* (Tübingen, 1989).

Hengel, M., *Property and Riches in the Early Church: Aspects of a Social History of Early Christianity,* (London, 1974).

——, *The Atonement, The Origins of the Doctrine in the New Testament* (London, 1981).

Héring, J., *La Première Épître de Saint Paul aux Corinthiens* (Paris, 1949).

——, *The First Epistle of Saint Paul to the Corinthians* (ET: London, 1966).

Hignett, C., *A History of the Athenian Constitution* (Oxford, 1952).

Hock, R.F., 'Paul's Tentmaking and the Problem of his Social Class', *Journal of Biblical Literature* 97, (1978), 555-64.

Hoehner, H.W., *Herod Antipas* (Cambridge, 1972).

Holladay, W.P., *Jeremiah 1—A Commentary on the Book of the Prophet Jeremiah, Chapters 1-25* (Philadelphia, 1986).

Holmberg, B., *Paul and Power: The structure of authority in the primitive Church as reflected in the Pauline epistles* (Lund, 1978).

——, 'Sociological versus Theological Analysis of the Question concerning a Pauline Church Order', in ed. S. Pedersen, *Die Paulinische Literatur und Theologie* (Århus, 1980), 187-200.

——, *Sociology and the New Testament* (Minneapolis, 1990).

Hooker, M.D., 'Beyond the Things which are Written': An Examination of 1 Corinthians 4.6', in ed. M.D. Hooker, *From Adam to Christ* (Cambridge, 1990), 106-112.

——, 'Were There False Teachers in Colossae?', in ed. M.D. Hooker, *From Adam to Christ* (Cambridge, 1990), 121-136.

Hopkins, K., 'Élite Mobility in the Roman Empire', in ed. M.I. Finley, *Studies in Ancient Society, Past and Present Series* (London, 1974).

Horsley, G.H.R., 'οἰκονόμος', *New Documents Illustrating Early Christianity* 4 (1987), 160-1.

Horsley, R.A., 'Pneumatikos vs. Psychikos: Distinctions of Spiritual Status among the Corinthians', *HTR* 69 (1976), 269-88.

——, 'Wisdom of Word and Words of Wisdom in Corinth', *The Catholic Biblical Quarterly* 39 (1977), 224-39.

Horst, P.W. van der, *The Sentences of Pseudo–Phocylides* (Leiden, 1978).

——, *Aelius Aristides and the New Testament* (Leiden, 1980).

Hyldahl, N., 'Den korintiske situation—en skitse', *Dansk Teologisk Tidsskrift* 40 (1977), 18-30.

——, 'The Corinthian 'Parties' and the Corinthian Crisis', *Studia Theologica* 45 (1991), 19-32.

Irenaeus, *Libros quinque adversus Haereses* II (Cambridge, 1857).

——, *Sancti Irenaei Episcopi Lugdunensis quae supersunt omnis* (Leipzig, 1853).

Jacobs, L., 'Greater love hath no man... The Jewish point of view of self-sacrifice', *Judaism* 6 (1957), 41-47.

Jeffery, L.H., *The Local Scripts of Archaic Greece: a Study of the Origin of the Greek Alphabet from the eighth to the fifth centuries BC* (Oxford, 1990).

Jewett, R., *The Thessalonian Correspondence: Pauline Rhetoric and Millenarian Piety* (Philadelphia, 1986).

Jolowicz, H.F. & Nicholas, B., *Historical Introduction to the Study of Roman Law* (ed 3: Cambridge, 1972).

Jones, A.H.M., 'Slavery in the Ancient World', in ed. M.I. Finley, *Slavery in Classical Antiquity, Views and Controversies* (Cambridge, 1960), 1-15.

——, *The Cities of the Eastern Roman Provinces* (ed 2: Oxford, 1971).

——, *The Greek City, From Alexander to Justinian* (Oxford, 1966).

——, *The Criminal Courts of the Roman Republic and Principate* (Oxford, 1972).

——, 'The Roman Colonate', in ed. M.I. Finley, *Studies in Ancient Society, Past and Present Series* (London, 1974), 288-303.

Jones, C.P., *Plutarch and Rome* (London, 1971).

——, *The Roman World of Dio Chrysostom* (Cambridge, Mass. and London, 1978).

Jones, N.F., *Public Organization in Ancient Greece: A Documentary Study* (Philadelphia, 1987).

Josephus, *Jewish Antiquities,* Loeb Classical Library (London, 1930-).

Judge, E.A., *The Social Pattern of the Christian Groups in the First Century: Some Prolegomena to the Study of New Testament Ideas of Social Obligation* (London, 1960).

——, 'Paul's boasting in relation to contemporary professional practice', *Australian Biblical Review* 16 (1968), 37-50.

——, 'The Social Identity of the First Christians: A Question of Method in Religious History', *Journal of Religious History* 11 (1980), 201-17.

——, *Rank and Status in the World of the Caesars and St. Paul* (Christchurch, New Zealand, 1982).

Jülicher, A., *Der Brief an die Römer* II (Göttingen, 1917).

Justinian, *The Digest of Justinian* II, edd. Th. Mommsen, P. Krueger (ET: Philadelphia, 1985).

Käsemann, E., *Perspectives on Paul* (London, 1971).

——, *Commentary on Romans* (ET: Grand Rapids, 1980).

Keck, L.E., 'The Post-Pauline Interpretation of Jesus' Death in Rom 5,6-7', in edd. C. Andresen and G. Klein, *Theologia Crucis—Signum Crucis, Festschrift für E. Dinkler* (Tübingen, 1979).

Kee, H.C., *Christian Origins in Sociological Perspective, Methods and Resources* (Philadelphia, 1980).

Kelly, J.M., *Roman Litigation* (Oxford, 1966).

——, *Studies in the Civil Judicature of the Roman Republic* (Oxford, 1976).

Kent, J.H., *Corinth—Inscriptions 1926-1950 Corinth: Results,* viii, Part III (Princeton, 1966).

Keppie, L., *Colonisation and Veteran Settlement in Italy, 47-14 BC* (London, 1983).

Klauck, H-J., *1. Korintherbrief* (Würzburg, 1984).

Kling, C.F., *The First Epistle of Paul to the Corinthians* (ET: ed 4: 1869).

Kubitschek, J.W., 'Aedilis', *Pauly's Real-Encyclopädie* I (Stuttgart, 1894).

Kümmel, W.G. & Kaiser, O., *Exegetical Method: A Student Handbook* (ET: New York, 1981).

Kunkel, W., *An Introduction to Roman Legal and Constitutional History* (ET: ed 2: Oxford, 1973).

Kuss, O., *Der Römerbrief* (Regensburg, 1963).

Lafaye, G. (ed.), *Inscriptiones Graecae ad res Romanas pertinentes* 4 (Paris 1927).

Lagrange, M.-J., *Saint Paul épître aux Romains* (Paris, 1950).

Landau, Y., 'Martyrdom in Paul's Religious Ethics: An exegetical commentary on Romans 5:7', *Immanuel* 15 (1952-3), 24-38.

Landvogt, P., *Epigraphische Untersuchungen über den ΟΙΚΟΝΟΜΟΣ: ein Beitrag zum hellenistischen Beamtenwesen,* dissertation (Strassburg, 1908).

Lane Fox, R., *Pagans and Christians* (Harmondsworth, 1988).

Lang, F., *Die Briefe an die Korinther* (Göttingen, 1986).

Larfeld, W., *Handbuch der griechischen Epigraphik,* II (Leipzig, 1902).

Larsen, J.A.O., 'Roman Greece', in ed. T. Frank, *An Economic Survey of Ancient Rome,* IV (Baltimore, 1938), 259-498.

Last, H., 'The Social Policy of Augustus', in edd. S.A. Cook, F.E. Adcock, M.P. Charlesworth, *The Cambridge Ancient History* 10 (Cambridge, 1966), 425-464.

Leenhardt, F.J., *L'Épître de Saint Paul aux Romains* (Geneva, 1981).

——, *The Epistle to the Romans* (London, 1961).

Lefkowitz, M.R. & Fant, M.B., *Women's Life in Greece and Rome* (London, 1982).

Lenschau, T., 'Korinthos', *Pauly's Real-Encyclopädie Supplementband* 4 (Stuttgart, 1924).

Lenski, R.C.H., *The Interpretation of St. Paul's Epistle to the Romans* (Columbus, 1936).

——, *The Interpretation of the Acts of the Apostles* (Minneapolis, 1961).

——, *The Interpretation of St. Paul's First and Second Epistles to the Corinthians* (Minneapolis, 1963).

Levick, B., *The Roman Colonies in Southern Asia Minor* (Oxford, 1967).

Liddell, H.G. & Scott, R., *A Greek-English Lexicon* (ed 9: Oxford, 1985).

Liebenam, 'Duovir', *Pauly's Real-Encyclopädie* V (Stuttgart, 1905).

Lietzmann, H., *An die Korinther* I, II (ed 4: Tübingen, 1949).

——, *Einführung in die Textgeschichte der Paulusbriefe an die Römer* (Tübingen, 1983).

Lightfoot, J.B., *Notes on epistles of St. Paul from Unpublished Commentaries* (London, 1904).

Lim, T.H., '"Not in Persuasive Words of Wisdom, but in the Demonstration of the Spirit and power" (1 Cor. 2:4)', *Novum Testamentum* 29 (1987), 137-49.

Litfin, A.D., *St. Paul's Theology of Proclamation: An Investigation of 1 Corinthians 1-4 in the Light of Greco-Roman Rhetoric,* unpublished D.Phil dissertation (Oxford University, 1983).

MacDonald, M.Y., *The Pauline Churches. A Socio-historical Study of Institutionalization in the Pauline and Deutero-Pauline Writings* (Cambridge, 1988).

Mackie, N., 'Local Administration in Roman Spain, AD 14-212', *BAR International Series* 172 (Oxford, 1983).

MacMullen, R., *Roman Social Relations, 50 BC to AD 284* (London, 1974).

Magie, D., *De Romanorum iuris publici sacrique vocabulis sollemnibus in Graecum sermonem conversis* I (Halle, 1904).

——, *Roman Rule in Asia Minor to the end of the Third Century after Christ* (Princeton, 1950).

Maier, H.O., *The Social Setting of the Ministry as Reflected in the Writings of Hermas, Clement and Ignatius* (Waterloo, 1991).

Malherbe, A.J., *Social Aspects of Early Christianity* (ed 2: Philadelphia, 1983).

Malina, B.J., *The New Testament World: insights from cultural anthropology* (Atlanta, 1981).

——, 'The Social Sciences and Biblical Interpretation', *Interpretation* 36 (1982).

——, 'The Gospel of John in Sociolinguistic Perspective', *Protocol of the Forty-Eighth Colloquy, Center for Hermeneutical Studies in Hellenistic and Modern Culture* (11 March, 1984).

Marcillet-Jaubert, J. & Vérilhac, A., *Index du bulletin épigraphique de J. et L. Robert* I, IV, V (Paris, 1972-1983).

Mare, W.H., '1 Corinthians', in ed. F.E. Gaebelein, *The Expositor's Bible Commentary* 10 (Grand Rapids, 1976).

Marshall, P., 'Hybrists Not Gnostics in Corinth', SBL Seminar Paper (Missoula, 1984), 275-87.

——, *Enmity in Corinth: Social Conventions in Paul's Relations with the Corinthians* (Tübingen, 1987).

Martial, *Epigrams,* Loeb Classical Library, (London and Cambridge, Massachusetts, 1961).

Martin, T.R., 'Inscriptions at Corinth', *Hesperia* 46 (1977), 178-198.

Mason, H.J., 'Greek Terms for Roman Institutions—A Lexicon and Analysis', *American Studies in Papyrology* 13 (Toronto, 1974).

McDaniel, W.B., *Roman Private Life and its Survivals* (London, 1925).

McDonald, W.A., 'Archaeology and St. Paul's Journeys in Greek lands, part III—Corinth', *Biblical Archaeologist* 5 (1942), 36-48.

Meeks, W.A., 'The Urban Environment of Pauline Christianity', *Seminar Papers: Society of Biblical Literature* (California, 1980), 113-23.

——, 'The Social Context of Pauline Theology', *Interpretation* 36 (1982).

——, *The First Urban Christians—The Social World of the Apostle Paul* (New Haven and London, 1983).

Meritt, B.D., *Corinth—Greek Inscriptions 1896-1927 Corinth: Results,* viii, Part I (Cambridge, Massachusetts, 1931).

Meurer, S., *Das Recht im Dienst der Versöhnung und des Friedens, Studie zur Frage des Rechts nach dem Neuen Testament* (Zürich, 1972).

Meyer, H.A.W., *Critical and Exegetical Handbook to the Epistles to the Corinthians* (ET: Edinburgh, 1877).

——, *Critical and Exegetical Handbook to the Epistle to the Romans* (ET: Edinburgh, 1879).

——, *Critical and Exegetical Commentary on the New Testament, Part VII, The Epistle to the Galatians* (ET: Edinburgh, 1884).

——, *The Epistles to the Corinthians* (ET: Edinburgh, 1892).

Michel, O., *Der Brief an die Römer* (ed 14: Göttingen, 1978).

——, 'οἰκονόμος', *TDNT* V (Grand Rapids, 1987), 150.

Miller, G., 'ἀρχόντων τοῦ αἰῶνος τούτου—A New Look at 1 Corinthians 2:6-8', *Journal of Biblical Literature* 91 (1972), 522-528.

Mitteis, L. & Wilcken, U., *Grundzüge und Chrestomathie der Papyruskunde* I (Leipzig and Berlin, 1912).

Mommsen, T., *Gesammelte Schriften* I (Berlin, 1905).

Morris, L., *1 Corinthians* (ed 2: Leicester, 1985).

——, *The Epistle to the Romans* (Leicester, 1988).

Morrison, C., *The Powers that Be: Earthly Rulers and Demonic Powers in Romans 13:1-7* (London, 1960).

Mott, S.C., 'The Power of Giving and Receiving: Reciprocity in Hellenistic Benevolence', in ed. G.F. Hawthorne, *Current Issues in Biblical and Patristic Interpretation* (Grand Rapids, 1975).

Moule, C.F.D., *An Idiom Book of New Testament Greek* (ed 2: Cambridge, 1959).

——, *The Birth of the New Testament* (London, 1962).

Moulton, J.H., *A Grammar of New Testament Greek* III (Edinburgh, 1963).

Moulton, J.H., & Milligan, G., *The Vocabulary of the Greek Testament: Illustrated from the Papyri and other Non-Literary Sources* (Grand Rapids, 1980).

Munck, J., *Paul and the Salvation of Mankind* (London, 1959).

——, '1 Thess. I.9-10 and the Missionary Preaching of Paul, Textual Exegesis and Hermeneutic Reflexions', *New Testament Studies* 9 (1963), 95-110.

Murphy O'Connor, J., *St Paul's Corinth—Texts and Archaeology* (Wilmington, 1983).

——, 'The Corinth that Paul saw', *Biblical Archaeologist* 47 (1984), 147-59.

Murray, J., *The Epistle to the Romans* I (Grand Rapids, 1959).

Mussies, G., *Dio Chrysostom and the New Testament* (Leiden, 1972).

Nygren, A., *Commentary on Romans* (ET: London, 1952).

O'Neill, J.C., *Paul's Letter to the Romans* (Harmondsworth, 1975).

Ollrog, W., *Paulus und seine Mitarbeiter: Untersuchungen zu Theorie und Praxis der paulinischen Mission* (Neukirchen-Vluyn, 1979).

Origen, *Opera omnia quae Graece vel Latine tantum exstant et eius nomine circumferuntur* VII, ed. C.H.E. Lommatzsch (Berolini, 1837).

——, *Contra Celsum* (ET: Cambridge, 1953).

——, *Commento alla Lettera ai Romani,* ed. F. Cocchini (Casale Monferrato, 1985).

Orr, W.F. & Walther, J.A., *1 Corinthians, A New Translation* (New York, 1976).

Oster, R.E., 'When Men wore veils to Worship: the Historical Context of 1 Corinthians 11:4', *New Testament Studies* 34 (1988), 481-505.

Pallas, D.I. & Dantes, S.P., ''Επιγραφες απο την Κορινθω', *Archaiologike Ephemeris* 1977 (1979), 75-76.

Pallis, A., *To the Romans* (Liverpool, 1920).

Pausanias, *Description of Greece,* Loeb Classical Library (Cambridge, Massachusetts, 1918).

Pearson, B.A., *The Pneumatikos-Psychikos Terminology in 1 Corinthians. A Study in the Theology of the Corinthian Opponents of Paul and its Relation to Gnosticism* (Montana, 1973).

Pesce, M., *Paolo e gli Arconti a Corinto, Storia della ricerca (1888-1975) ed esegesi di 1 Cor. 2,6.8* (Brescia, 1977).

Pfitzner, V.C., 'Purified Community—Purified Sinner: Expulsion from the Community according to Matthew 18:15-18 and 1 Corinthians 5:1-5', *Australian Biblical Review* 30 (1982), 34-55.

Philippi, F.A., *Commentary on St. Paul's Epistle to the Romans* (ET: Edinburgh, 1878).

Philo, *Loeb Classical Library* 12 vols (London, 1940-50).

Pliny, *Letters,* Loeb Classical Library (London, 1924).

Plutarch, *Moralia,* Loeb Classical Library (London, 1939-1968).

Polhill, J., 'The Wisdom of God and Factionalism: 1 Corinthians 1-4', *Review and Expositor* 80 (1983), 325-350.

Porton, G., 'The Traditions of Rabbi Ishmael III', in ed J. Neusner, *Studies in Judaism in Late Antiquity* XIX (Leiden, 1979).

Raditsa, L.F., 'Augustus' Legislation Concerning Marriage, Procreation, Love Affairs and Adultery', in ed. H. Temporini, *ANRW* II. 13 (Berlin, 1980), 278-339.

Rawson, B., 'Roman Concubinage and Other *De Facto* Marriages', *Transactions of the American Philological Association* 104 (1974), 279-305.

——, *The Politics of Friendship, Pompey and Cicero* (Parramatta, 1978).

Redlich, E.B., *S. Paul and his Companions* (London, 1913).

Reinhold, M., 'Usurpation of Status and Status Symbols in the Roman Empire', *Historia* 20 (1971), 275-302.

Reisch, E., 'Agonothetes', *Pauly's Real-Encyclopädie* I (Stuttgart, 1894).

Rengstorf, K.H., 'ὑπηρέτης', *TDNT* VIII, 542.

Reumann, J., 'Servants of God—Pre-Christian Religious Application of ΟΙΚΟΝΟΜΟΣ in Greek', *Journal of Biblical Literature* 77 (1958), 339-49.

——, 'οἰκονομία-Terms in Paul in Comparison with Lucan *Heilsgeschichte*', *New Testament Studies* 13 (1966/7), 147-67.

Reynolds, J., 'Cities', in ed. D. Braund, *The Administration of the Roman Empire 241 BC-AD 193* (Exeter, 1988), 15-51.

Rhodes, P.J., *The Greek City States* (London, 1986).

Richardson, P., 'Judgment in sexual matters in 1 Corinthians 6:1-11', *Novum Testamentum* 25 (1983), 37-58.

Richter, P.J., 'Recent Sociological Approaches to the Study of the New Testament', *Religion* 14 (1984), 77-90.

Robert, J. and L., *Bulletin Épigraphique* I-IX (Paris, 1972-1982).

Robertson, A. & Plummer, A., *A Critical and Exegetical Commentary on the First Epistle of St Paul to the Corinthians* (Edinburgh, 1914).

Robertson, A.T., *Grammar of the Greek New Testament in the Light of Historical Research* (ed 4: Nashville, 1923).

Robinson, T.A., *The Bauer Thesis Examined: The Geography of Heresy in the Early Christian Church* (Queenston, 1988).

Roos, A.G., 'De Titulo quodam latino Corinthi nuper reperto', *Mnemosyne* 58 (1930), 160-165.

Rosenmüller, D.J.G., *Scholia in Novum Testamentum* III (ed 6: Norimberg, 1829).

Roukema, R., *The Diversity of Laws in Origen's Commentary on Romans* (Amsterdam, 1988).

Runia, D.T., *Philo of Alexandria and the Timaeus of Plato* (Leiden, 1986).

Sahlin, H., 'Einige Textemendationen zum Römerbrief', *Theologische Zeitschrift* 9 (1953), 92-100.

Saller, R.P., *Personal Patronage under the Early Empire* (Cambridge, 1982).

——, 'Roman Dowry and the Devolution of Property in the Principate', *Classical Quarterly* 34 (1984), 195-205.

——, 'Patronage and Friendship', in ed. A. Wallace-Hadrill, *Patronage in Ancient Society* (London, 1989).

Salmon, E.D., *Roman Colonization Under the Republic* (London, 1969).

Sanday, W. & Headlam, A.C., *A Critical and Exegetical Commentary on The Epistle to the Romans* (Edinburgh, 1920).

Sanders, B., 'Imitating Paul: 1 Cor 4:16', *Harvard Theological Review* 74 (1981), 353-63.

Sänger, D., 'Die δυνατοί in 1. Kor. 1,26', *Zeitschrift für die Neutestamentliche Wissenschaft* 76 (1985), 285-91.

Sasse, H., 'αἰών', *TDNT* I (Grand Rapids, 1965), 197-209.

Savage, T.B., *Power through Weakness: An Historical and Exegetical Examination of Paul's Understanding of the ministry in 2 Corinthians,* unpublished PhD dissertation (Cambridge University, 1986).

Schlier, H., *Der Römerbrief* (Freiburg, Basel, Wien, 1977).

Schmithals, W., *Gnosticism in Corinth—An Investigation of the Letters to the Corinthians* (New York, 1971).

——, *Paul and the Gnostics* (ET: New York, 1972).

——, *Der Römerbrief, Ein Kommentar* (Gütersloh, 1988).

Schniewind, J., *Nachgelassene Reden und Aufsätze* (Berlin, 1952).

Schrage, W., *Der erste Brief an die Korinther (1 Kor 1,1-6,11)* (Zürich and Braunschweig, 1991).

Schreiner, K., 'Zur biblischen Legitimation des Adels: Auslegungsgeschichtliche Studien zu 1. Kor. 1,26-29', *Zeitschrift für Kirchengeschichte* 85 (1974), 317-57.

Schürer, E., *The History of the Jewish People in the Age of Jesus Christ (175 BC-AD 135)* II (ET: Edinburgh, 1979).

Schweizer, E., *Gemeinde und Gemeindeordnung im Neuen Testament* (Zürich, 1959).

——, *Church Order in the New Testament* (ET: London, 1979).

Scroggs, R., 'The sociological interpretation of the New Testament: The present state of research', *New Testament Studies* 26 (1979), 164-179.

Semler, J.S., *Paraphrasis epistolae ad Romanos cum notis, translatione vetusta, et dissertatione de appendice cap.,* XV, XVI (Magdeburg, 1769).

Seneca, *Moral Essays* III, Loeb Classical Library (London, 1975).

Shanor, J., 'Paul as master builder: construction terms in First Corinthians', *New Testament Studies* 34 (1988), 461-71.

Shear, T.L., 'Excavations in the Theatre District and Tombs of Corinth in 1929', *American Journal of Archaeology* 33 (1929), 515-546.

——, 'Discoveries at "The Wealthy City of the Double Sea"', *The Illustrated London News* (August 17, 1929), 286-7, 318.

Sherwin-White, A.N., *Roman Society and Roman Law in the New Testament* (Oxford, 1963).

——, *The Roman Citizenship* (ed 2: Oxford, 1973).

Smith, J.Z., 'The Social Description of early Christianity', *Religious Studies Review* 1 (1975).

Sohm, R., *Kirchenrecht* I (Leipzig, 1892).

Stambaugh, J. & Balch, D., *The Social World of the First Christians* (London, 1986).

Stanley, D.M., '"Become Imitators of Me": The Pauline Conception of Apostolic Tradition', *Biblica* 40 (1959), 859-877.

Staveley, E.S., *Greek and Roman Voting and Elections* (London, 1972).

Ste. Croix, G.E.M. de, 'Additional note on KALOS, KALOKAGATHIA', *The Origins of the Peloponnesian War* (London, 1972), 371-376.

Stein, A., 'Wo trugen die korinthischen Christen ihre Rechtshandel aus?', *Zeitschrift für die Neutestamentliche Wissenschaft* 59 (1968), 86-90.

Stephanus, H., *Thesaurus Graecae Linguae* I (Paris, 1831).

Stevenson, G.H., *Roman Provincial Administration till the age of the Antonines* (Westport, 1975).

Stillwell, A.N., *The Potter's Quarter xv, 1,* American School of Classical Studies at Athens (Princeton, 1948).

Stillwell, R., *The Theatre, Corinth* ii, American School of Classical Studies at Athens (Princeton, 1952).

Stowers, S.K., 'Social Status, Public Speaking and Private Teaching: The Circumstances of Paul's Preaching Activity', *Novum Testamentum* 26 (1984), 59-82.

——, 'The Social Sciences and the Study of Early Christianity', Approaches to Ancient Judaism V, ed. W.S. Green, *Studies in Judaism and Its Greco-Roman Context* (Atlanta, 1985), 149-181.

Strabo, *Geography*, Loeb Classical Library 8 volumes (Cambridge, Massachusetts, 1917).

Strack, H.L. & Billerbeck, P., *Kommentar zum Neuen Testament aus Talmud und Midrasch: Die Briefe des neuen Testaments und die Offenbarung Johannis* III (München, 1926).

Suetonius, I, Loeb Classical Library (London, 1970).

Syme, R., *The Augustan Aristocracy* (Oxford, 1986).

Tacitus, *Annals* I-III, Loeb Classical Library (London, 1962).

Taubenschlag, R., *The Law of Greco-Roman Egypt in the Light of the Papyri, 332 BC-640 AD* (ed 2: Warsaw, 1955).

Theissen, G., *Studien zur Soziologie des Urchristentums* (Tübingen, 1979).

——, *The Social Setting of Pauline Christianity: essays on Corinth* (Edinburgh, 1982).

Thistleton, A.C., 'Realized Eschatology at Corinth', *New Testament Studies* 24 (1978), 510-526.

Tholuck, F.A.G., *Exposition of St. Paul's epistle to the Romans* I, II (Edinburgh, 1833, '36).

Tidball, D., *An Introduction to the Sociology of the New Testament* (Exeter, 1983).

Tod, M.N., *Sidelights on Greek History: Three Lectures on the Light thrown by Greek Inscriptions on the Life and Thought of the Ancient World* (Oxford, 1932).

Vanderbroeck, P.J.J., *Popular Leadership and Collective Behavior in the Late Roman Republic (Ca. 80-50 BC)* (Amsterdam, 1987).

Vischer, L., *Die Auslegungsgeschichte von 1. Kor. 6,1-11* (Tübingen, 1955).

Waele, de, F.J., 'Erastus, oikonoom van Korinthe en vriend van St. Paulus', *Mededeelingen van het Nederlandsch historisch Instituut te Rome* 9 (1929), 40-8.

——, 'Die Korinthischen Ausgrabungen 1928-29', *Gnomon* 6 (1930), 52-7.

Wallace-Hadrill, A., 'Family and Inheritance in the Augustan Marriage-Laws', *Proceedings of the Cambridge Philological Society* 207 (New Series, 27) (1981), 58-80.

——, 'The Social Structure of the Roman House', *Papers of the British School at Rome* LVI (1988), 43-97.

Weaver, P.R.C., 'Social Mobility in the Early Roman Empire: The Evidence of the Imperial Freedmen and Slaves', in ed. M.I. Finley, *Studies in Ancient Society, Past and Present Series* (London, 1974), 121-140.

Weber, M., *The Theory of Social and Economic Organization* (ET: London, 1947).

——, *Economy and Society: An Outline of Interpretive Sociology,* (ET: Berkeley, 1968).

——, *On Charisma and Institution Building,* ed. S.N. Eisenstadt (London, 1968).

Weerd, H. Van de, 'Een Nieuw Opschrift van Korinthe', *Revue Belge de Philologie et d'Histoire* 10 (1931), 87-95.

Weiß, B., *Kritisch exegetisches Handbuch über den Brief des Paulus an die Römer* (ed 7: Göttingen, 1886).

Weiß, J., *Das Urchristentum* (Göttingen, 1917).

——, *Der erste Korintherbrief* (ed 10: Göttingen, 1925).

——, *The History of Primitive Christianity* I (London, 1937).

Welborn, L.L., 'On the Discord in Corinth: 1 Corinthians 1-4 and Ancient Politics', *Journal of Biblical Literature* 106 (1987), 85-111.

West, A.B., *Corinth—Latin Inscriptions 1896-1920 Corinth: Results,* viii, Part II (Cambridge, Massachusetts, 1931).

Westermann, W.L., 'Slavery and the Elements of Freedom in Ancient Greece', in ed. M.I. Finley, *Slavery and Classical Antiquity, Views and Controversies* (Cambridge, 1960), 17-32.

Wettstein, J.J., Ἡ ΚΑΙΝΗ ΔΙΑΘΗΚΗ, *Novum Testamentum Graecum* II (Amsterdam, 1752).

Whitby, D., *A Paraphrase and Commentary on the New Testament* II (ed 7: London, 1760).

Wilckens, U., *Der Brief an die Römer* I (Zürich, 1978).

Wink, W., *Naming the Powers, The Language of Power in the New Testament* I (Philadelphia, 1984).

Winter, B.W., 'The Lord's Supper at Corinth: An Alternative Reconstruction', *Reformed Theological Review* 37 (1978), 73-82.

——, 'Providentia for the Widows of 1 Timothy 5:3-16', *Tyndale Bulletin* 39 (1988), 83-99.

——, *Philo and Paul among the Sophists: A Hellenistic Jewish and a Christian Response,* unpublished PhD dissertation (Macquarie University, 1988).

——, 'The Public Honouring of Christian Benefactors, Romans 13:3-4 and 1 Peter 2:14-15', *Journal for the Study of the New Testament* 34 (1988), 87-103.

——, 'The New Testament as Commentator on the Cultural Setting of First Century Roman Corinth', lecture delivered to The Society for Early Christianity, Macquarie University (December, 1989).

——, 'Secular and Christian Responses to Corinthian Famines', *Tyndale Bulletin* 40 (1989), 86-106.

——, '"If a man does not wish to work ...": A Cultural and Historical Setting for 2 Thessalonians 3:6-16', *Tyndale Bulletin* 40 (1989), 303-15.

——, 'Theological and Ethical Responses to Religious Pluralism—1 Corinthians 8-10', *Tyndale Bulletin* 41 (1990), 209-26.

——, 'In Public and in Private: Early Christian Interactions with Religious Pluralism', in edd. A.D. Clarke & B.W. Winter, *One God, One Lord in a World of Religious Pluralism* (Cambridge, 1991), 112-34.

——, 'Civil Litigation in Secular Corinth and the Church, The Forensic Background to 1 Corinthians 6.1-8', *New Testament Studies* 37 (1991), 559-572.

Wiseman, J., 'Corinth and Rome I: 228 BC-AD 267', *ANRW* II.7.1 (Berlin, 1979), 438-548.

Wisse, F., 'The Righteous Man and the Good Man in Romans V.7', *New Testament Studies* 19 (1972-3), 91-93.

Woodward, A.M., 'Archaeology in Greece 1928-9', *Journal of Hellenic Studies* 49 (1929), 220-39.

Wüllner, W., 'The Sociological Implications of 1 Corinthians 1.26-28 Reconsidered', in ed. E.A. Livingstone, *Studia Evangelica* VI (Berlin, 1973), 666-72.

——, 'Greek Rhetoric and Pauline Argumentation', in edd. W.R. Schoedel, R.L. Wilken, *Early Christian Literature and the Classical Intellectual Tradition—in honorem Robert M. Grant* (Paris, 1979), 177-88.

——, 'Ursprung und Verwendung der σοφός-, δυνατός-, εὐγενής- Formel in 1 Kor 1,26', in edd. E. Bammel, C.K. Barrett, W.D. Davies, *Donum Gentilicium—New Testament Studies in Honour of David Daube* (Oxford, 1978), 165-184.

——, 'Tradition and Interpretation of the "Wise-Powerful-Noble" Triad in 1 Cor 1,26', in ed. E.A. Livingstone, *Studia Evangelica* VII (Berlin, 1982), 557-62.

——, 'Paul as Pastor, The Function of Rhetorical Questions in First Corinthians', in ed. A. Vanhoye, *L'Apôtre Paul—Personnalité, Style et Conception du Ministère* (Leuven, 1986), 49-77.

Yarbrough, O.L., *Not like the Gentiles: Marriage Rules in the Letters of Paul* (Atlanta, 1985).

Zaas, P.S., '"Cast out the evil man from your midst" 1 Cor 5:13b', *Journal of Biblical Literature* 103 (1984), 259-61.

Zahn, T., *Der Brief des Paulus an die Römer* (ed 3: Leipzig, 1925).

Ziesler, J.A., *The Meaning of Righteousness in Paul, A Linguistic and theological enquiry* (Cambridge, 1972).

——, *Paul's Letter to the Romans* (London, 1989).

INDEX OF ANCIENT AND MODERN AUTHORS

INDEX OF SCRIPTURE REFERENCES